RAISING MONEY-WISE KIDS

RAISING MONEY-WISE KIDS

Judith Briles

NORTHFIELD PUBLISHING
CHICAGO

The *Value Line Investment Survey* on page 197 is © 1995 by Value Line Publishing, Inc. Reprinted by permission. All rights reserved.

The following terms used in this book are registered trademarks: Abflex, Apple, Barbie, Big Mac, Cabbage Patch, Cap'n Crunch, Classic Coke, Cocoa Pebbles, Cocoa Puffs, G.I. Joe, Game of Life, Girls Can, Golden Books, Happy Meal, Hot Wheels, Keds, Looney Tunes, Maserati, MasterCard, Mercedes, Monopoly, My First Sony, Nike, Ninja Turtles, Nintendo, Oreos, Pepsi, Ping Pong, PlaySkool, Porsche, Post-it Notes, Power Foam, Power Ranger, Quicken, Rollerblades, Sega Genesis, Smart Mop, SpaghettiOs, Tonka Toys, Wheaties, Young AmeriTowne.

ISBN: 1-881273-59-8

1 3 5 7 9 10 8 6 4 2

Printed in the United States of America

For Robin
Who parents from the heart

Also by Judith Briles

GenderTraps
The Briles Report on Women in Healthcare
The Confidence Factor
Money Sense
Woman to Woman
The Workplace
When God Says NO
Judith Briles' Money Guide for Christian Women
The Dollars and Sense of Divorce
Faith and Savvy Too!
Money Phases
The Woman's Guide to Financial Savvy

Contents

Acknowledgments

You are about to read a book that has been in my heart for two decades. *Raising Money-Wise Kids* was first seeded in the late seventies. When I proposed it to a publisher in the eighties, there was little enthusiasm. When *Money Sense: What Every Woman Must Know to be Financially Confident* was published in 1995, Northfield Publication's then managing editor Linda Holland finally matched my enthusiasm for *Raising Money-Wise Kids*. With Linda's support, the *Money Sense* series was birthed. It's a practical, "let's roll up our sleeves and talk about money" how-to. Linda has accepted a promotion with another company, but her vision is intact. I thank her—and miss her.

Master editor Cheryl Dunlop dug into the manuscript. She suggested adding the chapters on weddings, wheels, and leaving the nest. She was right—each add so much to the book. Thank you, Cheryl, for your keen eye and attention to detail.

The marketing team at Northfield—Bill Thrasher, Suzanne Dowd, and Judy Tolberg—instantly saw the value of a parents' book that was no-nonsense. Ragont Design has done a wonderful job of laying out the text for reader friendliness.

Friend and neighbor Robin Bunger worked a zillion hours transcribing my tapes (all my books are dictated for the first draft). With her great sense of humor and parenting skills honed by raising five kids, her participation and voice were invaluable. I couldn't have done this book without her. Thank you.

My family has continued to be a tremendous support and study in motion for all my work. Daughters Shelley and Sheryl, son Frank, grandson Frankie, and husband John have been there through the years as my work sometimes enveloped me. I know they have wondered, "What is she writing, now, about us?"

Thank you to all the professionals whose energy is for parenting and kids. My only regret is that there was so little for teaching kids about money when I was an active parent—today there are wonderful resources that are available to everyone.

Introduction

My kids were young in the sixties and early seventies. Their concept of getting money was that Mom could write a check or go to the bank. Voilà—cash was abundant. Today's child has the same idea about the ATM: put the card in and voilà—cash is abundant.

As a mother of four, the grandmother of one, the auntie to numerous nieces and nephews, the sister to three brothers, and the daughter of a father (who, at the age of eighty-four, *still* does not think it is appropriate to talk about money), I have had plenty of frontline experience in delivering *Money $ense* to my loved ones.

The catchphrase of the nineties has been family values. A definite faith in family values includes an understanding of right and wrong and the ability to respond correctly when these values are challenged. Your family's value system probably includes yielding respect to those who are older (and probably wiser!) and other simple truths. *Raising Money-Wise Kids* deals specifically with one of these truths, which is that money attitudes and the ability to manage money are critical kernels in rearing a child.

Of my four children, two are alive today. Shelley, at thirty-two, has always been responsible about money. When she was sixteen, we allowed her to use a credit card (which she paid off monthly) and we cosigned on a car loan for her (her payments were always on time). Then there is her sister Sheryl, who is twenty-nine and the mother of my fabulous grandson, Frankie. She has finally gotten her money act together, but until recently, her attitude was: have credit card—will travel.

My two sons, Frank and Billy, died many years ago. Billy, who died as a baby, certainly didn't receive any money-wise training. His death, though, did impact us financially. Medical costs were many thousands of dollars. Our savings were wiped out.

Frank died when he was nineteen. He drowned when he fell from an old, abandoned bridge he was descending with several of his friends. I can remember the chain of events just before and after his death today as clearly as when it happened in 1983. There were costs related to memorials and the mortuary, and there were emotional costs as well. "Emotional" meaning that as a self-employed individual, I was a mess. I couldn't think or talk straight.

As someone who makes a living needing both my brain and my mouth, I wasn't doing well. When a person doesn't have full use of the assets that create funds that are the primary support for his or her family, there's a big problem. For almost a year, I did not function at 100 percent. I forgot to pay bills. Electricity was cut off, newspapers were stopped. We ended up selling what remaining assets we had to cover the expenses of living, because I just could not work at the level that was needed.

Frankie is the son of my daughter Sheryl. As of this publication, he is a delightful nine year old. He is named after Frank, the uncle he never met, and he is so much like him. He is one of God's "yeses" in life. You will read and hear about Frankie, my daughters Shelley and Sheryl, and my son Frank and what they taught my husband, John, and me about how to pass along information about money and life.

Have I always been right on and perfect about money? Of course not! In the late seventies and early eighties, I could have been nominated the consumer of the year. We had *all* the material things: a big home, a pool, a thriving business, two Mercedes, and kids in private schools—many could envy what we had built.

There were times when unlimited vacation dollars were available to my family; for example, after Christmas we routinely spent a week in Hawaii. And each of the kids was allowed to take a friend along. Then there were times when we lost everything: house, cars, and many of our clothes. Ironically, the best lessons in money understanding and knowledge that were passed on to my children came from the disastrous times.

In 1981 one of my business partners got into trouble. Her troubles dominoed and directly impacted my family. In the end, we lost more than a million dollars. We were broke: no home, no cars, minimal furniture. Even jewelry was sold. I felt that God had dropped me on my head. Gone were the spiffy vacations and all the goodies attached to them. We couldn't even afford to take the kids on a camping trip—gasoline was too expensive. In the end, that bad time became a blessing. A major change (for the good this time) occurred in our family. It was because of that bad time that we finally sat down with our kids and talked about money.

The purpose of *Raising Money-Wise Kids* is to pass along some of the advice that I obtained through this thing called living, as well as the sound money advice I received from others. All parents meet financial challenges with their kids—it doesn't matter if they're young or have matured to adulthood. I have shared many of my frustrations, even the absurdities, that go along with teaching kids about money. After all, we parents need to band together when we tell our kids why they can't have the $140 pair of sneakers they covet.

Money $ense kids begin with the parent(s) in their lives—you. Let's see where you stand by taking the following short quiz.

Money $ense Quiz

1. Your son started mowing your lawn, at no charge, at age ten. At thirteen, he wants to make some money. He proposes that he approach the neighbors about mowing their lawns. He will continue to mow your lawn, but at a discount.

You:

   a. Tell him no and hire your son's friend because he's offered to do the job for less.
   b. Tell him that mowing the lawn is part of his responsibility as a family member—the answer is no.
   c. Offer him a deal: Since your son will be using your mowing equipment, you will pay him half the amount he charges the neighbors and he must pay for all the gas used.
   d. Tell him you will pay the same rate he charges the neighbors, he can use the power mower, and you will pay for the gas.

2. It's your four-year-old daughter's birthday, and she has received a lot of presents from friends and family members. She becomes bored with unwrapping presents and goes off to do something else.

You:

   a. Gather the remaining unopened gifts and put them away for a rainy day.
   b. Do as in "a," and if friends and family ask what to give on the next occasion, suggest that since there is always too much, just come. If they persist, suggest a small contribution to the child's college fund.
   c. Finish opening the gifts. Why waste the festivities?
   d. Teach your child a lesson—give the unopened gifts to less fortunate children.

3. Your eleven year old has a paper route. He says he's tired of getting up

at five in the morning and doesn't see why people can't wait until a more reasonable hour, like 7:30 A.M., to get their paper. He's already received a warning from his manager that he's on probation for delivering the papers late.

You:

R a. Remind him of the words of your father: "Do the job right or don't do it at all."
   b. Agree with him that 5:00 A.M. is an outrageous hour and tell him that you will get up early to help him fold and deliver the papers so he won't lose his route.
D c. Tell him that it is his choice: He can get up early to deliver the papers on time and keep his job and the money he makes, or quit so he can sleep later. You will support either choice.
   d. Ask one of your other kids or one of his friends if they want to help out or take over the job.

4. Your kids have been bugging you for Sega Genesis and you have repeatedly said no. Your brother shows up on your doorstep with goodies for everyone, including Sega Genesis for the kids.

You:

R D a. Bite your tongue, smile, and thank him for his generosity.
   b. Tell the kids you need to test it first and proceed to take it over.
   c. Thank your brother for his generosity and ask that in the future he consult you before giving the kids expensive gifts.
   d. Immediately tell your brother they can't have expensive gifts and return the gifts to him.

5. Your young kids, ages five and seven, are preoccupied with death, particularly yours. They want to know where they would live and who would take care of them if you and your spouse died tomorrow.

You:

   a. Ask them if they would like to live with Aunt Debbie (your current will identifies Debbie as their guardian until they are adults).
D b. Tell them that most likely they would go to live with Aunt Debbie (this is your druthers, but you haven't had time to write it up in a will).

R c. Ask them if they would like to live with Aunt Debbie (again assuming your will states this). Then write a letter to Debbie stating how you want your kids raised if you die and outlining what insurance you have set aside for their financial support and education.

    d. Tell them that there is no need to talk about such a morbid topic, because you're not going to die while they are young.

6. Your sixteen-year-old daughter gets a weekly allowance for chores she's expected to do around the house. She has called a strike but still expects to get her allowance.

You:

    a. Cease paying the allowance.

    b. Give it to her anyway, but remind her that when she's eighteen she will be on her own.

RD c. Discuss with her what the value in dollars is to you for each of the chores she has been doing. Be firm in telling her that she will no longer receive an allowance, and let her know that she will be paid for only those chores done on a timely basis and without reminder.

    d. Tell her that you will hire someone else to do her work.

7. Uncle James gave your eight-year-old son ten dollars for his birthday. He has lost the money.

You:

    a. Tell him that he is irresponsible and should have put the money in the bank.

R D b. Allow him to do extra chores so that he can earn $10 to replace the money that he lost.

    c. Tell him "Tough, you should have been more careful."

    d. Call Uncle James and ask him to replace the lost $10.

8. Your four year old has developed the "gimmes." On a visit to the toy store, he begins to make a scene and will not be satisfied with what you previously agreed to buy for him.

You:

    a. Decide that you won't go anywhere with him until he's eighteen years old.

b. Buy him whatever he wants so you can exit the store quickly.

c. Talk to him calmly and tell him that he can choose one item within a certain price range that is close to what you had planned to spend anyway.

d. Remind him that you are bigger and stronger and that you will win. Ignore his crying.

9. When your daughter was a little girl, you told her that when she was a teenager, she could pick out and buy her own clothes. Yesterday, she turned thirteen. Today, she arrives home with her new purchases, and they are some of the most hideous things you have ever seen.

You:

a. Bite your tongue; she loves the clothes and bought them within the clothing allowance you gave her.

b. Tell her that her taste in clothes is horrible and, further, that she needs a lesson in the quality of clothing.

c. Tell that she has to return all the clothes—immediately.

d. Compliment her on staying within the budget. Remind her that you will not advance her any more money for clothing beyond the amount agreed to, so if she's not sure about any of her choices she should take them back while they are still new. (And say a prayer of thanks that she doesn't like *your* clothes.)

10. Your seventeen-year-old son is using the family car for his big date, and as he goes out the door, he asks you for an extra $20.

You:

a. Tell him to have a great time. Loan him $20 plus an extra $5 for gas.

b. Remind him that all gas and date money was to come out of his allowance and his earnings from his part-time job. The answer is no.

c. Don't give him the full amount. Offer him $5—take it or leave it.

d. Remind him that when *you* were dating, you could go to a movie and get a soda for $5. Ask him where he's going that he needs that much money.

11. Your fifteen-year-old daughter receives a $25 birthday check from her grandmother.

You:

    a. Make her sign it, then deposit it in the savings account you set up for her.

    b. Tell her she must put $10 in her savings account and that she can spend the rest on whatever she wants.

    c. Call the grandmother and remind her that $25 doesn't go very far these days. After all, a CD costs $15.

    d. Bite your tongue, and use what she does with it as an example to affirm (or alter) future discussions on money.

12. Your twelve year old saves a portion of his allowance and any money he's earned from outside jobs, as well as gift money. He has his eye on getting his own CD player.

You:

    a. Remind him that you didn't have toys like that when you were twelve years old and that if LPs were good enough for you, they should be good enough for him.

    b. Tell him that he should be using his savings only for important things.

    c. Offer to buy it for him so he can save his money.

    d. Congratulate him on his ability to save that much money and allow him to buy it.

13. You are at the video store and your kids insist that they will "just die" if they can't get the $50 video game that goes with the Sega Genesis that Uncle Jeff gave them.

You:

    a. Give them the money to get the video they want, but tell them that they have to save up to buy any additional ones.

    b. Tell them no, they must save their money.

    c. Suggest borrowing the neighbor's copy or renting a copy to make sure that this is really what they want before you fork over any cash.

    d. Give them the money to avoid making a scene at the store.

14. The big day has arrived, and your daughter tells you that she wants to be first in line to get her driver's license. It dawns on you that the cost of

your insurance premiums will increase when you add her to your policy.

You:

a. Gladly pay the increased premium because she is an important part of your family.
b. Calculate the increase in your premium, and tell her that she will have to pay this amount herself if she wants to drive.
c. Welcome her to the responsibility of driving. Tell her that you will split the increased cost of your insurance premium with her and also that she will have to pay for all the gas she uses.
d. Remind her of the health benefits of riding a bike and walking.

15. Your twenty-three-year-old son has lost his job and has moved home "temporarily."

You:

a. Remind him that he is an adult and tell him he has two weeks to get his act together.
b. Dismantle your sewing room so that he can have his old room back and be comfortable during this painful time.
c. Tell him to pitch and in help around the house for as long as he's there.
d. Set up an agreement that states when he will move out— no matter what—and what financial contribution he will make toward the household expenses (which may have to come from future earnings) and what household work he will do while he is there.

Answer Key:

1.	a. (0)	b. (1)	c. (3)	d. (2)
2.	a. (2)	b. (3)	c. (1)	d. (0)
3.	a. (2)	b. (1)	c. (3)	d. (0)
4.	a. (2)	b. (0)	c. (3)	d. (1)
5.	a. (2)	b. (1)	c. (3)	d. (0)
6.	a. (2)	b. (0)	c. (3)	d. (1)
7.	a. (1)	b. (2)	c. (3)	d. (0)
8.	a. (1)	b. (0)	c. (3)	d. (2)
9.	a. (2)	b. (0)	c. (1)	d. (3)

10.	a. (1)	b. (3)	c. (2)	d. (0)
11.	a. (1)	b. (2)	c. (0)	d. (3)
12.	a. (0)	b. (2)	c. (1)	d. (3)
13.	a. (1)	b. (2)	c. (3)	d. (0)
14.	a. (1)	b. (2)	c. (3)	d. (0)
15.	a. (0)	b. (1)	c. (2)	d. (3)

To Score: Total the values of your answers. Your Total _____
What your score means:

0–15   Don't plan on getting a smaller house when your kids are adults—you've lavished them with your money while rearing them, so why should they leave?

16–34   You are in the middle of the class—your kids know how to "push the right buttons" to get what they want. But there's still hope (and a prayer or two might not hurt). You might want to read *Money $ense*, the first book in this series, for some help.

35–45   Congratulations! You are developing *Money $ense* for both you and your kids. With continued fine-tuning, you will launch a savvy new generation of future *Money $ense* adults.

Your challenge as the primary adult(s) in your children's lives is to prepare them to live in the world as it really is. You have the task to shape and empower them with solid principles, values, and strategies. That will enable them to thrive and grow strong—an awesome responsibility.

Part One
FOR YOU, THE PARENT

Chapter One

THE GAME PLAN
FOR PARENTS

Most likely, your parents used Dr. Benjamin Spock as their guide to your medical needs when you were a baby. You probably turn to "Dr. Mom" or to pediatrician Dr. T. Berry Brazelton. Unlike Dr. Spock in his early years, today's medical and psychological gurus are proponents of setting limits. Syndicated columnist Ann Landers has stated many times in her columns that kids who have everything they want soon lose respect for money—and for their parents! Yet the reality is that setting limits is often difficult. When kids develop the "gimmes" and are given *things* to counteract their demands and temper tantrums, parents rarely want to admit that they are responsible for the outcome.

When it comes to kids and money, it is a rare parent who can't remember saying something like "When I was a kid, the tooth fairy brought only a dime"—or in some cases a quarter. When you say something like this, think back to what "then" was. "Then" meant that for a dime you could buy a candy bar, a pack of gum, or a treat from the ice-cream truck. In the nineties a candy bar or pack of gum costs fifty cents. Penny bubble-gum machines have gone the way of the dinosaur. Comic books are at least one dollar. It's easy to say to our kids, "You don't know or appreciate the value of the dollar." At the same time, we as their parents forget that the value of the dollar does tend to change. The dollar is worth less now than when we were kids, and the trend continues.

The nineties parent is busy, and most admit to being overcommitted. It's guesstimated that many parents only spend fifteen minutes each day one-on-one with their child. When a family has more than one child, that one-on-one time is reduced. Few families sit down together for a meal, either breakfast or dinner, all at the same time. Everyone is going in different directions, to lessons, school, out with friends. You name it, we're a scattered lot.

Parents know they need to talk to their kids about money, but the mañana syndrome hits. Tomorrow is another day. Talking to your kids and teaching them the principles of money is as exciting as cleaning out your "Fibber McGee" closet. You know it's there, but it has got all kinds of ghosts and skeletons. It even has some good stuff hidden away behind the boxes, but it's easier just to keep the door shut and hope that it will go away or that someone else will clean it up.

With the publication of *Raising Money-Wise Kids*, I reached my fiftieth birthday. When I was a kid, it was taboo to talk about money. My brothers and I didn't have a clue about our family's money situation, how much or how little was in our house. Somehow, there were meals on the table and clothes were bought in September for the new school year. We did not know how much money my father made (or what he actually did for a living), how much was paid in taxes, or how much we had in the bank (if anything). My family was not atypical: That was the normal approach to money in the fifties and sixties. The majority of my friends didn't have a clue about their parents' money situation either. I suspect you didn't know much about your parents' income and expenses.

Families are more open today. They talk about sex, drugs, and the perils of both, yet they still hold back about money. After all, money is a powerful weapon. Parents use it to cover their guilt or to display their affection. They can withhold money or they can give it—and they should reserve the option to give it generously or with strings attached. But if parents have trouble managing money and it runs out before the end of the month, their children's ability to live within their means and manage their money needs and desires becomes a mirror image of the training they received.

Money-Wise Tip

Set aside one day each month to talk about family money.

More than two thousand teens between the ages of twelve and nineteen participated in a survey in the early nineties that was conducted by Teenage Research Unlimited. They were asked how they spent their money. (Their answers did not include items received as gifts.) They reported:

- 14% bought a home stereo
- 13% bought a portable radio
- 11% bought a CD player
- 11% bought a small personal stereo with headphones
- 7% bought a home video game system
- 5% bought a portable CD player
- 5% bought a personal computer

KIDS' REALITY

The Northbrook, Illinois, company of Teenage Research Unlimited monitors the $90+ billion spending group of twelve to nineteen year olds. When it comes to spending, boys and girls are fairly equal in their spending habits. They spend $62 a week on average! For every $2 of their own money spent, they are matched with an additional $1 from their family. The primary areas for the expenditures are clothes, movie tickets, snacks, and cosmetics. Then of course there is the amount of money spent on electronic equipment. Today, because more kids drive and even own cars, it's not uncommon for them to pick up small grocery orders between their parents' routine bulk grocery shopping trips. Those "pickups" are of great interest to the nation's advertisers.

When you add the four- to twelve-year-old market into the financial pie, an additional $14 billion is spent. With the younger group, a greater percentage of the money comes from their parents. In the four- to twelve-year-old range, 40 percent, or roughly $6 billion dollars, goes toward savings, and the remainder is spent. What does "spent" mean? It means that more than $2 billion is spent on candy, sodas, frozen desserts, and snacks; more than $2 billion is spent on toys and games; $1 billion is spent on clothing; $600+ million on movies, sports, and live entertainment; $500+ million on video arcade games; and more than $300 million on CDs and telephones. A lot of money!

There's no doubt about it, money brings incredible power to kids. This power enables them to purchase items they think they need and items they want. As a parent, you are in control of your children's spending up to about the age of three. After that, most kids are given choices, such as what type of ice cream cone they want or which toy they wish to play with.

From about the age of three on, children are recognized as a consumer force. Just look at the commercials on children's TV programming. At age four, kids get to pick things they want and watch their parent(s) paying for the items. At five, they make the selections and are also often given the money to pay to the cashier. Between the ages of seven and eight, kids routinely make unassisted purchases when they are out shopping with their parents.

James McNeal is a marketing professor at Texas A&M University and is an expert on children and their finances. He estimates that kids between the ages of four and twelve influence adult purchases in sixty-two product categories—everything from canned pasta (60 percent of these sales are influenced by kids—hello, SpaghettiOs) to bicycles (40 percent) and athletic shoes (20 percent), for a total spending power of more than $130 billion each year. This amount includes the $14 billion cited earlier.

In the end, what you don't teach your kids will be taught to them, and the most likely instructors are their peers and the media. In the past, the children who are today's adults were told that money didn't grow on trees. Nineties kids have a different slant to this old cliché. They believe that money grows out of an ATM machine. Few really understand that a parent had to put money into a bank account as the source for the money that comes out of the machine. Kids today are growing up with the belief that credit cards can satisfy every need and whim, which include, but are not limited to, at least one VCR and video game program, the latest fashions in clothing, and the most recent fad item. Not only do they have this belief, but they believe that their right to satisfaction is a God-given birthright.

COPING WITH TV ADVERTISING

Frankie is my nine-year-old grandson. In school he has struggled with math at times. But I am fascinated by his ability to memorize the infomercials and their corresponding 800 numbers that flash on the TV screen. Within the past month, he's called to tell me about Abflex, the Smart Mop, and Power Foam. Not only does he know how much each item costs, but he can also describe the benefits and recite the 800 number to call.

With the billions of dollars that kids spend annually, it's impossible to ignore their buying power. As a parent, you know that you are zapped from almost every corner to buy this and buy that. When kids watch their favorite shows on TV, the commercials bombard them with the message to buy, buy, buy. More money may be spent on the commercial than on the actual production of the show. And for good reason.

Just take a stroll in your favorite grocery store and note the types of items that are kept on the lower shelves (at kids' eye level), especially in the cereal aisle. Also note the amount and variety of frozen foods. When Swanson introduced its first TV dinner, I suspect the company had no idea how big the "already cooked/heat 'em up" food industry would be one day. In my local grocery store, I have found everything from Looney Tunes Meals to Power Ranger juices. There are special clothing stores for kids, such as The Gap. Sony was not to be denied a piece of the kids' market, so in the nineties it came out with the My First Sony line of electronic products.

It used to be a chicken in every pot and two cars in every garage; now it's at least one VCR in every home. With the VCR, a whole new industry evolved around videos: decades-old movies (*The Wizard of Oz*), the latest *Batman*, and Disney classics. Megamillions of dollars are spent on videos. These videos are seen dozens and dozens of times. The distributors have tuned into this fact and preface the feature film with several commercials about upcoming or already distributed films. After all, they have a captive audience.

GENDER MARKETING

The Zandl Group is a New York City research company that specializes in studying the youth market. They found that, over the years, boys are far more likely to respond to commercials and ads that are sports-oriented and aggressive; girls respond to commercials that are cute and sentimental.

Shoes are a very hot item. Those in the shoe business have learned that boys like Nike and girls buy Keds. When it comes to the huge soda market, girls prefer diet sodas and flavored filtered water, and boys prefer root beer and Classic Coke. *Seventeen* magazine is still a favorite with girls, and boys look for *Sports Illustrated*. When "Beverly Hills 90210" was introduced, it quickly became #1 with teenage girls; boys preferred "Cheers."

What's a parent to do? The first reasonable thing you might consider doing is to sit down and watch TV with your kids. Pollsters say that kids in the U.S. watch from two to three hours of TV programming per day. Within a thirty-minute program, commercial time can range from eight to thirteen minutes. A great majority of those commercials are specifically targeted toward your kids. Advertisers are not dummies; they know that kids have money of their own (billions!).

Kids know that they are *masters* of influence on what their parents buy; and their parents know it too, as do advertisers. Many believe that commercials on *all* children's programming should be banned. I don't think so, because they offer parents an opportunity to explore how commercials and their products pitch to the viewer, opening a dialogue on presentations, manipulation, even values.

Here's a game we played with Frankie. He loves cereal, and he has developed expertise in getting me to try every brand that he sees on TV. I confess that as a doting grandmother, I did it for a while, but then I got smart. Try playing our TV Commercial Comparison Test in your home. Not only will it teach the strategy of being a *Money-Wise* consumer to your young one, but it will stimulate some refreshingly new and interesting dialogue between you and your child about truth in advertising and which product is the best deal.

TV COMMERCIAL COMPARISON TEST

Your goal: To teach your kids to be *Money-Wise* consumers.

Tools you will need: Any kid show on TV, preferably an afternoon or Saturday morning program. A pad of paper and a pencil. A visit to the grocery store after viewing the show.

For the test: Three "testers" work well—friends or family members. All testers should be potential consumers of the product.

Rules: Watch a TV program with your child, with specific emphasis on commercials. Ask the child before the show if he or she can remember what kinds of products are on the rows in the grocery store. If he or she remembers, explain that because there are so many different product choices, the people who design and make commercials try to convince you that their product should be in your home. Ask your child to select one of the products shown in the commercials for a test.

The prize: The "winning" item from your test will be stocked in the cupboard.

How to proceed: I did this with cereal. Fruit snacks and sodas are also ideal candidates. We went to the supermarket, and Frankie found the product he had selected for our test (it was Cocoa Pebbles). The grocery we go to has rows that are six shelves high. Our test product was found on the second shelf from the bottom—kid level. We purchased one box each of Cocoa Pebbles, Cocoa Puffs, and a similar generic or store brand. When we got home we did a taste test.

Three bowls of cereal were poured, milk was added, and each of our three testers was blindfolded. The taste testers then picked the product that they liked the best. In your test, if it is the one that was promoted in the commercial, your child wins. You will buy the product for regular family consumption. If the product flunks the test (the majority of our testers didn't rank #1), then you won't buy it. After you do this a few times, your child will learn that what is seen in the commercial is not necessarily as good as it appears and that getting what you ask for is not always satisfying.

As an added note, you can ask: How did our product comparison go? (Substitute your test product.)

Cocoa Pebbles cost _____, Cocoa Puffs cost _____, and the generic or store brand costs _____.

Our taste test put the generic brand in the lead, which allowed me to take the lesson one step further. Assuming that two boxes of cereal were eaten every month for twelve months, twenty-four boxes would cost _____.

If Frankie had insisted on staying with his preferred Cocoa Pebbles at _____, the yearly cost would have totaled _____. Thus a yearly difference in cost between the Cocoa Pebbles and the generic brand totals _____. I told him that since we were going to buy the generic brand, we would put the cost savings into his bank account, his reward for being a *Money-Wise* consumer.

THE POWER OF KIDS

When I was a kid, every Wednesday was bank day at school. Religiously, I deposited twenty-five cents in my bank savings envelope. After the deposits were posted in our bank books, the school delivered the deposits to the bank. Granted, twenty-five cents was worth a lot more in 1952 than it is in the 1990s. Yet that weekly deposit introduced the concept that my accumulated pennies, nickels, dimes, and quarters (all those wonderful coins) added up to a tidy sum by the end of the year, at least in my child's eye. And it was mine. I could add more or withdraw money whenever I wanted. School banking programs were everywhere in the fifties and then disappeared. Today they are making a comeback.

I didn't get an allowance when I was a kid, but I was able to earn my share of nickels for jobs around the house. I had a bonus too. Dad said I could keep any pennies I found lying around. So, sometimes my twenty-five-cent deposit per week was all I had; at other times it was a fraction of my money. I thought I was rich until I discovered some huge dill pickles that cost a nickel apiece. Once a month I withdrew five cents from my growing savings account and treated myself to a pickle.

A few years ago, the American Express Company and the Consumer Federation of America sponsored a nationwide test of the consumer knowledge of high school seniors. The results weren't terrific. Only 18 percent knew that the annual percentage rate (APR) is the best indicator of the true cost of a loan. Eighteen percent knew that rates for automobile insurance that were offered by different companies to consumers with comparable driving records in the same area could vary in premium cost.

At the same time, the National Council for Economic Education did a survey that included the general public, as well as high school and college students. Their results weren't so terrific either. Only 36 percent knew what a profit was. These statistics stress the importance of teaching your children all you can about money. Your *Money $ense* needs to be as sharp as possible to meet the challenges you have ahead with your children.

Kids are gullible and are easily roped in by the TV commercials that bombard them on a regular basis. One way to help them learn to be discerning consumers is to subscribe to *Zillions: Consumer Reports for Kids*. *Zillions* appeals to the ten- to fourteen-year-old crowd and routinely does comparison tests on items that kids spend their money on—from hamburgers to sneakers. It follows the advice and reputation of its well-known parent publication, *Consumer Reports*. Another excellent and current resource is *Money for Kids*, created by the folks who publish *Money* magazine.

Throughout this book, you will find series of Money-Wise Tips that are meant to enhance the commonsense approaches you already have in place. Use of that common sense and being consistent with your children will dramatically enhance the money sense you all are developing.

THREE POWERFUL *MONEY $ENSE* PARTNERS

Zillions: Consumer Reports for Kids

Encourage your kids to develop *Money-Wise* consumer habits by subscribing to *Zillions*—six issues per year—$16 annually. Contact: The Subscription Dept., P.O. Box 54861, Boulder, CO 80322, or call (800) 234-1645.

Young Americans Bank

The ideal bank for young people is Young Americans Bank, 311 Steele Street, Denver, CO 80206, (303) 321-2265. Write or call for information.

Money for Kids

A quarterly publication full of games, profiles of athletes, and music and movie stars who pay attention to money. Easy for kids to relate to because of the "star" quality. Lots of "how-to's." Write P.O. Box 30626, Tampa, FL 30630-0626.

Repeated studies and dialogue with parents shows that when kids are given information and the incentive to learn about money, they are quite astute. In my hometown of Denver, the Young Americans Bank was established several years ago. Customers come from every state in the country and range up to twenty-two years of age, with the average age being nine. The bank offers banking by mail, checking and savings accounts, credit cards, and loans. It also offers a variety of newsletters and summer classes. Kids learn to work in the shops of Young AmeriTowne and the Girls Can programs.

The Young Americans Bank carries more than 17,000 savings accounts, with an average balance of $357. The most common reasons their customers give for saving are: to buy a car, a computer, or Nintendo and Sega games. The bank has more than three hundred certificate of deposit holders, with an average balance in excess of $2,200. The average CD holder age is fifteen. The most common reason for buying CDs is for college funds.

The bank carries more than one thousand individual checking accounts, with an average balance of $390, average depositor age of sixteen, and the average check written for $35. The most common reason given for having a checking account was "experience." This "experience" is exercised most commonly by writing checks for shopping, mail orders, and pizza.

When kids hit the age of twelve, peer pressure becomes a primary factor in their decision making. That means you will have approximately ten years (ages two to twelve) to directly influence monetary behaviors and strategies. One of the most important things for you, as a parent, to do is to develop a type of strategy that fits with your personal family values and lifestyle. What works for your neighbors may not work for you. Your strategy has everything to do with income levels, the characteristics and traits of you and your kids, as well as spending and savings habits that you have brought to the party. The second part of finding the right strategy is to commit the necessary time to your child in teaching him or her your principles and values.

If you work for pay (everyone works—some get a paycheck, some don't), encourage your employer to subscribe to *Loose Change*. This is a bimonthly newsletter that is chock-full of information about money—yours and your kids'. Employers get a deep discount for volume purchases, paying as little as 26 cents an issue. As an individual, you can also subscribe—the cost is $30 per year. Created by the Financial Literacy Center and endorsed exclusively by the Institute of Certified Financial Planners, *Loose Change* has the best visual and content presentation I've come across. For information (and to get a sample copy) call: (800) 334-4094; fax: (616) 343-6260; or write to: Financial Literacy Center, 350 East Michigan Avenue, Suite 301, Kalamazoo, MI 49007-3851.

By challenging yourself (and your kids) with strategies to guide them through the money maze, you will have a far clearer understanding of what your family comprehends and needs.

Chapter Two

MODELING MADE EASY

Children are all ears and eyes when it comes to money, especially yours. The financial atmosphere in your home will play a major role in their monetary attitudes and behaviors. It's time to ask some questions. If you are married, do you and your spouse talk about money? If so, is it positive or negative? Does one scold the other about spending too much or not enough? Within your family, is money a taboo topic, or do you talk about it freely? Does having money, or the lack of money, create tension?

Adolescence and hormone changes start around age twelve, and kids begin to turn to their peers for advice, no matter how good the advice is, or how bad. You can be confident, however, that your earlier attitudes and practices will most likely continue to shape their decisions as they mature into adults.

 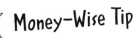

Money-Wise Tip

Don't ever underestimate the impact of your hard work in these years. Your youngsters' "bad attitudes" during the adolescent years rarely indicate permanent trends, even though many parents believe that what you see is what you get from now on.

MOM AND DAD MAY HANDLE MONEY DIFFERENTLY

Quick. Would you rather spend money or save it? Let's find out. Below is the *Money $ense Personality Quiz*. Part 1 is for you, and Part 2 is for your kids. (You will answer about them.)

Parents' Money $ense Personality Quiz

1. Is it important to own the "right things"?   Yes ___ No ___
2. If Aunt Martha left you a lot of money, would you put most of it in the bank?   Yes ___ No ___
3. Are you always in debt at the end of the month?   Yes ___ No ___
4. Are you afraid of being broke when you are old?   Yes ___ No ___
5. Do you usually say "we can't afford it," when your spouse says "we need it"?   Yes ___ No ___
6. Do you think about money a lot?   Yes ___ No ___
7. Do you use your credit cards to the limit?   Yes ___ No ___
8. Does having money give you a feeling of power or being liked?   Yes ___ No ___
9. Do you know how much money is in your purse or wallet, within $1?   Yes ___ No ___
10. Do you reward yourself for a good day or an achievement by going shopping?   Yes ___ No ___
11. Do you feel inadequate financially in comparing yourself to your friends?   Yes ___ No ___
12. Do you love watching investments and bank accounts increase?   Yes ___ No ___
13. Is it hard for you to make decisions about how to spend your money?   Yes ___ No ___
14. Do you use a shopping trip to make yourself feel better?   Yes ___ No ___
15. Do you buy unneeded items simply because they are on sale?   Yes ___ No ___

Transfer your Yes answers as Xs to the table below and total.

Spender: 1_____3_____7_____10_____11_____14_____15_____

Total *Spender* *Yes* Answers _____

Saver: 2_____4_____5_____6_____8_____9_____12_____13_____

Total *Saver* *Yes* Answers _____

So, how did you do? How do you think your child might answer those questions as an adult? To get a peek, answer the questions from the *Kids' Money $ense Personality Quiz* and see what may be in the future.

Kids' Money $ense Personality Quiz

If you have more than one child, make extra copies of the quiz or answer for each child with a different colored pen or pencil.

1. When given money, does your child save most of it? Yes ___ No ___

2. Does your child routinely save his money for special things he wants? Yes ___ No ___

3. When you go on trips, does your child want to buy souvenirs for friends? Yes ___ No ___

4. Does your child misplace or lose money? Yes ___ No ___

5. Does your child like to put money in his bank account? Yes ___ No ___

6. When you say "no" to a stop for pizza, does your child offer to pay for it? Yes ___ No ___

7. Is "Frankie has one" a reason your child uses for buying something? Yes ___ No ___

8. Is your child hesitant about spending any of his money? Yes ___ No ___

9. When shopping, does your child begin a lot of sentences with "I want"? Yes ___ No ___

10. When your child has a bad day, do you suggest a shopping trip?   Yes ___ No ___

11. If your child sees money on the ground, will he pick it up?   Yes ___ No ___

12. Does your child often ask for merchandise related to the latest "hot" movie?   Yes ___ No ___

13. Does your child like to collect things?   Yes ___ No ___

14. Does your child pay attention to sale ads or coupons in the newspaper?   Yes ___ No ___

15. Do you think your child is too generous?   Yes ___ No ___

Transfer your *Yes* answers as Xs to the table below and total.

Spender: 1_____ 3_____ 7_____ 10_____ 11_____ 14_____ 15_____

Total *Spender Yes* Answers _____

Saver: 2_____ 4_____ 5_____ 6_____ 8_____ 9_____ 12_____ 13_____

Total *Saver Yes* Answers _____

If either you or your kid(s) scored extremely high in any one category, it doesn't mean that you will be either tightfisted or a spendthrift for the rest of your life. Ideally, what you'd like to be is a careful and prudent spender, as well as a consistent, committed, and disciplined saver. Throughout *Raising Money-Wise Kids*, you will find quizzes and games that can be used as examples for teaching money behaviors and to modify existing behaviors. Not only will your kids learn some things, but you might too.

Money Opposites Attract

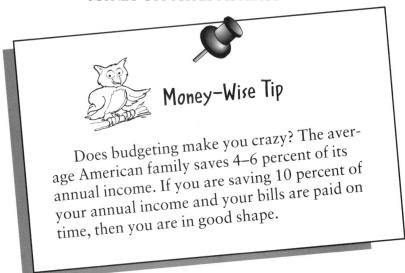

Money-Wise Tip

Does budgeting make you crazy? The average American family saves 4–6 percent of its annual income. If you are saving 10 percent of your annual income and your bills are paid on time, then you are in good shape.

It's well documented that disagreement about money is one of the top three leading causes of divorce in the U.S. (The others are sex and children.) Knowing whether you are a *spender* or a *saver* is important. Let's go a step further. See if you recognize yourself among the very general money personality classifications identified below.

- *The Bookkeeper.* You get charged up when your savings and investments grow. You balk whenever your spouse and/or kids want to spend anything. You also know, to the penny, what funds you have in bank accounts, as well as in your wallet or purse. For sure, you won't die broke. That's the good news; the bad news is that most people think you are a royal tightwad, when what you are really doing is keeping track.

- *The Good-Deeds Doer.* A saver, you're not. You are inclined to get rid of your money as fast as possible. You pick up meal checks routinely, and when there is a cause, you are there with your checkbook. Having the ability to spend money is directly tied in with receiving affection or acceptance from others.

- *The Chief.* Most likely, if there is a new toy on the market, you own it. Savings is not your thing, and you routinely plan what you'll buy with your next bonus. You believe that someday, if you work hard enough, your ship will come in. You also buy lottery tickets when the "pot" is worth many millions. To you, success means having money. The more, the better.

- *The Celebrator.* The last thing you want to do is balance your checkbook. You routinely plan the parties at work and in the neighborhood, and you pick up the majority of the bills for these parties. In doing this you make your spouse, who is probably a Bookkeeper, crazy. Your friends and co-workers think you are a hoot and are glad they have such a grand friend.

Any one of the money personalities is not necessarily bad; each has positive and negative sides. You can have traits of more than one personality, too. The objective is to get in balance. If you are married to a Celebrator and your finances appear out of control, action is called for. If you have always paid the bills and bought the groceries—switch. Let the Celebrator take over these responsibilities. You may have to step forward and agree to loosen up a little bit. But only if your spouse will agree to cut back.

Money-Wise Tip

If your spouse is disorganized, find a shoe box. It's the first step in getting him or her to gather receipts into one spot. Next, decide who is going to balance the checkbook and monitor the use of the credit cards to avoid abuse. Try this for a three- to six-month period and then switch responsibilities. You will probably find that both of you felt better about finances during one of the trial periods, and that person should then be in charge of those duties on a regular basis.

If you feel that things are seriously out of control, there is always help available, whether the problem is mounting debt or just spending too much. Here are several sources for help and credit counseling assistance.

The National Foundation for Consumer Credit
8611 Second Avenue, Suite 100
Silver Spring, MD 20910; (800) 388-2227

Family Service America, Inc.
11700 West Lake Park Drive
Milwaukee, WI 53224; (800) 221-2681

Christian Financial Concepts
601 Broad Street S.E.
Gainesville, GA 30501; (404) 534-1000

Consumer Credit Counseling Service
8611 Second Avenue, Suite 100
Silver Spring, MD 20910; (800) 388-2227
(This number will refer you directly to the nearest CCCS office.)

Consumer Fresh Start
601 Pennsylvania Avenue N.W., Suite 900
Washington, DC 20004; (800) 933-2372
(A national nonprofit organization that provides information and support for those going through or recovering from bankruptcy)

Bankcard Holders of America
560 Herndon Parkway, Suite 120
Herndon, VA 22070; (703) 481-1110
(Provides a credit and financial referral service and information about low interest/no annual fee and secured credit cards)

Do You Do As You Say, or Do You Do Something Different?

Kids need to hook into your chain of thought and logic. It makes no sense for you to lecture them about their extravagance and wastefulness when they want to replace their Sega Genesis or Nintendo video systems with the latest version if you borrow to buy a new car every year. When it comes to money and your kids, a critical *Money-Wise* rule is to be consistent. If you pay your kids an allowance and you have made a rule that there will be no advances on next week's allowance—hang tight. Your kids must learn to live within their own spending plans. If you regularly give in to their pleas for advances, wait a few years and see what they will do with credit cards.

THE PUPPIES OF THE YUPPIES BELIEVE THAT LOVE = THINGS

I'm not quite sure how it all began, but I believe a factor in a child's belief that love equals things started when both parents went to work. Perhaps, because of less time spent with the kids, guilt came into play. Some parents found that one surefire way to temporarily relieve guilt is to buy something. An Ann Landers column I clipped years ago contained this statement: "If you worry that your child doesn't have as much stuff as other kids in the neighborhood, the problem isn't your child, it's you."

So, what do you do when your kids badger you for more and more things? Or, how do you deal with the issue when your kid *must* have a $140 pair of sneakers—"all the other kids' parents bought them"? I can remember when a pair of Keds, the only sneakers available, was under $5. Let's hear it for the TV commercials and celebrity endorsements—they have greatly increased the cost of products that your kids covet.

The best answer is so simple that I'm almost embarrassed to say it: *Just Say No!* No doubt about it, your kids are going to be ticked at you, but in the end you're still Mom and Dad, and they are going to love you despite your refusal to give in to every whim they have. Remember, you are the adult, it's your house, and you pay the bills. Therefore, you're supposed to be in charge.

Most people think that $100+ for any pair of shoes is extravagant. However, if just plain No doesn't appeal, you can offer a compromise. Tell your son or daughter how much you allocate toward their shoes, and tell them that you will contribute that much to the overall cost. They had better start working and saving. It's interesting how individuals of all ages often reevaluate a financial situation when they realize that their own money must go into the pot to make it work. It wouldn't hurt to remind your kids that their feet are still growing and they may not be able to enjoy wearing their $140 investment in a few months.

When my younger daughter was fourteen, she was obsessed with brand labels. It was designer this and designer that—from the name on the back of her favorite jeans to the coveted $100+ purse she felt was essential to carry to school. My answer was a resounding NO! Today, when Frankie wants something he has seen on TV or something his friends have, she looks at me and rolls her eyes and says, "It's payback time."

Kids are astute in deciphering who is the easier mark, Mom or Dad. For the parent who is the soft touch (it's usually Mom) it might make sense to say something along this line: "That's an interesting idea to spend money on; let's talk to Dad and see if we agree that this will fit our spending plan." After they hear that a few times, most likely they will back off. If you are a single parent, try, "Let's get our calendar and mark off two weeks. If, at the end of two weeks, you and I *both* feel that you *need* this, then we will make a plan on how to budget for it."

MISTAKES TO AVOID

Above all, be candid with your kids about money. When they ask questions, answer them. That doesn't mean you have to tell them the exact family income. Most kids who are mid teens and younger can't comprehend the difference between $20,000 and $220,000 anyway. Either way, it sounds to them like a lot of money, and with that much money they think you can buy whatever they want. If money is tight in your home, let them know it. Explain why you can't buy the new Rollerblades and why you can't spend the money to go to McDonald's a couple of times a week like their friends do.

One of the smartest things I did with my kids was instituted when they were in their teens. When each one hit the age of sixteen, he or she got to be Mom's Personal Assistant. He or she did all the shopping with me and helped me pay all the bills. For the three-month summer period, the child wrote checks for the mortgage, cleaning, insurance, gasoline, entertainment, etc. Anything that demanded a check, the child wrote it. This hands-on experience showed them the reality of how much money was required to operate our household. They never forgot that.

In the early eighties, our family went through a financial disaster that impacted us for the next ten years. As soon as we recognized the depth and the seriousness of it, my husband and I called a family meeting. We told the kids what was going on—that, in the end, we could lose our home, our cars, even our business. We wouldn't be taking vacations, going out to dinner— good times *and* things that cost money would be deleted from our lifestyle. As it turned out, we lost everything.

What happened? I had a partner who got into trouble and drew money against a credit line that I had personally guaranteed through our business. When it was over, we lost in excess of a million dollars. It was a devastating time, but it could have been far worse if we hadn't called our family together and explained the circumstances. We made the upside and the downside of our new life together perfectly clear. The kids all pitched in—Amazing! Demands ceased and help was overflowing. They knew we were fighting for our lives; mentally, physically, financially, and even spiritually.

Tell the truth to your kids. If you are in trouble with money, let them know. If things are OK, they need to hear the good news too. It's amazing what young minds can construe to be a problem in a household when there is no problem. Keep your children posted. Sharing with your kids about how much things cost and how to use money brings you closer to each other. Soon, you will see your values growing in them. Values that they will, in turn, plant in their own kids.

The Money-Wise Parent's Creed

Teaching youngsters about money in their formative years can promote their intellectual development. It also helps adults rethink the basics of the value of money and the importance of making it grow. Children need to understand that we seldom receive anything for free. We work for what we receive. But if we work, we have a right to expect to benefit.

The Money-Wise Parent's Creed reads:

Parents provide their child with a hands-on learning experience while maintaining an atmosphere of trust and communication that is critical to the learning process. The parent teaches through experience, and the guiding principle is clear: Learn by doing.

If children function as responsible, cooperative, giving family members, and if they understand and accept the "game rules," they should participate in the benefits. Gifts of knowledge, understanding, and self-discipline can have their own rewards for you as a parent.

Chapter Three
YOUR INSURANCE IQ

Contrary to popular belief, life insurance is for the living—the folks who are left behind when you die (and you will, someday). There are three key reasons to buy life insurance:

1. To replace income if you die prematurely and family members depend on that income.
2. To provide money to buy out a business partner, repay business loans, or hire a successor in case of an owner's death.
3. To provide immediate, liquid money to pay estate taxes and burial costs.

The first reason should flash blinding lights at you. Unless you have megabucks, your family will need some financial protection if you are no longer in the picture. It doesn't matter whether you are the primary bread-winner or a homemaker. Either role, and all the ones in between, have a significant financial value to them.

As you begin to probe the maze that is insurance land—and believe me, it is a land unto itself—keep two rules in mind:

- Keep it simple. It is easy for your brain to go numb when considering insurance. If you don't understand the concept of an agent's proposal, ask for clarification. Don't invest unless and until you understand what is being offered, no matter how urgent the agent tells you it is.
- Frugality wins. Buy the lowest-cost insurance you can. Stretch your dollar and get the most for the least.

Life insurance is death protection—protection for those you love and care for. Other types of insurance go beyond pure death protection. They may have savings and investments attached to the policy—as well as a hefty price tag.

WHO NEEDS IT?

Not everyone. Below are a few scenarios. See where you fit:

You're married, with children. You need insurance, lots of it. Those kids have to be raised and educated, and it's not cheap. But you probably need the coverage only until they're on their own. Then this portion of your insurance can be canceled. Applause, applause for the income boost you feel after the kids go out on their own.

Money-Wise Tip

A rule of thumb for the dollar amount of life insurance coverage: Carry seven times your current annual earnings.

You're single with dependents. Dependents come in all age ranges: babies to elderly parents. Insurance alert! What happens if you die . . . tomorrow? If you are divorced and you have children, the kids may go to their father. Would he need to pay for child care, housekeeping, and other services if you weren't there? If so, a term policy of $50,000 to $100,000 on your life makes sense. What about the elderly parents? Who will provide care and supplement their income? A policy makes sense.

If you have children from a prior marriage, it can get complicated when it comes to money. A life insurance policy could be placed in a trust that would designate disbursements—your lawyer, insurance agent, or financial planner will help here after you tell him what you want.

If relatives or friends will become guardians, do your kids *and the guardians* a huge favor by having insurance proceeds to fund living expenses and education needs.

Money-Wise Tip

If you are under fifty and a nonsmoker, you can get a term insurance policy worth $100,000 for less than $200 a year—that's $16 per month!

You're rich. You may need money to pay estate taxes. If your investments are illiquid (real estate and privately owned companies fit here) you need money—ready cash.

Money-Wise Tip

If you are wealthy, you should consider setting up an irrevocable trust that will keep the insurance proceeds out of your estate. (See Wilson J. Humber, *Saving the Best for Last*, Moody.)

SURPRISE . . . SOCIAL SECURITY HAS SOMETHING FOR THE KIDS

If you (or your spouse) pay into Social Security, you have extra coverage. When Social Security was started in the 1930s, no one foresaw that kids would be covered . . . but guess what, those under nineteen are. There's more.

Social Security will pay an income to:
- surviving spouses age sixty and up.
- disabled spouses age fifty and up.
- a spouse who remarries a Social Security recipient. She can still collect on the previous spouse's account if it pays more.
- a single, surviving spouse caring for a child under sixteen or one who was disabled before twenty-two.
- unmarried dependent children under eighteen.
- unmarried dependent children under nineteen if still in secondary school.
- parents at least sixty-two and older who got at least half their support from the worker who died.

There is also a lump-sum death benefit of $255 to the surviving spouse.

Money-Wise Tip

Make sure you check your Social Security record every few years. The form PEBES—for Personal Earnings Benefit Estimate Statement—is quite easy to read. Call (800) 234-5772 for Form SSA-7004.

WHAT'S WHAT IN INSURANCE

There are two types of life insurance and a zillion hybrids. *Term* and *whole life* are the most common. *Universal life* was introduced several years ago and combines aspects of the two (kind of). Then there are variations of all three.

Term insurance works well to replace lost income. The key parts of term insurance are:

- You pay premiums every year (monthly, quarterly, or annually). Insurance stays in force until you stop paying. There is no cash build-up or savings benefit.
- With ordinary term, your premium increases slightly each year. You can buy a level term, which keeps the premium fixed for several years.
- Costs are determined by age, whether or not you smoke, and gender (usually women pay less, although some insurance companies use unisex rates).
- Companies vary in what they charge. A policy with the same dollar amount of coverage can cost twice as much at another company.
- It should be guaranteed renewable—which means you don't have to requalify with a physical every year.

Whole-life insurance has a savings account attached to it. The longer you are in it, the more savings you will have. In order to achieve this, whole-life premiums are much greater than term premiums. When whole life is proposed it is always accompanied by illustrations, the "What-ifs." Projections for growth on the savings side are *always* inflated. They are *never guaranteed!*

It's easy to be misled by interest rates that are quoted to you. Insurance companies routinely announce high interest rates to keep policyholders at bay, then they increase their operating expenses and charges for mortality (the death benefit). These expenses are deducted from your cash value before any interest is paid.

Universal life offers some flexibility. You can get a guaranteed policy amount for when you die; you can accumulate tax-deferred cash; you can pay extra premiums early on so that extra cash will build up (theoretically), and pay future premiums. Here's the catch: If the interest rates projected in your illustration are not achieved (after all, rates do vary), your cash won't build up to pay the premiums down the road.

Once you are into a universal life policy, it can be quite expensive to cancel it. In fact, you can lose 100 percent of the money you put up on the savings side . . . and this is insurance?

Pay the Piper

How much should you pay for life insurance? The amount you pay each year is called a *premium*. After you decide how much life insurance you need in your particular situation, the amount of your annual premium is based on four calculations.

- Your age
- Your current state of health
- How much money the insurance company can earn by investing your premium dollars until your death
- The insurance company's expenses for paying the agent's commission and mailing you bills.

How Much Cheaper Is Term Insurance?

Picking only from lower-cost companies, the following table shows dramatically how much more coverage you get for your money with term insurance. The premiums quoted are for a $100,000 policy for a nonsmoking male. Rates for women will be less. The term premiums rise as you get older; those for cash-value policies can stay level for life. But in terms of what's affordable at any given age, term insurance wins hands down.

Remember, your objective is *life insurance*. Any $100,000 policy will pay $100,000 to your beneficiaries if you die. If you die after ten years of paying premiums, wouldn't you rather have paid ten years of term premiums and invested the difference? Universal life and whole life also include the option of borrowing against the money you've paid—it's not just insurance; it's an investment. But as an investment, it stacks up poorly. The recommendation: Buy term insurance for your insurance needs, and invest the difference elsewhere.

Yearly Premiums for a $100,000 Policy			
Age	Term Insurance	Universal-Life Insurance	Whole-Life Insurance
30	$136	$ 590	$ 875
35	140	746	1,095
40	163	950	1,391
45	205	1,217	1,776
50	320	1,583	2,311
55	440	2,078	3,038
60	610	2,741	4,717
65	980	3,665	5,376

Source: National Insurance Consumer Organization

How to Find Cheap Insurance

There are two ways to find the companies whose rates will fit your spending plan.

1. *Check out the National Insurance Consumer Organization (NICO).* In early 1991, it set out the *maximum* rates that consumers ought to pay for annual renewable term insurance (see page 49). Use NICO as a guideline to what your insurance should cost. Their guidelines are updated annually. If your coverage costs more, it's too expensive. You can probably find lower rates than these, however, by checking the insurance-quote services indicated below.

   Write NICO at:
   121 N. Payne St.
   Alexandria, VA 22314

2. *Locate a computerized price-quote service.* All you provide is your age, gender, and health status, and the computer starts to crunch. It's a good idea to recheck every three to five years.

- *Insurance Information* (800) 472-5800. For $50, Insurance Information sends you the names and phone numbers of the five insurers that offer the lowest term rates for someone with your stats. Your $50 will be refunded if you don't find a policy more than $50 cheaper than the one you presently have. Insurance Information does not sell insurance.

Other price-quote services are offered by insurance agents. There is no obligation to buy, and *no salesperson* will call to sell you a policy. In other words, you are in charge.

- *TermQuote* : Dayton, OH (800) 444-8376
- *SelectQuote*: San Francisco, CA (800) 343-1985
- *InsuranceQuote*: Chandler, AZ (800) 972-1104

Caution. Price quotes are accompanied by brief descriptions (not with great detail) of the policies. Make sure you ask for *annual renewable term* quotes. Many will give a reentry or revertible term, which means you have to requalify in a few years (as in health).

Two groups that will connect or refer you to individuals who sell low-load or no-load policies are:

- *Fee for Service* (800) 874-5662. This service is located in Tampa, Florida, and will direct you to financial planners who sell low-load cash value insurance. The fees for consultation or analysis of current policies run about $100–$150 an hour. The policies they offer typically charge less than 20 percent of a usual agent's commission on similar policies.
- *Life Insurance Advisors' Association* (LIAA) (800) 521-4578. LIAA is a national association consisting of fee-only advisors. Members' objectives are to offer unbiased life insurance; low cost, non-commissioned insurance; and independent reviews of policies currently held. Any policy recommended is not commission motivated. You will pay the advisor an independent fee. Remember, there is no free lunch.

As a guideline, the following is a table of rates supplied by NICO:

THE MOST YOU SHOULD PAY FOR TERM INSURANCE*

Nonsmokers' Annual Premium			Smokers' Annual Premium		
Age	Male	Female	Age	Male	Female
18-30	$ .76	$ .68	18-30	$1.05	$ 1.01
31	.76	.69	31	1.10	1.05
32	.77	.70	32	1.15	1.10
33	.78	.71	33	1.21	1.15
34	.79	.72	34	1.28	1.20
35	.80	.74	35	1.35	1.25
36	.84	.78	36	1.45	1.31
37	.88	.82	37	1.56	1.38
38	.92	.86	38	1.68	1.45
39	.97	.90	39	1.81	1.52
40	1.03	.95	40	1.95	1.60
41	1.09	1.00	41	2.12	1.73
42	1.17	1.05	42	2.30	1.89
43	1.25	1.10	43	2.50	2.05
44	1.34	1.15	44	2.72	2.22
45	1.45	1.20	45	2.95	2.40
46	1.59	1.29	46	3.22	2.59
47	1.74	1.41	47	3.52	2.79
48	1.91	1.53	48	3.85	3.01
49	2.10	1.66	49	4.21	3.23
50	2.30	1.76	50	4.60	3.50
51	2.49	1.90	51	4.97	3.79
52	2.70	2.06	52	5.38	4.10
53	2.96	2.22	53	5.82	4.44
54	3.40	2.40	54	6.29	4.80
55	3.40	2.60	55	6.80	5.20
56	3.66	2.79	56	7.31	5.58
57	3.94	3.00	57	7.87	5.99
58	4.23	3.22	58	8.46	6.43
59	4.55	3.46	59	9.10	6.90
60	4.90	3.70	60	9.80	7.40
61	5.43	3.98	61	10.83	7.95
62	6.02	4.28	62	11.98	8.54
63	6.67	4.60	63	13.25	9.18
64	7.40	4.93	64	14.65	9.86
65	8.20	5.30	65	16.20	10.60

* Per $1,000 of coverage, per year. Source: National Insurance Consumer Organization

Notes to the table:
- The table shows the premium rate per $1,000 of coverage. If you're buying a $100,000 policy, multiply the cost by 100 and add $60 (for the insurer's fixed policy expenses) to see the most that you should pay.
- Policies smaller than $100,000 cost a little more. Policies written for $500,000 and up cost a little less.
- Nonsmoker rates are for preferred health risks.
- The relative rates for smokers keep rising as insurers see how fast smokers are dying.
- Rates and companies may have changed by the time you read this.

For an update, check the latest NICO guide: *Taking the Bite Out of Insurance: How to Save Money on Life Insurance*, available at bookstores or by contacting NICO, 121 N. Payne St., Alexandria, VA 22314.

Finally, one other way to cut out the middleman (agent) is to buy a no-load policy directly from the insurance company. No-load means no commissions are paid, which becomes attractive when whole-life or cash-value insurance is your choice. Two of the best are:

- USAA Life, San Antonio, TX (800) 531-8000

Individual representatives, not commissioned salespeople, will answer your questions and send you policy quotations based on your individual needs. The only policies they offer are underwritten by USAA Life Insurance, which is rated A++ by A. M. Best; AAA by S&P; and AA-1 by Moody's.

- Ameritas, Houston, TX (800) 552-3553

Individual representatives, not commissioned salespeople, of Ameritas Life Insurance respond to your questions. The company is highly rated: A+ by A. M. Best; AA by S&P; and A by Weiss Research. Note: Ameritas offers other policies that are sold by agents, but to get the direct sales office you must use the toll-free number listed above.

Who's the Fairest in the Land?

Most insurance companies quote their A. M. Best rating when queries are made about safety. When Executive Life failed in 1991, A. M. Best was still rating the company A+! Go ahead and fake a yawn if you get the Best rating. What you want is the Weiss Research rating. Weiss Research is the newest rating kid on the block—and the most conservative. Before Executive Life went belly-up, the Weiss rating had been reduced to D.

To date, libraries don't carry Weiss. You can contact Weiss directly at (800) 289-9222. Your cost will be $15.

Agents won't tell you if the insurance company they are illustrating/promoting is unsafe. Nor will they tell you that any investment projections are unrealistic. You may get a low quote for future premiums, and they may be dependent on the company making a 15 to 20 percent profit on its investment portfolio. That just isn't realistic, so forget it. And it is a rare agent who will tell you that you can get a better deal someplace else.

To protect yourself, *you* must be informed and take responsibility. Insurance moneys are very serious dollars. If I were in your insurance shoes, here's what I would do:

- Buy annual, renewable term insurance.
- Stop smoking. If you are weed-free for two years, you are considered a nonsmoker. You save big on premium dollars each year.
- When the kids are gone and financial responsibilities decline or disappear, you retire, and your spouse is self-sufficient, cancel your policy. And congratulate yourself.

Most Need It . . . Few Have It

Of all the insurances, disability is the one that is the most ignored. Too few carry it; those who do, often don't carry enough. If you get a serious illness or are in an accident that prevents you from doing your work, where will the money come from to pay your bills? Rents and mortgages have to be paid. And your family would appreciate it if the heat stayed on and there was food on the table.

Insurance companies have three definitions of "disabled." They are:

- Totally incapacitated and confined to bed
- Unable to work at any occupation
- Unable to work at a specific occupation

Being totally incapacitated and confined to bed means just that. You cannot leave your bed, your room, your home. You are stuck. Someone who fits in this category could have a terminal disease or could have been involved in an accident that has left him paralyzed. It could also involve a situation where one has to remain immobile so that bones or surgery can heal.

Being unable to work at any occupation could involve either a physical problem or a mental disease. Many people are able to work at a variety of occupations. Usually, what they need is the training to qualify them.

The third definition of disability relates to a specific occupation. A person who makes her living as a concert pianist and is in an accident in which she loses the use of her right hand has a problem.

Two-thirds of the work I do involves speaking. If I were to get a disease or suffer an injury that impacted my vocal cords, I might not be able to speak. If I couldn't speak, who would hire me to give a speech? No one. In fact, the disability policy I carry covers exactly that.

As a rule, the sooner the benefits of a policy begin, the more costly it will be. According to data, most people who are temporarily disabled return to work after an accident or illness within twenty-one days of the onset of the disability. With that in mind, explore the costs of policies that commence ninety days after a disability, versus a thirty-day wait. Why? You will save big bucks in premiums. And if you have three- to six-months' living expenses in the bank, as you should, you won't need the money until then anyway.

Money-Wise Tip

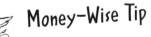

USAA in San Antonio, Texas, is one of the few disability underwriters that will sell direct to the consumer without working through an independent agent. Call them for a direct quote at (800) 531-8000.

What It Says Is What You Get

Contract language is critical, especially when it comes to insurance. Any disability policy that you purchase should have a *noncancelable clause*. This means that as long as you pay the premiums on time, the insurance company cannot cancel it.

A *guaranteed annual premium* is a must. It means that the insurance company cannot increase the premium that has already been declared within the policy. As a rule, the younger you are when you purchase your policy, the less the premium costs will be.

If you become disabled, a *waiver of premiums clause* is most welcome. It says that if you are disabled, you don't have to pay the ongoing premiums to keep the policy in force. This option will cost extra money.

An excellent disability policy also includes a *residual benefit disability payment*. This means that the policy will pay the difference between the income that you are able to earn after you are disabled and the original amount of your guaranteed monthly payment.

What You Don't Need

There are two insurances that you probably don't need. The first is children's insurance. If Grandma tells you that she is going to buy her favorite grandson a policy to pay for his college education, tell her to pass on it. She would get a better return putting her money into a passbook savings account.

The other insurance deals with school. It is quite common to have your child come home with information on student policies at his school. Pass on this if you already have adequate health insurance coverage.

Insurance—life, disability, health, and others—must be purchased with a *Money-Wise* awareness. If it isn't, you will overpay. You could buy the wrong type at the wrong time and not know until years have passed. Not good. Having the right insurance coverage for your particular needs is imperative in building your financial security. This is one area where it makes sense to hurry. The appropriate insurances set a strong foundation in your home.

Chapter Four

WHERE THERE IS A WILL, THERE IS A WAY

In *Money Sense: What Every Woman Must Know to Be Financially Confident*, I wrote about my friend Nicole. Nicole had come for dinner and spent the night. In my kitchen is a large unframed oil painting of geraniums. She loves it and asked me if I died before she did, would I leave it to her? "Absolutely" was my response.

Knowing that I wouldn't be rushing to my attorney the next day to change my will, I immediately wrote a note to give the painting to Nicole if I died and taped it on the back of the canvas for my family. I then told my husband that it should go to Nicole. Until I redid my will, my family was told that this is what I wanted done with the painting.

If you were to die tomorrow, does your family know what you want done with your assets, your treasures, and most important, your kids? You will die someday. If it were tomorrow, is your financial house in order, or are you like 75 percent of America—tomorrow is another day?

Your daughters may love your jewelry. If you leave your jewelry to both of them, what happens if one moves a thousand miles from the other? Who decides who gets what, or how do they share? Few people can reach perfect accord over what to do with mutually owned property.

Anything that can't be divided should either be left to one person or sold and the proceeds split. Few really plan for death or for those they leave behind. If no planning is done, those who are left behind may end up living with a monster.

I came across this column several years ago, saved it, and now pass it on to you. It has been repeated numerous times in Ann Landers's syndicated column and is reprinted with her permission:

DEAR READERS: If you want to do something nice for your family, get your affairs in order.

I came across this gem in *The Survivor*, a splendid magazine for widowed people. I obtained permission from the author, Judge Sam Harrod III, of Eureka, Illinois, to reprint it.

IF YOU DON'T HAVE A WILL, YOUR STATE HAS ONE FOR YOU

The Statutory "Will" of John Doe

I, John Doe, make this my "will," by failing to have a will of my own choice prepared by my attorney.

1. I give one-half of all my property, both personal and real estate, to my CHILDREN, and the remaining one-half to my WIFE.

2. I appoint my WIFE as Guardian of my CHILDREN, if she survives me, but as a safeguard, I require that:

   a. my WIFE make written account every year to Probate Court, explaining how and why she spent money necessary for the proper care of our CHILDREN;

   b. my WIFE file a performance BOND, with sureties, to be approved by Probate Court, to guarantee she will properly handle our children's money;

   c. when our CHILDREN become adults, my WIFE must file a complete, itemized, written account of everything she has done with our children's money;

   d. when our SON and DAUGHTER become age 18, they can do whatever they please with their share of my estate;

   e. no one, including my WIFE, shall have the right to question how our CHILDREN spend their shares;

3. If my WIFE does not survive me, or dies while any of our CHILDREN are minors, I do not nominate a Guardian of our CHILDREN, but hope relatives and friends may mutually agree on one, and if they cannot agree, the Probate Court can appoint any Guardian it likes, including a stranger.

4. I do not appoint an Executor of my estate, and hope the Probate Court appoints someone I would approve.

5. If my WIFE remarries, the next husband:

   a. shall receive one-third of my WIFE'S property;

   b. need not spend any of his share on our CHILDREN, even if they need support, and

   c. can give his share to anyone he chooses, without giving a penny to our CHILDREN.

6. I do not care whether there are ways to lower my death taxes, and know as much as possible will go to the Government, instead of my WIFE and our CHILDREN. In witness whereof, I have completely failed to make a different will of my own choice with the advice of my attorney, because I really do not care to go to all that bother, and I adopt this, by default, as my "will."

(no signature required)

Sounds pretty bleak, doesn't it? Without writing one, everyone has a will. If you don't choose one on your own, you get the one your state picks for you. Would you choose the one from the Ann Landers column? I think not.

Rarely do I see people under forty with a will that is properly put together, but I do believe that wills should be written as soon as you begin to acquire any assets or *if you have children.*

The average working person spends more than 10,000 days making money. It seems shortsighted not to spend one day making a determination of where your assets should go when you die. Unfortunately, more than 80 percent of those who will die today leave no will. When you leave no will, the state in which you reside will step in and assist your heirs in determining exactly where the assets will go.

Make It So

Wills are important, and yours should be written now. If you are shopping around for an attorney, by all means sit down and make a holographic will that will work until you can get a formal document drawn up. A holographic will is merely one which is handwritten by you. In it, you will recite who you are, your permanent address (and, if applicable, secondary address), your place of birth, and your marital status.

Your spouse should do the same. If there are any previous marriages, make sure that information is included, and include the names and addresses of your immediate family, which would include your sons, daughters, siblings, and parents.

If you have ever created a trust, make sure you indicate the appropriate title for that. If you are entitled to any pensions, profit sharing, or other funds, include that information. If you have insurance policies, include the numbers and beneficiaries—both primary and secondary—and the necessary information if you are covered under any group policies. Have a complete list of all your assets, as well as their current market value. If any of your assets are held under a name different from your present one, make sure that it is specified. If you have any safe deposit boxes, state where they are located.

You should indicate the name and address of an executor or executrix of your estate, as well as a guardian if you have children under eighteen. You also may need a trustee for the management of your assets until your beneficiaries reach the age in which the actual distribution will be granted.

If you have any stocks, bonds, limited partnerships, retirement accounts, passbooks, time deposits, or any other marketable assets, make sure they are included, as well as the location of your tax returns for the last three years.

Finally, make sure that you spell out exactly what your plans are for your beneficiaries.

Then sign it.

This document acts only as a temporary instrument. It is much preferred that you have an attorney who specializes in estate planning look it over and make whatever changes are necessary. If you have already listed the location of your various assets, that should reduce your bill substantially. Remember, changes can be made as the circumstances warrant, and an addendum, or codicil, can be added to your new will.

If you have made any previous wills, state in your new one that it revokes any previous testaments. In addition, to be safe, destroy all copies of old wills. If you have out-of-state assets, make sure you deal with them correctly. Some states will demand that you go through a separate probate in their state. It might be wise to liquidate your assets and bring them into the current state in which you reside and/or set up a separate will that covers that state's laws.

If you have any personal belongings of sentimental value, attach to the will a letter of intent that states exactly who gets which belongings. If the majority of your property is divided by percentage, the items covered in your letter of intent will be excluded from a distribution of the primary estate.

DOING IT YOURSELF VS. PAYING A LAWYER

You are probably wondering, if you have done all this, why you need an attorney. For two reasons: First, the tax laws that deal with estates and trusts keep changing. Unless you are in the legal profession, it is highly unlikely that you are going to be up-to-date on the current laws.

If your last will is dated prior to September 13, 1981, and you are married, call your attorney today to revise it. Any wills dated before September 13, 1981 pay more in estate taxes. Anything written after that date is covered under current law. The current law says that no gift or estate taxes will be due on property left to your spouse. Second, there are often inaccuracies in your wording, which could actually change your intent.

Homemade wills may be quite clear to you but vague to others. A trip to the local court may be necessary to determine what you really meant. That's only one reason it makes more sense to have an attorney draw yours up. For a fairly simple will, an attorney should charge from $150 to $300—you can pay big dollars if it is complex. Here's why an attorney, who specializes in wills, makes money sense:

- To say exactly what you mean: is it niece Mary or Aunt Mary who gets your jewels?
- To advise you on how to hold property.
- To reduce death taxes. If your estate is under $600,000, you owe Uncle Sam nothing; but not all states match the federal $600,000 floor for exemption.
- To advise you on any twists in the law—i.e., if you leave Aunt Mary your home and there is a mortgage on it, your estate may be required to pay off the mortgage, thus leaving niece Mary out of getting the cash you thought would go her way.
- To ask you questions you might not think about—do you want a beneficiary's share to go to her children or her spouse if she dies before your treasures get to her . . . or do you want it to go to a battered women's shelter?
- To make your will challenge-proof. Believe me, challenges arise. You need the right number of witnesses (this varies from state to state) who could testify that you signed it, you were in sound mind, etc.

For the do-it-yourselfers, one of the best guides is Nolo's *Simple Will Book* by Denis Clifford. It's available in many bookstores, or you can contact Nolo Press at 950 Parker St., Berkeley, CA 94710.

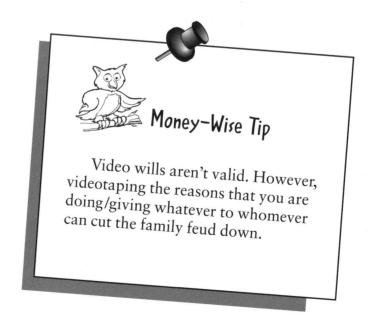

Money-Wise Tip

Video wills aren't valid. However, videotaping the reasons that you are doing/giving whatever to whomever can cut the family feud down.

CHANGING YOUR WILL

When should you update your will? One time to do so is when you move from one state to another. It is important to check whether the probate laws are comparable in your new state. If you have moved, play it safe and have a local attorney check your will.

Another reason to update your will would be that the executor you have selected is no longer acceptable or has died; in this case you should name a new one. (It is often a good idea to choose an executor or executrix who is younger than you are.) In addition, if you have divorced or remarried or if the number of children you have has increased or decreased, this should be noted in your will. And if your family size has increased with grandchildren and in-laws, you may want to include them.

If the value of your estate has risen or substantially declined, it may make sense to look over the details of distribution you previously stated. Or if you have disposed of any real property listed in your previous wills, you should adjust the documents accordingly. I recommend an overhaul of your will approximately every three years. With the way our laws keep changing, as well as our own personal objectives, it makes sense. If you have only a few changes, it is not necessary to have the whole will rewritten. Changes can be handled with a codicil. A codicil is merely an afterthought added to the will and then initialed or signed separately.

You should change your will when:

- You have children—either by birth, adoption, or marriage.
- Your net worth takes a jump, or a dive.
- Your child(ren) marries, separates, or divorces.
- One of your heirs dies.
- You have a child who has an illness that may go on forever.
- There are any changes in the inheritance or property laws—federal or the state you live in.

Money-Wise Tip

To change a will you can (1) make a new one that revokes all wills and codicils before it; or (2) tear it up. If you choose #2, do it in front of witnesses and state that the will is no longer valid. Make sure you track down any copies and destroy those too.

If you have only one child, do a will, and then have another child, what happens? Without being specifically mentioned, the second child will get something. It could be the same . . . or different. The deciding factor is dependent on what state you live in and what its laws are. Both birth and adopted children are treated the same. Stepchildren aren't. Unless you specifically say your stepchildren are to have something, they won't.

Money-Wise Tip

Whenever there is a new tax law, ask your attorney if the new laws impact you.

No Excuses, Please

People come up with plenty of excuses for not having a will—from "I'm not dying this year" to "I have nothing to leave anybody" to "It's too morbid to think about death" to "Tomorrow is another day."

You and your will:
- You can/should have a will even if your financial affairs are a mess.
- When you do yours, only you and the attorney who writes it up will know the contents. Everyone else finds out when you die (unless you tell before).
- You don't have to have any of your assets appraised—just say which person you want to have it. (Note: I said "which person," as in singular. Don't do sharing with your favored folks . . . it just doesn't work.)
- No one has to know what you own—again, unless you tell them.
- If you change your mind about whom you want to have what, change your will—the only time it becomes permanent is when you die.

Doing a will can be fun. Let's do a little visionary work. Imagine how grateful your niece will be when she receives the treasure she has always told you she loves. This is your chance to have the last word . . . a tactic many love and rarely get to act on.

When I wrote *Money Sense,* I knew that I was long overdue in doing another will. My excuse . . . tomorrow was another day. When my friend Nicole said she would love one of my paintings, I ended up calling my children and several close friends and asking if I had any item that they might like if I died. After the initial shock at my question, we brainstormed about my various treasures. From my library to my pearls, from the lead toy soldiers to an afghan I had made, each found a home. What homes do you want your memories and treasures to go to?

To recap, without a will, here's how the courts will deal with your former life:
- Depending on state law, not all of the property may go to your spouse.
- Your grown children may get some of the money that was meant for your spouse, leaving your spouse with too little to live on.
- A court will choose your children's guardian.

63

- Stepchildren usually get nothing.
- Your friends get nothing.
- Your family might battle with the courts.
- Your family will battle with each other.
- A fight might break out among your relatives over who gets the kids and who runs their inheritance (if there is one).
- A bigger fight breaks out over the kids if there is no money to raise them.
- There probably won't be a trust to take care of your young children's money (if there is any).
- Part of the money that you meant for your spouse may go to your young kids. Your spouse, as guardian, can use it only for their support. The court will have to approve certain expenditures and will require an annual accounting.
- Part of the family might be cut off from the family business.
- A closely held business may have to be sold fast, because the estate might not be permitted to run it or your family needs money to pay estate taxes.
- You can't leave your favorite things to your favorite people.
- Your unfavorite people could end up with your favorite things—this is a bummer!
- The state bends over backward to keep money safe for young children—then hands it all over to them when they reach majority, usually age eighteen. If they're not ready for the responsibility, too bad.
- You can't leave a contribution to a church or charity.
- Your retarded or handicapped child may inherit money, disqualifying him or her from government aid.
- Everyone will be mad at you.

Most of you think that even without a will, property passes to the person who most ought to own it. What's "right" under state law may be all wrong for your family and friends. What happens if you and your spouse both die in an accident? Now, who gets your property, your treasures, your kids? Wouldn't you want to select the child care provider—now called a guardian? Laws vary, but the following table gives you a general idea of what could happen if you die *intestate*. This means you left no will—at least, no one could find one.

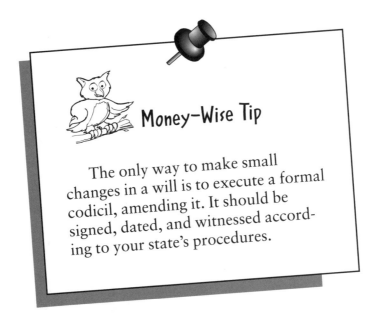

Money-Wise Tip

The only way to make small changes in a will is to execute a formal codicil, amending it. It should be signed, dated, and witnessed according to your state's procedures.

Here's what's in store for you if:

You are:	*And die without a will, your property will go:*
• Married, with children	Depending on the state and the size of the estate, all to the surviving spouse, or part to the spouse, part to the children. The spouse may get one-third or one-half of your separately owned property, part or all of the community property, and all of the joint property you held together.
• Unmarried, with children	To your children but probably not to stepchildren. The court appoints a guardian for your minor children and their funds.

WHY BOTHER ... ?

You may think, *If I tell my friends and relatives who will get what, why bother with the will stuff?* Here are a few good reasons:

- To name a guardian for your children and your children's inheritance.
- To give away property you didn't expect to own. This usually happens with accidents. If your spouse dies and you die a few days, months, even a year later, the state will decide what's what with your property and your kids.
- To dispose of any property you get after your death. You actually can get rich when you're dead. If you die in an accident, a court might bring in a big judgment payable to your estate. What do want done with the money?
- To avoid family uproar.
- To avoid all the problems of joint ownership and named beneficiaries.
- To dispose of your half of jointly owned property, if both you and the other owner die in the same accident.
- To make sure that your probate-avoiding tactics work. If you set up a living trust, you need a "pour-over will." It guarantees that any property you forgot, or that comes to you after your death, will be added to your trust.

Money-Wise Tip

Get it in writing. The only time "oral wills" will be valid is if you are in imminent danger of death, there isn't much property involved, and several witnesses have heard you.

WHO SHOULD GET THE CHILDREN?

The first response is usually Grandma. Certainly, grandparents want the best for their grandchildren. But if Grandma is seventy-five, this is not such a hot idea. First, she has raised her family—no parent in his or her right mind covets raising kids through the teen years again. Second, you are setting your kids up for losing their new parents in a fairly short period of time. Grandma could easily die naturally within the next five to ten years.

Now, if Grandma is young (under fifty-five), that's another story. But your better bet is a sibling. Or if you have a "second family," an older married child, even a close friend who shares your values and way of life, they might be the best choices.

If your kids are old enough to understand the question, ask them who they would want to live with if something happened to you. The older your kids are, the more critical it is that they be involved in the decision. But if they disagree, you need to decide—don't split them up.

In addition to the "care" guardian, you need someone to handle the money side. Usually, the care guardian does both. But if he or she is not great at handling money, it may be *Money Wise* to get someone who has common sense in the money department.

If you are divorced, the kids usually go to the ex-spouse if he or she wants them. Courts rarely step in if the other parent is fit (unfit could mean abandonment, no contact or financial support for at least two years, drug addiction, etc.).

Put in your will why you chose the person to be the guardian of your kids. Spell it out clearly so that your kids are protected. The last thing they need is to be Ping-Pong balls.

How to Leave Money for Young Children

1. Name a legal guardian for the children's funds. State law determines what can be spent on the children and what investments can be made. The guardian makes an annual accounting to the court. When the child comes of age—at eighteen or twenty-one, depending on your state—he or she gets the money.
2. Use the Uniform Gifts to Minors Act (UGMA). In most states, you have to make the gift during your lifetime, rather than by will. The funds are left to an adult who acts as custodian for the child. The law determines how the money can be spent and invested. A custodian usually has more flexibility in handling money than a guardian does, such as not having to go to court every time something is bought or sold. The funds go to the child when he or she comes of age, usually at eighteen.
3. Use the Uniform Transfers to Minors Act (UTMA), if your state has adopted it. UTMA allows transfers by will, as well as gifts during your lifetime. The custodian can hold the assets until the child is eighteen or twenty-one (twenty-five in California). This is much better than the UGMA—a few years extra in maturity can do wonders in preserving a nest egg.
4. Leave the money in trust. This is the best solution for sums over $20,000 or so. Your trustee—a relative, friend, attorney, or bank—manages the inheritance and pays it to the child according to your instructions. Money can be doled out as needed for the child's education and living expenses. The remainder is turned over to the child at the age you set—it could be twenty-five or thirty.

You can state that the child gets the money all at once or in installments—say, at ages twenty-five and thirty. You might want to give the trustee the power to withhold payments, if it seems to be in the child's best interest. (Young people have been know to join cults—is this where you want your money to go?) You might make the child co-trustee in his or her early twenties. Sharing in investment decisions without yet having to handle the money solo makes sense. It's a good learning tool for his future.

Set up a single trust for all the children. If one child has big medical bills, they can be paid out of common funds without looting that child's basic inheritance. Or, if you have already financed two kids through college, you may want to designate a greater amount to your third one for college costs, then do a split. Typically, all the money stays in trust until the youngest child reaches an age you specify. Then the trust dissolves, and everyone gets his or her appointed share.

You probably feel that assembling all those bits and pieces is a tedious and time-consuming chore. But you can be assured that it will be time well spent should the unforeseeable occur. Do yourself a favor, as well as your heirs, and make sure you have this base covered.

Providing for your family means planning ahead . . . for whatever. Any person who cares for his or her spouse, children, parents, friends, church, and community will not put off any longer this critical document. There is only one time that will work. *It's called now.*

Nothing Is Free

When an attorney prepares your will, you will sign it in the presence of witnesses. You receive a copy, and your attorney keeps a copy in his or her vault. That's the one service an attorney offers free—vault storage for your will. Granted, your will won't take up much space, but there's a reason behind the freebie.

Your attorney bills you for the legal expenses of drawing up your will. When you die, your heirs will need an attorney to take your will through the court process of *probate*—changing the names on all your assets as directed by your will. Who best to do it but the folks who drew it up? Ah, a method behind his/her madness!

The legal fees for handling an estate through probate can be many times the fees charged for writing the will. In many states, probate fees are based on a percentage of the gross value of the estate. If you have a young attorney, he or she will hope to outlive you and earn the probate fees. An older attorney will have shelves of wills in the vault, waiting to be probated by a younger partner.

Alas, there's never a free lunch. Your attorney may have a breakfast on what he made preparing your will. When you die, he takes a vacation!

PROBATE

Probate has nothing to do with taxes. It is the legal process of changing the title on assets you own into the names of your heirs when you die. The probate court resolves disputes, pays off creditors, inventories your estate, and distributes your assets. If there's no will, it distributes your assets according to state law. Now, this can be scary. The reprint of Ann Landers's column is a real wake-up call!

This process presents a double whammy:

1. It's expensive—legal fees can be as much as 10 percent of the total value of your gross estate. In states where the gross valuation of assets is the basis for determining legal fees, the court does not deduct the amount of any loans—including mortgages—from the asset side. Ouch!
2. It can take a long time (it shouldn't, but it often does). It's not uncommon for estates to take more than two years to process. If you own property in states other than your residence, the process is repeated in each state where you own real estate.

When probate is prolonged, it's rarely a defect of the court—probate courts are fairly efficient. The snag is usually with the lawyer. If the lawyer gets off the dime and hustles, a will can be admitted in a week. Most wills are declared valid almost immediately. And if you are a surviving spouse with hungry mouths to feed, you want access to your money pronto.

If you are married, it makes money sense to have accounts titled properly. If you have any joint moneys, have accounts read "JTWROS." This means "joint tenants with right of survivorship"—if one of you dies, the other can immediately access any funds. If you live in a community property state and hold title to your accounts as "community property," then the survivor will also have immediate access.

THE LIVING TRUST (A.K.A. INTER VIVOS TRUST)

A trust is a legal entity that can own, buy, and sell assets. When you personally transfer items to a trust, you no longer own them. The trust does. Have you lost control? Nope. Name yourself trustee and you are in charge.

A living trust is like a will—it's revocable, meaning that you can change it as often as you want.

Here's what a trust can do, in a nutshell:

1. It allows for continuity of your personal finances and business.
2. Privacy is maintained after you die. Wills are public documents; trusts aren't. This is why very wealthy people are rarely reported to have zillions of dollars at their deaths. The great majority of their assets are buried in trusts . . . for theirs, their family's, and their attorney's eyes only.
3. All assets in the trust bypass probate.

The cost of creating a living trust can range from $500 to $2,500, depending on your needs and the attorney's fees. The living trust is not the answer to all estate planning issues, but it certainly does create flexibility in managing estate issues. The living trust, by itself, *does not* save federal or state death taxes. But it *does* save all the costs of probating your will, while giving your estate a high degree of privacy both in death and during your lifetime, should you become incapacitated and require a conservator to look after your financial affairs.

Money-Wise Tip

Work with a lawyer who specializes in estate plans, not business plans.

LEAVING MONEY IN TRUST

A *testamentary trust* is set up by your will. Instead of leaving money directly to the beneficiary, you leave it in trust, to be managed by a trustee. Funds can be paid out for various purposes. At some point, the trust dissolves and the money is distributed. You get to decide when.

A trust can hold money until a child grows up. But don't try to control from the grave. By the time he or she is thirty, the child should be able to get the money and swim . . . or sink.

A trust can save estate taxes. If your net worth is over $600,000, talk to a lawyer about how to cut federal taxes. Also read Wilson J. Humber's *Saving the Best for Last* (Moody). Often you can do it without using a trust. The state may levy taxes on net worths less than $600,000—not all match the $600,000 federal exclusion.

A trust can manage money left to a spouse. A trustee manages the money. Your spouse receives the income and, if needed, payment out of principal. When your spouse dies, the remaining money goes to whomever is named. A family member, bank, or investment advisor is usually the trustee.

The spouse should be able to change trustees if the relationship isn't working. Again give the option—many surviving spouses do a better job than the friendly bank. Don't lock up *all* of your money in trust. Your spouse may have ignored managing money when you were alive but could thrive when you're gone. Allow some flexibility.

YOUR DISABLED CHILD

A trust can provide for retarded or disabled children. State and federal programs cover basic medical and residential care, but only if the child has almost no money. This presents parents with a catch-22: Money left to the disabled child will be consumed by the institution, guaranteed. If there's no money, the child will get only bare-bones support. Either scenario is a parental nightmare.

Middle-income parents may feel that they have little choice. They leave their modest assets to their healthy children and let the handicapped one get government aid. If you want to do this, you should specifically disinherit the handicapped child (and tell your relatives to do likewise). You hope and pray that your healthy children will provide the extra comforts that their institutionalized sibling needs.

Do your entire family a huge favor and call a powwow. Be blunt about the situation and get their commitment that they will be there for their sibling. Promises made at times like these usually glue for life. Don't assume—tell them what you expect. If they can't commit, you know who to leave your money to.

If you have money, set up a trust. The disabled child (having little or no money) can usually qualify for government aid. The trust supplies extra maintenance and support, not dependent on siblings' generosity. For advice on how to do this, call your state or local Association for Retarded Citizens. Ask for the names of lawyers experienced in your state's public-assistance laws. For the booklet *How to Provide for Their Future*, send $8 to the Association for Retarded Citizens, P.O. Box 1047, Arlington, TX 76004.

A trust can assure that the children of a prior marriage will inherit. If you leave all your money to your new spouse, he or she can do anything with it, including cutting your children out. A trust prevents this. If you want, you can give your spouse an income for life while guaranteeing that your children will ultimately inherit when he or she dies.

As you have read through this section, you may have thought, "Well, this doesn't sound too overwhelming." One of my missions in writing *Money Sense* and *Raising Money-Wise Kids* is to demystify the money maze. Wills and trusts are loaded with potholes. Please, please get legal advice, and use an estate planning attorney to guide you.

Part Two
PRESCHOOLERS THROUGH PRETEENS

Chapter Five

PRESCHOOLERS: THE BEGINNING YEARS

Quick, what do preschoolers do that their older siblings usually don't? Answer: They get to watch more TV. Advertisers are in heaven because they know they have a captive audience—TV is often put in a baby-sitter's role. Your preschooler is blitzed; TV advertisers know how pliable young minds are. They can pitch just about anything, and your youngster can "parrot"— verbatim—much of the verbiage dedicated to commercial messages.

When Frankie was three years old, we discovered the Berenstain Bears books. This series covers a variety of topics. Among them, we read about baby-sitters, doctors, Mom going to work, and sibling rivalry. One of Frankie's favorites was about the "gimmes." We all know that scene; if you haven't personally experienced it, you have seen and most definitely heard such an episode.

The stage is set at any retail or grocery store. Children learn quickly that they have a big audience to play to. Your own home works too. Ever notice how they act up when company arrives? Usually, it begins innocently enough with "please, Mommy." A negative response increases the loudness of the young one's voice and even the number of his demands. Birthdays and holidays seem to inspire peak performance. The message from the Berenstain Bears rings true for just about every adult; it says clearly that preventive medicine is your starting point.

LAY OUT THE RULES

Before you go on any outing, discuss the agenda for this event with your child, and be clear about the possibility of a treat (if there is one). The treat could be edible or it could be material. I found that it made sense with

Frankie to be specific about the range of choices and dollar amount. He knows in advance what I will *not* buy. In the three- to four-year-old range, he first discovered the Ninja Turtles. Later his interests evolved to the X-Men, Batman, Power Rangers, and now his latest love, at the age of nine, is the Star Trek series.

When I had laid out the ground rules before we left on a store adventure (believe me, they were often adventures) and the "gimme" song began, I could easily say that these weren't items that I had agreed to buy. Frankie has always liked gum, and when the agreed-upon item for the outing was a pack of gum, it was amazing how easy it was to direct his shopping time to the selection of the most perfect pack of gum. Happily, most stores have several brands.

The same thing happened with cereal and fruit snacks. He loved to look over all the boxes. If a box of cereal was the treat, this was all we took home with us—no more. If he acted out, with a pushy attitude, nagging, or whining, he was told no. If any of the undesirable behavior continued, he was told that he would not go on the next outing, and he didn't. Kids really do keep a careful ledger of what you say, so be consistent.

Sizes, Shapes, and Colors

Kids like to handle money, and they love coins. When they evolve from putting them in their mouths to putting them in their pockets or on the counter to pay for something at the store, you're ready to take their hand and start them through the money maze. Until kids really grasp numbers, paper currency doesn't have much significance to them. They do, though, *love* coins: The sizes, shapes, and colors fascinate them.

If you were to set out a penny, a nickel, and a dime, most likely they would select the nickel. Why? It's bigger. Kids have no trouble discerning value when you put out a quarter, a half dollar, and a silver dollar. They go for the bigger and heavier silver dollar—size and weight speak loudly. Think about it—when you were a kid, which package under the Christmas tree did you go for first? I suspect that it was not the one with the size and shape of a ring box.

Two years ago, Frankie was enthralled with the Mighty Morphin Power Rangers. His mom's best friend bought him one of the Power Ranger action figures and wrapped it in a huge Barbie dream playhouse box. The box was beautifully wrapped and strategically placed under his Christmas tree. He drooled as he looked at the biggest package under the tree, counting the days, even the hours, until he could rip into the wrappings. On Christmas morning, we could barely hold him back until everyone was in place for the big event.

Frankie's first choice—you guessed it—The Big Box. When he unwrapped it, and saw what he thought was a Barbie toy, he was crushed. He couldn't believe that "Aunt" Becky would give him such a thing. Tears started to well up. We encouraged him to continue opening the box and not to judge the gift by the wrapping. He reluctantly forged ahead. Eventually, he found the treasured action figure. He learned several lessons: (1) "Aunt" Becky has a sense of humor; (2) Don't judge what's inside by what's on the outside; and, most important of all, (3) Bigger is not always better. Since that time, we have a Christmas tradition in which everyone wraps treasured things in goofy boxes—and Frankie laughs the loudest.

THE COIN GAME

Here is a game you can play with your child to begin to teach him or her about coins. Gather one of each of the different coins. Even track down a silver dollar. Give your kids paper and pencil and begin to teach them math by using coins. Have them outline the coins as follows: first, outline the penny five times, put in an equals sign, and outline the nickel (five pennies equals a nickel), next have them outline five nickels, add an equals sign, and then outline a quarter (five nickels equals a quarter); have them do the same with dimes, half dollars, and so forth.

I can't emphasize enough the need to imprint the concept of the value of money in your preschooler's mind. Be prepared, they will ask why a dime is smaller than a penny yet is worth more. Play this game often, so they will be comfortable with the inconsistencies of the U.S. coinage. You might also want to take this a step further. Have them outline the number of coins it takes to buy their favorite edible treat and draw the treat after the equal sign.

Once they learn which coins are which, the Treasure Chest Game introduces exchanging pennies for nickels, dimes, and quarters—that one coin may actually be worth more than a larger number of another type of coin.

THE TREASURE CHEST GAME

For eight years, my daughter Sheryl worked with me. When Frankie's preschool had a teachers' day off or he had a fever or a case of the sniffles, it wasn't uncommon for him to come to work with Sheryl. My offices are in my home, so we have all the creature comforts he needed.

We usually receive deliveries for our business on a daily basis. One day Frankie's route and the delivery man's route converged at the same point—the front door. A very large package arrived that day, full of packing peanuts. Frankie wanted to keep the box for his own because he was fascinated by its size and especially by the peanuts. He was also just learning about coins, their sizes and their values.

So, we turned the box with its gallons of peanuts into the Mystery Treasure Chest. I dropped a handful of pennies, nickels, dimes, and quarters into the chest and gave the peanuts a stir. Then I challenged Frankie to reach his hand into the box. Each time he came up with coins in his hand he had to identify the name of each coin, tell its value, and then total them all up.

At this point, he began to learn that he could switch five pennies for one nickel and ten of them for a dime. Those shiny little dimes had greater value than the bigger brown pennies.

SHOPPING ALERT

My younger brother Terry has three kids. When Cristen and Jimmy were three and a half and one and a half years old (Patrick was yet a gleam in his parents' eyes), my brother wanted to surprise his wife with an anniversary weekend getaway; my husband and I agreed to keep the kids as our anniversary gift to them. Under the pretense that they were coming for dinner, the four of them arrived at our doorstep late one afternoon. Then a limousine arrived.

As we all waved good-bye, it dawned on me that my brother's prior planning didn't match his enthusiasm. He hadn't brought much of the necessary kid hardware—T-shirts, diapers, toddler food items, and the like. It had been quite a few years since I had had the twenty-four-hour-a-day responsibility of little ones, and our larder was devoid of wee kid necessities. So, off I went to the grocery store with the two very active youngsters in tow. What a fiasco!

I had totally forgotten about busy little hands and the distance a grocery cart, loaded with two toddlers, needed to be from the shelves. As I was getting diapers and T-shirts for Jimmy, I glanced down. To my dismay, I found the two of them sharing a purloined box of chocolate cookies. Most of the cookies were gone, some to their tummies and a lot to their faces, hair, clothes, and even toes.

What a mess! Crissy and Jimmy didn't agree—going to the store with Aunt Judy was great fun! Unfortunately, with young ones, too much of a good thing proves the old saying—what goes in, must come out. The cookies were running through little Jimmy by the time we got home.

The moral of the story might be to leave the kids at home, but that is not always realistic. What to do? If I had had my wits about me, I would have made a game of going to the store (Rule #1: stay in the center of the aisle so little hands can't reach anything). So, the next time I had to take them to the store with me, I told Crissy that I would pay her a nickel—remember that is a *big* coin for a three year old—for sounding out if Jimmy grabbed anything off the shelves. She truly earned her pay.

You can extend this game by taking advantage of the terrific recall system kids develop early from the TV bombardment of commercial images. I told Crissy that for another nickel I needed more help. When we got to the cereal aisle, I told her that I was in pursuit of Cap'n Crunch. I described the Cap'n Crunch cereal box a little bit, and, sure enough, her face lit up. She began to scan the aisle, looking for the desired package. Since there are several flavors of this brand of cereal, Crissy got to choose. (When she dropped the box in the basket, little did I know that this was just the beginning of her talent of putting what she wanted in a "basket." She graduated from high school this year, and she is a very "hot" item with coaches for college women's basketball.)

By allowing her to have a choice, I avoided any "gimme" episodes, plus she felt like she was part of the shopping trip. Also, if you have the time as you shop with preschoolers, you can point out items (unbreakable only) you need to buy and let them take them off the shelves and put them in the basket. Encourage them to build on their math skills by having them count the number of items they put in the basket.

Money-Wise Tip

A terrific book is *Money Skills: 101 Activities to Teach Your Child About Money*, by Bonnie Drew (Career Press).

A good way to introduce children to the savings that coupons offer is to turn over kid-related coupons to your four year old (only for those products that you would normally buy). When you get to an aisle that has one of the coupon items, hand the child the coupon and tell him or her to spot it for you. Have the child walk, not ride. Most kid-oriented products are placed on shelves at their eye level, not yours, and not above basket level. I was surprised to find that even my grandson's favorite frozen macaroni and cheese dinner was found at kid-eye level.

TV Pitch

Programs that are targeted to the preschooler contain commercials with a lot of flash and glitz—dancing peanuts, stars, raisins. Kids love them. In the cartoon venue, it's often difficult for a preschooler to recognize the difference between the program and the commercials. His recall of the program will show that it has all blended together.

Take the time to sit down with your child to watch a half-hour program. Ask questions when it is over—you will probably be amazed. There's an excellent guide entitled *A Parent's Guide: Advertising and Your Child* published by the Children's Advertising Review Unit (CARU). The guide recommends ways that you can monitor, interpret, and explain the different advertising that is directed at your kids. To order, write to: CARU, 845 Third Avenue, New York, NY 10022, or call (212) 754-1354.

Allowing Allowances

From a very early age kids learn that there is only one way for Mom and Dad to take things out of the store—and that is by paying for them with money. At the age of three, kids began to grasp this concept, so this is the time to begin to introduce the concept of saving. It's quite difficult to save if there isn't a source of income (there aren't many Help Wanted ads for three to four year olds). Outside of grandparents, you are their primary income source. This may be the time to introduce a small allowance, but not before the age of three and not a large amount of money. Generally, allowance is paid weekly, but you can tie it to your pay periods if this works best. When you decide to start an allowance program, you need to ask yourself some questions:

- Long term, what can you reasonably afford? (Watch what you spend on your child for incidental goodies for a few weeks, and base the allowance roughly on this amount.)
- Should you tie the performance of household chores to an allowance? (This is a good idea—if you will be consistent about monitoring.)
- How much of the allowance do you want your child to save? (Be reasonable.)

With the allowance in place, you can begin to step away from instant gratification (the "gimmes") and reinforce the concept that saving money is essential to the *Money-Wise* kid. You will have the answer to your child when he sees something on TV that he wants NOW. The answer is "Let's see how we can help you save for this treasure." You have to be realistic about savings with the three to four year old because he doesn't understand the difference between wanting a two-dollar toy and twenty-dollar toy. With patience from you, your child will begin to understand just how far a dollar can—or can't—stretch.

Here's another use for the coin drawings: Have your child outline the coins that relate to the amount of his/her allowance, then explain to him how many of these drawings it will take to buy a desired item.

Play on the young child's fascination with coins by supplying a clear plastic container (easy to open and close) to bank the money at home and let him see the coins and bills multiply. Resist the cute piggy bank. With most, he can't see his money or handle it without the danger of hurting himself when his curiosity gets the best of him—and it will.

 Money-Wise Tip

Try the kitchen section of a nearby store (where there are canisters and spice containers) for a bank that will suit you both. Encourage your child to apply artwork and his name to the container. As the money builds, you can get coin wrappers from the bank.

Parents debate whether or not an allowance should be tied to household chores. Some believe that a regular allowance, in and of itself, will begin to teach a child about money and its usage. Others believe that allowances should be tied to the performance of specific chores. I am a member of the latter school that believes in the work ethic—if you work, you are rewarded. I also firmly believe that a clear line has to be drawn between chores that need to be done as a responsible family member and chores that are to be rewarded with money.

If you choose to give an allowance with no strings attached, don't get yourself in the position of being overly generous. It may make sense to offer chores that they can choose to do for extra money—this is far more likely to occur with older children.

If you tie allowance to your preschooler's performance of chores, be sure that they are simple and reasonable tasks. You don't want to knock him out and down when he is just beginning to walk the money maze. More on allowances in chapter 7.

INTRODUCING A LIFELONG SPENDING PLAN

You need to determine how much allowance to give. Again, your spending plan is the first consideration. If you are considering an allowance amount for the older child, you will do well to determine how much you shell out to each child over a month's time before you make a final decision. With the three to four year old, the range of one dollar up to one dollar times the child's age in years per week (four dollars for a four year old per week) works for most. Granted, giving a four year old four dollars per week might appear to be going overboard. So let's open the door to what kids do with allowances. This is the time to introduce the concepts of saving, spending, and charity.

Savings. Most kids love to spend money. When you let them know that they will *always* get to spend a portion of what they receive, you are on solid ground. Telling your younger children that they are saving for their college education will probably get a 0–2 rating out of a possible 10. If you tell them they can save for a desired toy, game, or outing, you are playing their tune. Preschool-age kids can only think short-term. The bigger ticket items (cars and college) can't be dealt with successfully until the middle years, say twelve and up.

Americans are horrible savers. The average American saves between 4 and 6 percent of his or her income. Teach your children to save early, and reinforce it. Encourage them to save 20–25 percent of all the money they receive from allowances, gifts, and work.

Spending: This is discretionary money that your child should be allowed to spend as he or she sees fit. Of course, every household has limitations on what money can be spent on. In our house, an X-rated item is cotton candy; no money can be spent on it. This is something Frankie wants at Rockies baseball games, and the answer is always no.

If your child spends all his money and then begins the begging, whining, and badgering, be firm and continue to say no. Many times, a young child experiences "buyer's remorse." He has blown his spending money on what you always considered to be junk. Now, he agrees because he has spied what he *really* wanted all along.

Remind him he had his choice on how he spent his money. Then you could involve him in a discussion of the enjoyment, or lack of same, that resulted from his spending. Follow up by encouraging him to save his money so he can buy something that may give him more lasting enjoyment. Maybe, with time, his periods of dissatisfaction won't occur so often.

Often a parent gives in to a tantrum. This only reinforces the child's belief that he knows how to push your button and turn you into his personal ATM machine. Don't get into the habit of giving in, especially when you are out in public, or this will be something you will have to deal with for years to come, perhaps until your "child" has passed his thirtieth birthday.

Your preschooler catches on fast to your concepts about money. As your child's primary role model, you can help him start building sound money habits that will work for the rest of his life.

Charity: Children don't need a Ph.D. degree to learn that there are destitute people out there. They may not know what the word *destitute* means, but they have seen commercials for Save the Children, TV broadcasts about disasters such as the Oklahoma City bombing, and homeless people on the street. Encourage them to allocate some of their money on a regular basis to an individual or group that is less fortunate than they are.

Generally speaking, a child is not born with a charitable nature when it comes to his money; thus charitable giving will require some nurturing from you. When you both see something that touches the child, ask him what he would like to do with his money to help the situation. One great, child-oriented charity is the Ronald McDonald House.

A year ago, I spoke for the Oncology Camps of America, an association of camp counselors and directors who work with kids who have cancer and their families. The Ronald McDonald House is a big supporter of this program. I was so touched by the scope of the work done by this group that I vowed to find the time to donate my services again. When kids see other kids in trouble, most want to help. Encourage yours to allocate 5 to 10 percent of their spending dollars to help others.

Money $ense Resource Center:

BOOKS AND SOFTWARE FOR YOUNGER KIDS

There are lots of books and specially designed software programs for computers that can help you in your efforts to educate your child about money. Consider adding some of them to your library.

Books:

- *The Berenstain Bears Get the Gimmes* by Stan and Jan Berenstain (Random House)
- *Trouble with Money* by Stan and Jan Berenstain (Random House)
  The Berenstain Bears books are part of an ongoing series with new titles added on a regular basis. Check with your favorite bookstore for new additions.
- *Freckle Juice* by Judy Blume (Dell)
  This is a story about a young boy who uses several weeks of his allowance to buy a secret freckle formula and learns a valuable consumer lesson.
- *Every Kid's Guide to Intelligent Spending* by Joy Berry (Living Skills Press)
- *Every Kid's Guide to Making and Managing Money* by Joy Berry (Living Skills Press)
  Both of the Every Kid's books teach kids about advertising and how to be savvy consumers.
- *If You Made a Million* by David M. Schwartz (Lothrop, Lee & Shepard)
  A magician shows the reader what money looks like and introduces the concept of a million dollars.

- *The Monster Money Book* by Loreen Leedy (Holiday House)
  Shows young kids how to manage and spend their Monster Club dues and also how to be good shoppers.
- *The Money Book: The Smart Kid's Guide to Savvy Saving and Spending* by Elaine Whatt and Stan Hinden (Tambourine Books)
  Lots of good tips about budgeting, saving, banking, and earning.

Software:

- Treasure MathStorm (The Learning Company)
  A computer software program that is in a game format. It teaches math skills using the concepts of money and time.
- Money and Time Adventures of a Lollipop Dragon (Society for Visual Education)
  Kids are taken through their paces and learn the basics of money skills.

Chapter Six

BEYOND BARNEY: THE MIDDLE YEARS

A great learning tool for kids age six and beyond is an American classic—the garage sale (or tag sale in some regions). Last spring, Frankie burst into my kitchen with the announcement that just around the corner one of my books was on sale for a dollar. He insisted that I drop everything and get right over to pick up the bargain. After plunking down my dollar to pick up a book that sells for twenty-three dollars, but is impossible to find at any price, we scouted the other tables at the sale for other great finds.

Garage sales are a terrific environment for you to introduce your child to a comparison of buying used versus new. There is another plus factor—you can teach them about bargaining on the price. Garage sales offer a potpourri of merchandise. Kids' toys and clothing are usually a staple, but the range of items for adults is almost limitless.

Granted, there's going to be a lot of junk that the seller seems to value beyond reason. But, with a little probing, some great bargains can be found. Haven't you seen a news item pop up now and then that recounts the purchase of a dirty old painting at a garage sale? Subsequent removal of the grime of years of neglect brings a surprising result—the face of a masterpiece shines back.

Frankie has trooped to many garage sales with me or his mom. And he has astutely realized that he too could participate in such entrepreneurial events. So, he decided to sell his ho-hum Power Ranger stuff at his mom's next garage sale. The next step for him was to price the items he planned to sell. Since they were his toys, the money made by selling them would be his.

The light bulb of understanding about bargains lit his face when I emphasized that his expensive toys (thirty- to forty-dollar original cost) would bring in only five to ten dollars each. He didn't like it much, but he learned that the bargains flow both ways—if you can buy something you absolutely love that has only a few hours of wear and tear on it for five dollars, so can someone else.

Frankie now is interested in Star Trek and all the related memorabilia for the Next Generation, Deep Space 9, and the latest in the series, Voyager. He realizes he can have the treasured items from this multiple series, and at a fraction of their retail price, if he is patient and diligent in his scouting at garage sales. What a big step for a nine year old!

COMPARISON SHOPPING

From the ages of six to ten you can have a tremendous impact on your kids. They are at their peak of receptiveness to your guidance. From age six on, kids know that ten dimes are a lot better than ten pennies or even ten nickels.

This is a great time to teach them about pricing. Show them what unit pricing is all about (source: the item labels on grocery shelves) and have them help you determine whether a sale price is really the best bargain. Have them point out an item in the store that they saw pitched on TV and see how it compares price-wise to similar items. This age group is prime for learning about the differences between brands: cost, size, quality, and quantity. The middle year kids are readers, and they are anxious to show you what they can read. Encourage them to read labels, ads, etc., to you.

They are also a visual bunch.

A fun project for a rainy day is to put together a list of the "necessity" items that are used around the house. Start with the kids' area to get them going.

- *The kids' bathroom:* the most logical inclusions would be toothpaste, soap, shampoo, and toilet paper. For some, bubble bath would be considered a necessity.
- *Your bathroom:* to the items above, you most likely will add deodorant, hand lotion, cotton swabs, dental floss, conditioner, razor blades, etc.
- *Kitchen:* offer suggestions such as sugar, flour, cereals, coffee, tea, spaghetti, rice, raisins, cocoa, and so on.
- *House:* dishwashing detergent, garbage bags, light bulbs, vacuum bags, laundry detergent, fabric softener, etc.

The purpose of these lists is to help identify the basic necessities needed to run your family's household. The kitchen and house in general are primarily your domain, but don't exclude the kids' input. You will be surprised at their interest in learning about what is needed. Favored foods should be included—for Frankie, macaroni and cheese and fettuccine were at the top of our list for two solid years.

A final note about compiling the lists with the kids: Work with them on the difference between: "do we need this" versus "do we just want it, but really can live without it for now." As you look over the list and ask those questions, they may respond, "No, I don't need the bar of soap, but I do need the sweets." Remember, you are the adult and get to give the final yea or nay on each item listed.

Once you have established what is essential and what is not, your shopping will be made much easier. So now let's turn your kids' attention to the food advertising supplements from the newspaper that come midweek and on weekends. Grocery stores spend a lot of advertising dollars putting these coupon sections together to get your attention. They can be a wonderful resource for you and your child.

These supplements often contain terrific pictures that will snag your visual six to ten year old's interest. And they contain pricing in general, notations on cents-off pricing, and most important—the dates for the sale. They are *the* way to introduce your child to comparison shopping. Now, it's time to put the kids to work.

With the help of the ads, they can see what fits with your already prepared "necessity" list. You can also let them search for what fits the "if we have extra money, it would be nice to have this" list. If you live where there are competing grocery stores, comparison shopping opportunities are even more challenging for your kids. Using more than one store's ads could, however, create more of a challenge for you at shopping time than you bargained for. So you will probably want to pick the one store (or perhaps two) that has more of the listed items on sale or has better prices on them.

With scissors in hand, your assistant(s) are ready to go to work. Have them clip coupons or price quotes for items from the necessity list (later you can work on the "extra money" list). Then, have them put the clippings in alphabetical order, using the general name for each—not the brand name. For example, put an ad for Oreos in the pile for the letter C—cookies—not under the letter O.

The next step is to put the alphabetized clippings into general categories:

fresh fruits and veggies in the produce pile, soaps and cleaning needs together, etc. Then proceed to compare prices to see which coupons win the price competition and discard the rest. The same steps can be taken with the "extra money" list.

You might want to further organize the coupons according to the store's general layout. If several kids are involved, you might want to assign them each an area and its respective coupons to avoid total pandemonium at the store. When kids have done this several times, they can probably rid you of this chore for years to come.

Now you're ready to go to the store (but is the store ready for all this efficiency in comparison shopping?). Appoint yourself the captain of the grocery cart, direct the traffic, and put the kids to work. Have them hunt down the items for you. It is essential that you emphasize the necessity of sticking to the shopping list. It is easy to get off target and be swayed by impulse buying.

As the kids pick up each item that has a coupon, have them note the regular price and the coupon price on a pad of paper. (These days, most store receipts list individual grocery items by name, but they don't get more specific than "grocery coupon" on the subtraction portion of the receipt.) When you get home, tally the differences so all can see what the total savings were for the shopping trip. If you think the kids will tire of doing this, here's an incentive to keep them going. Put the savings total in a kitty for a special family outing such as miniature golf, the latest kid movie, or pizza. Or, you could reinforce the *Money-Wise* kids by putting the money in their savings accounts.

Money-Wise Tip

Most stores place featured items at the ends of each aisle. Rarely are they buried mid-aisle. If your list is short and you intend to shop only the sale items, skip going up and down every aisle—shop the perimeter instead. You will save plenty of money by avoiding impulse temptations.

BUDGETED FUN

Last summer, Frankie took his friend A. J. along with us to see a Rockies baseball game. When the invitation was issued to the boys, they were told that we would have a ballpark-type dinner—translation: hot dogs, sodas, and most likely some other gooey type of concoction. Upon arrival at the stadium, the boys were told that they had some choices for food that evening. They could pick from the food booths we passed on the way to our seats (purchases to be made later, after several innings had been played) or take a chance on potluck by selecting from the concessionaires who pass through the stands.

They were each given a budget of $10 for the evening. They added up the cost of items they thought they wanted as they filled their tummies. Between the two of them, they made it a game—how much could they get with their combined pool of $20? By the end of the game, the boys had spent approximately $18.

Instead of just doling out dollars, put a few strings on the "gift." Tell them that there is just so much money allocated to a particular event, and they must work within the proposed budget. As an incentive, you can offer to put the difference in their savings account if they come in under budget.

SPENDING PLANS AND KIDS: A LIFETIME ROAD MAP

Kids and spending plans go hand in hand. You can help your kids by devising a simple method of keeping track of their expenditures: what they spend their money on and how much (if any) is left over at the end of the week. Here's a spending plan that Frankie's mom, Poppa, and I put together for Frankie.

FRANKIE'S SPENDING PLAN

Month_____ Week _____

Money Received	Sat.	Sun.	Mon.	Tues.	Wed.	Thurs.	Fri.
Allowance	—	—	—	—	—	—	—
Gifts	—	—	—	—	—	—	—
Odd Jobs	—	—	—	—	—	—	—
TOTAL	—	—	—	—	—	—	—

Money Spent	Sat.	Sun.	Mon.	Tues.	Wed.	Thurs.	Fri.
Arts & Crafts	—	—	—	—	—	—	—
Books & Tapes	—	—	—	—	—	—	—
CDs & Videos	—	—	—	—	—	—	—
Charity	—	—	—	—	—	—	—
Church	—	—	—	—	—	—	—
Clothes	—	—	—	—	—	—	—
Clubs/Scout Dues	—	—	—	—	—	—	—
Gave to Friends	—	—	—	—	—	—	—
Gifts	—	—	—	—	—	—	—
Holiday Costumes	—	—	—	—	—	—	—
Lunch Money	—	—	—	—	—	—	—
Movies	—	—	—	—	—	—	—
Parties	—	—	—	—	—	—	—
Pets	—	—	—	—	—	—	—
Savings	—	—	—	—	—	—	—
School Events	—	—	—	—	—	—	—
Snacks	—	—	—	—	—	—	—
Toys/Games	—	—	—	—	—	—	—
Other	—	—	—	—	—	—	—
TOTAL	—	—	—	—	—	—	—

Total Money Received $_____
Total Money Spent $_____
Over/Under $_____

This is the first step in establishing a lifelong habit of planned spending as well as dealing with expected income. It's a simple spending plan, but you can expand or shrink it to meet your child's needs. Just make sure that you take into account that, like adults, children have fixed and variable expenses and income.

By the time a child is six years old, his or her allowance should include provision for some "walking around" money that can be spent on whatever he or she desires. As your child approaches the age of ten, the ability to match income with expenses should become evident. Your son or daughter should have a good grasp of the sources of his or her income and outgo.

Your ten-year-old child should understand which expenses are fixed—such as school lunches and supplies. A grasp of amounts to put toward savings and donations to charities and the church should also be evident. Your shining hour as their top role model is here. Kids at this age are very tuned in to how you save money (do you need to start saving now for next summer's vacation?) and how you spend it—ongoing family expenses. The key here is to give your children a road map to planning their spending. Discuss your family's spending plan: the hows and whys of the income and outgo, the successes and the failures in keeping to the spending plan. A monthly family spending plan session is an excellent tool to use for regular reinforcement for the concepts you are teaching your kids.

POCAHONTAS, BATMAN, AND YOU

By the time most kids reach age eight, they have some suspicions about phony TV commercial promises, what rings true in them and what doesn't. The summer that I worked on this book, TV blitzed kids with commercials relating to *Congo*, *Batman*, *Pocahontas*—you name it. Any movie that cost multimillions of dollars to produce also has a handsome advertising budget. Watches, cups, and toys beckon youngsters. All this marketing was directed toward your youngster; reaching you, other than indirectly through your child, was never a part of the equation. Since the "hype" of these advertising blitzes is directed solely at your kids, it opens an important window of opportunity for your joint investigations of the truth and fiction in a TV commercial.

Before your child wises up to the manipulations of Madison Avenue, he will be inexperienced and naive about advertising. Thus it is normal for him or her to expect a product to perform exactly as it does on TV. This brings up the subject of enhancers. If you don't know what an enhancer is, the nauseating details of some follow. Enhancers are used to demonstrate a product, to make it look better or more accurate (such as perfect). You have a great opportunity to discuss how they're done and, more important, *why*.

Don't forget celebrity endorsements. Today, basketball is one of the hottest sports in our country. McDonald's paid millions to Michael Jordan, Larry Bird, and Charles Barkley for the commercial that shows all three taking a shot with a basketball, including one from the moon to the earth. The prize for the winner—a McDonald's Big Mac. Use ads like these as examples of how ridiculous or impossible some feats portrayed on TV really are. To get the dialogue going, ask your kids such questions such as:

- How did Michael Jordan and Larry Bird get to the moon?
- Can Michael Jordan really shoot a basketball that far?
- Why do you think these players want to be in the commercial? Money or fun?
- Do you think any of the players did the commercial for free? (Some give money to charity, and pointing this out is an opportunity for positive emulation of a celebrity.)
- Do you think they would have done the commercial even though they might not like McDonald's Big Macs?

For the older child, you can even open up the values drawer. If Michael Jordan got into "trouble," would McDonald's still use him as an endorser?

Ask your kids if they can remember how the hamburger looked on the TV spot, and then ask them to compare this image to the next one they bite into. It's rare that the TV burger looks anything like one in real life—why? As a rule, the meat in the burgers in commercials is basically raw. The burger has been seared for only a few seconds on each side (to avoid the shrinkage that occurs when the meat is cooked well done, as it should be). Those terrific looking barbecue grill marks are painted on by hand. The seeds on sesame seed buns are glued in place, one by one and the more the merrier. Ask your kids if they have ever gotten a hamburger with a soggy bun. In the commercials, the buns have cardboard slipped into them for stability so they won't collapse from the moisture that accumulates during the "shoot." After all, those filming lights are hot!

The *Consumer Reports* folks have produced three behind-the-scenes videos that expose what really goes on when a commercial is produced. They are entitled: *Consumer Reports: Buy Me That, Buy Me That Too,* and *Buy Me That Three.* They're not inexpensive to own, but they could save a lot of your family's money because of the education they provide. If you have other friends with children, you could pool your resources to build a communal film library. That's smart parent *Money \$ense.*

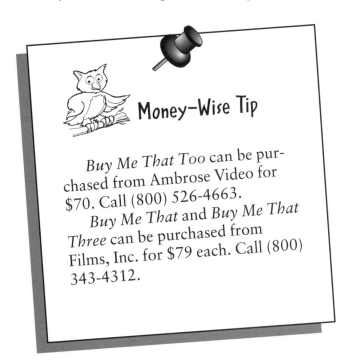

Money-Wise Tip

Buy Me That Too can be purchased from Ambrose Video for $70. Call (800) 526-4663.
Buy Me That and *Buy Me That Three* can be purchased from Films, Inc. for $79 each. Call (800) 343-4312.

Zillions: Consumer Reports for Kids publishes its annual ZAP awards. A panel is made up of twelve of its readers, and they evaluate all the nominations from other readers. ZAP means to zap it off the air. What are they zapping? Various commercials and pitches that don't live up to their promises or are downright misrepresentations.

DEALING WITH PEER PRESSURE

When your kids reach the age of eight or so, they become increasingly aware of their friends' and peers' inventory of things, as well as the degree of "in-ness" that is attached to each one of these things. Every parent has felt the subtle pressure or has been subjected to the outright demand to buy something because a friend has one. You might hear one of these statements: "I'll just die if can't have that" or "What will the other kids think?" Once in a while, there can be a legitimate reason for your child to want to "keep up with the Jones kid," so don't tune him out as a matter of principle.

I don't mean to suggest that kids' complaints are never legitimate or that parents have a right to merely ignore the issue of whether or not the choices they make for their kids' clothes (or other possessions) might unnecessarily alienate the kids from their peers. After all, most parents make an effort to wear the "right" clothes to the office, even if they need to be creative and go with less expensive versions of the right clothes.

One of my friends pointed out that her parents had taken the cheap and easy route when it came to kids' clothing, to the social detriment of herself and her siblings. She told me, "I went through eighth grade (and earlier, but it was very important by then) trying to answer kids' rude questions about the way I dressed. When other kids bought their own designer blue jeans, my mom bought me 'old lady' pants from the catalogue. I owned *two* pairs of pants, both of them elastic-waisted slacks with a sewn-in 'crease' down the middle of each leg. My parents wondered why I had no friends, but I don't think the way I dressed helped me any. We had other minor luxuries, so I think it was an issue of priorities more than purely a money question. And we lived in a lower middle-class neighborhood, so I wasn't vainly trying to keep pace with rich kids."

Once you have determined whether a need is real or imagined, give your child an answer. It is very important to make your value system—what you think about the acquisition of things—clear to your child, as well as what you can afford to buy. Kids either forget or they may not be aware that it takes your hard work, and sometimes pressure-induced sweat, to provide them with the lifestyle they are presently enjoying.

If they want something that's inappropriate, because of its cost or because you are categorically opposed to having such a thing in your home, let them know why. You might tell them: "I don't have the money to spend on this right now" (also make clear when or if the money will be available) or "I believe this is dangerous . . ."—whatever your rationale may be. Beware—parents often do their children a disservice when they either give in to or actually foster the duplication of what their peers have, so they will "fit in." You might want to try out a toy swap with your child's friends so that this need for duplication diminishes.

If your kid whines anytime you say no to a request, have you ever said to your child—vive la différence—*everyone is different, and being different is definitely OK?* If your kids learn early that they don't have to be like everyone or do what everyone else is doing, they will have an easier road to travel. As teens, they will find that saying the important word "no" comes naturally. Most kids can accept their financial status in life if you have been clear in stating the facts to them. An excellent resource on this topic is the book *What Makes You So Special?* by Edna LeShan (Dial Books). LeShan deals in a commonsense manner with the subject of giving your child the resources to deal with peer pressure.

There are two classic games that teach children about money: *Monopoly*, the old stand-by, and the *Game of Life*. It takes much more time to complete a game of *Monopoly* than to play a *Game of Life. Monopoly, Jr.* can be completed in an hour. Even though this game was designed for middle kids, adults like it too.

Money-Wise Tip

For $2, you can get *Money: Book Store Catalog*, which lists financial games and books that are available for varied age groups of kids. Write to: the National Center for Financial Education, Dept. KK, P.O. Box 34070, San Diego, CA 92163, or call (619) 232-8811.

Paul Richard developed his money catalog because so many parents wanted more information for their kids. If you call or write, tell him you saw this in *Raising Money-Wise Kids*. He will send you a free copy of *Eighteen Ways to Teach Your Children and Grandchildren About Money*.

Money $ense Resource Center:

Newspapers and Magazines

- *Zillions: Consumer Reports for Kids*
  Subscription Dept., P.O. Box 5177, Boulder, CO 80321
  Encourages kids to be savvy consumers.
- *Money for Kids*
  P.O. Box 30626, Tampa, FL 33630
  For games, inspiration, kid-level features covering careers,
  role models, school study habits, etc.
- *Mini-Page*
  Many newspapers include the weekly *Mini-Page,* which is circulated
  by the Universal Press Syndicate. A mini-newspaper for kids can
  include riddles, games, experiments, and money tips. Check your
  local paper. If the paper doesn't carry one of these, crusade for it or
  check out-of-town papers at your local newsstand.
     In a recent edition, young readers learned about the real Pocahon-
  tas, what life was like for kids and teens in 1612, and several
  Powhatan words with meanings and pronunciations. The issue also
  included several pictures of paintings and sculptures of Pocahontas, an
  Advent calendar, a drawing maze, a hidden word game, a blurb from
  one of the Denver Nuggets basketball team members challenging readers to get good grades and stay in school, some jokes, and a series of
  questions to be used by teachers and parents.
- *Ask Dr. Tightwad*
  This is a syndicated column that addresses a variety of money issues
  for parents. Dr. Tightwad is the editor of *Kiplinger's Personal Finance
  Magazine.* Terrific common-sense and humorous responses to readers' questions.

Books

- *Surviving the Money Jungle*
  By Larry Burkett (Christian Financial Concepts). A guide for twelve
  and up on managing their personal finances. Done in workbook format. A teacher's (parent's) guide can be purchased separately.

- *Coping with Money*
  By Richard S. and Mary Price Lee (Rosen Publishing Group). All about allowances, designing budgets, even saving for college—best for teens.
- *Kiplinger's Money Smart Kids*
  By Janet Bodnar (Kiplinger). Based on many of the *Dr. Tightwad* columns, this is a excellent resource filled with scenarios of today's families.
- *Making Cents: Every Kid's Guide to Money*
  By Elizabeth Wilkinson (Little, Brown). Lots of money-making ideas for the middle years child.
- *Smart Spending: A Young Consumer's Guide*
  By Lois Schmitt (Charles Scribner's Sons). Presents budgeting, consumer fraud, advertising, and how to deal with consumer complaints—best for teens.
- *Henry and the Paper Route*
  By Beverly Cleary (Dell). Young boy faces the problems of starting his own business. Excellent fun for your budding entrepreneur.
- *Your 1st Book of Wealth*
  By A. David Silver (Career Press). Teen's guide to starting one's own business, collectibles, and investing.

Software—Games

- *Hot Dog Stand*
  This is part of the Survival Math series that includes the Smart Shopper Marathon and the Travel Agent. Players will learn how to manage a business and operate a hot dog stand at several football games. (Sunburst Communications)
- *Whatsit Corporation*
  Participants develop whatsits production (the name of a product) for six months, making decisions that a normal business owner would encounter. For middle children to teens. (Sunburst Communications)
- *DinoPark Tycoon*
  Kids learn how to build their dinosaur theme park as a business, managing concession stands and staff. (MECC)

- *The One and Only Common Cents Series*
  Designed for the kindergarten to second grade level and to be used in the classroom, this delightful series teaches kids about where money came from, why it was invented, and why savings are important. The series was created by Neale S. Godfrey, chairman of the Children's Financial Network, and released in 1996 through Modern Curriculum Press at (800) 321-3106. Each kit contains play paper and coin money, several copies of each booklet, and a teacher's guide. Cost per kit is $47.85.

New games and educational programs are being created as you read this. Video stores rent computer games. A *Money $ense* parent should "test" (rent) the product before buying. Don't forget your local library as an additional source for testing before buying books, tapes, computer games, etc.

Chapter Seven

ALLOWANCES: WHO, WHAT, WHERE, WHEN, & WHY

Contrary to the belief of many, an allowance doesn't make your kids spend more money. And it doesn't necessarily make you spend more on your kids than you would otherwise. I believe that giving an allowance—regularly—is a great way for you to begin teaching your flock how to handle money.

The debate among child experts on the wisdom of giving a child an allowance continues. Those who agree on the concept cannot agree on whether an allowance should be tied to the performance of jobs around the house or whether it should be given with few or no strings attached. I believe allowances should be tied to jobs.

Here's my definition of an allowance: money that a child receives on a regular basis (usually weekly) as a payment for being a participating and working member of the family.

Most parents raise their children to be self-sufficient. Let's not forget that they will go out in the world one day and work for pay. In the gentle environment of your home, you have the opportunity to show your children that if they do the job right they will get paid *and* keep their job. Another step toward becoming a successful *Money-Wise* adult is the "salaried and employed kid."

Earning an allowance is one of the first "grown-up" financial steps for your kids. Statistics show that the "unemployed" kid (a child who doesn't get an allowance) has access to and spends the same amount of money as the "salaried" kid. But the big difference is that the "salaried" kid is empowered through control of his own money. Let's look at what allowances can introduce to you and your child:

- For *You*: control of the amount of money your child gets from you. For *You* and *Your Child*: reduce the stress of "gimme" attacks for both of you.

- For *You*: an easy way to open the door of the money-taboo cupboard. For *You* and *Your Child*: an introduction to healthy money concepts—money is part of the work/reward system. It is *not* a cure-all for being sad, a substitute for quality family time, or a means of "buying" status with peers.

- For *You*: a perfect place to begin serious dialogue about what a specific amount of money does and does not do. For *You* and *Your Child*: the concepts of spending plans and saving flow naturally for you both through the discussion of allowances—you can share your successes (failures too).

- For *You*: a terrific opportunity to discuss the realities of your child's spending needs. For *You* and *Your Child*: quickly identify what is needful and what is wishful thinking.

- For *You*: a starting point, a foundation for your child's attitudes toward spending and saving. For *You* and *Your Child*: less friction about money issues—you both know the rules that the allowance is based on.

- For *You*: a great way to create and foster the responsible *Money $ense* child. For *You* and *Your Child*: your child completes jobs that create cash flow for him, and you pay him regularly—a new word: *accountability* (which does go both ways).

Finally, allowances cannot be a money cure-all, especially when emergencies arise. You may have to dip down in your pocket once in a while, so be flexible but firm in your approach.

How Much: You're Part of the Family, Aren't You?

I'm for starting a very simple allowance for mature three year olds, although your child may not be ready until age four or five. Here are some tips to identify that perfect moment in time.

- Does your daughter understand that a nickel is the same as five pennies? Or that a quarter is the same as five nickels?
- Most preschoolers think that bigger is best, so their logic tells them that a nickel has more value than a dime. Once they grasp that there is a difference, they're ready.
- Does your daughter understand trading? When you take her to McDonald's and she orders a Happy Meal, does she expect to give money to receive it?
- Do a test allowance. If you give her a dollar, does she understand that this money needs to last for several days? (Young children often have trouble grasping the concept of an entire week.)
- Does your daughter understand that the grocery store will not take Monopoly play money or those chocolate coins covered in gold foil? If the answer is yes, she's ready.
- Has you daughter started the "gimme" phase? If the answer is yes, she is ready to start an allowance. (Then she can save and pay for her own "gimmes.")

If your child meets all the criteria above, it's time to start talking money. First, make sure that you take charge of the amount given to your children for an allowance. They can choose how they receive it. For example, they can have fifty cents in nickels or dimes, or they can have a dollar in two quarters, four dimes, and two nickels, etc. Then, talk with them about what they will use the allowance for and when they will get it. Make a commitment to be consistent—your child needs to know she can count on having her allowance, whatever the amount or timing.

Money-Wise Tip

As a rule, jobs should be completed before allowance money is paid.

Once you agree on the amount of the allowance and when it is to be paid, be fully aware that the money is not yours anymore—it belongs to your children. They get to decide what they will spend the money on. Believe me, they will make mistakes. Don't chide them too much at first. Also, don't be surprised if they lose the money a few times. Little children don't have any idea how to keep their money safe at first. Let them know about holes in their pockets. All of these new experiences will give both of you opportunities to discuss their first money successes and failures. And make sure praise is given so they will know what you like about their spending practices. At this age, your child delights in pleasing you by being a big girl or boy and exhibiting responsibility.

For years, we had a job checklist on our refrigerator door. Jobs were rotated monthly. Assignments were based on age and amount of time estimated to complete a task. We lived in the country when the chart on the opposite page was used. Our backyard had many mature oaks and other trees in it. Whoever got the "sweep" duty spent a few hours doing the cleanup—it was a big job.

In order for our kids to get their allowance (pay time was Saturday morning and was based on jobs completed the preceding week), each task they were assigned had to be marked "Done." The "Done" box had to have as many Xs as days required to complete the individual tasks. If not, they would not get their allowance.

Older children will need more money because they are more active outside of the home. When hot lunches were introduced at my school, I begged my mother to let me buy my lunch. I admit to an ulterior motive: Trading or bartering items from school lunches goes way back in kid history, and my usual lunch from home, a peanut butter and mayonnaise sandwich, had no value in this marketplace.

Success—I got my way and was given lunch money, and I became a budding entrepreneur. With cash in hand, I had choices: (1) I could buy a portion or all of someone else's lunch. (2) I could purchase the cafeteria offering for the day. (3) I could bank all or some of my lunch money—I would eat a couple of apples I brought from home.

Every parent wonders how much allowance really is enough. Studies have shown that, as a rule, family income has little bearing on the amount given out (especially to the preschool child). Age is one factor, and parental education level is another. *Youth Monitor* is a syndicated service of Nickelodeon and Yankelovich, Clancy and Schulman. In the early nineties, they did a survey of the amount kids received weekly for an allowance.

106

JOB CHECKLIST   Month of _____

	Water garden	Feed Gillie & Sam	Dirty clothes to washer	Clean cat box	Clean up after dog	Unload groceries	Dinner dishes	Take out trash	Unload dish-washer	Set table	Clear table	Sweep backyard
Shelley Age 11			X		X	X		X		X		
Frank Age 10	X		X				X					X
Sheryl Age 8		X	X	X					X		X	
Complete on/by	Tues., Sat.	A.M. & P.M. daily	Sat. A.M.	Wed., Sat.	Wed., Sat.	As needed	As needed	Each day	Each day	Each day	Each day	Sat.

The results:

Age 6–8 ....$1.99
Age 9–11 ....$4.17
Age 12–13 ....$5.82
Age 14–15 ....$9.68
Age 16–17 ....$10.80

Keep in mind that these are national averages and that parents actually give their kids even dollar amounts for allowances. Some parents tie the amount of allowance to either the age of the child or the grade in school. For example, a second-grade child would receive two dollars per week, or a seven year old could receive seven dollars per week.

In our home, our kids had a list of chores that had to be completed prior to the disbursement of allowance. If they didn't arrange for a substitute or just plain skipped doing the chore, they got no allowance at all. It was as simple as that—all or none. Granted, this policy created some grumbling, but it only took a few skips to understand the responsibility tied to their allowance payout.

Other ideas that can work include a point system. You and the kids identify chores around the home and the pay rate for each. Make a chart or use a bulletin board (the kind that accepts pushpins—reusable) with the kids' names at the top and the chores/rate of pay down the side. When the jobs are completed, use a star or pin to designate completion. Tally them up at the end of the week and pay for what has been done satisfactorily.

If your child's allowance must cover some expenses, be sure he knows what those expenses are. Most parents take the responsibility of covering the costs of school clothes and supplies. You might want to plan ahead and decide when or if your kids will receive a clothing allowance. Older children should be allowed to exercise some of their preferences in clothing styles (a good opportunity to teach them about the extra cost of brand-name clothing). It is reasonable to expect kids to pay for snack foods that are not part of your normal pantry stock, recreational games (including video arcades), movies, CDs, tapes, and so on.

Frankie's Spending Plan, from the preceding chapter, includes money being spent on charity and church, as well as savings. One way to set an early habit of portioning out money is to get a checkbook-size expandable file for coupons. Make labels for each "envelope" in the file to include all the items from your child's personalized list of budgeted expenses—toys, movies, and gifts. Don't forget savings, church, and charity.

Let's suppose that today is allowance payday, and your child expects his three dollars. Instead of giving three one-dollar bills each Saturday, give him a combination of bills, quarters, nickels, and dimes. This way your child has the change he needs to disperse his allowance to the budgeted "envelopes." Encourage your child to put in 5 to 10 percent for a charity of his choice and 20–25 percent into savings. The rest is his to spend in any way he wants.

Most kids are very visual, and they want to see where their money goes. By placing the money in a holder, they can have the pleasure of counting and recounting their moneys. You can also use clear jars (plastic, please) that are labeled Spending, Savings, and Charity.

When Is It Time for More—or Less?

Most adults like to be paid more when they do a good job. Kids are no different. So, count on it, they're going to ask for a raise sometime. Revisit the allowance issue several months down the road from the time you start it—this is especially important for the preschooler. For instance, if your five year old has been a little Trojan and completed her work the way you want her to do it—give her a raise. Every dime counts. For older kids, an allowance evaluation is appropriate about every six months. When you re-evaluate the allowance for your eleven year old, be realistic about what you expect him or her to spend funds on—tune in to his or her cost of living. Bite your tongue if you are thinking "When I was a kid . . ."

If your child spends or gives away the greater portion of his or her allowance, it doesn't always mean that you are giving too large an amount. You must respect your child's choices. Simply devote a little more time to guidance if you feel that you have a budding spendthrift on your hands. If, however, the assigned jobs are not done satisfactorily and/or not on time, you have a problem.

Let's look at an example: Each week your daughter is supposed to dust the front room, collect the dirty clothes, and empty the trash. She has decided that once a month is adequate for dusting, dirty clothes can be worn wrong side out so the dirt doesn't show, and the trash doesn't really smell that bad. Does this sound familiar? If so, it's time for a joint meeting of parent and child. In fact, call it what it is: a business meeting. This is salary review time—employer meets with employee.

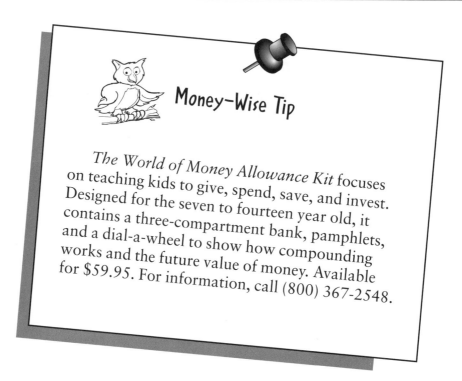

Money-Wise Tip

The World of Money Allowance Kit focuses on teaching kids to give, spend, save, and invest. Designed for the seven to fourteen year old, it contains a three-compartment bank, pamphlets, and a dial-a-wheel to show how compounding works and the future value of money. Available for $59.95. For information, call (800) 367-2548.

You may have to consider docking your child's paycheck (allowance) or even go so far as to put him or her on leave without pay if your meeting doesn't result in a better level of performance. Sometimes, kids get bored with the same ol', same ol'. Try being creative by varying the job description (new jobs and chores for a while). But above all, be firm. I come from the philosophy that a bargain once made must be kept. If your child isn't keeping up his part of the bargain, you don't pay the allowance.

THE CASE OF THE MISSING BUCK

Today is Wednesday, and allowance is paid on Saturday. Your child's allowance is already gone. He doesn't know where it went; he claims it died and went to "Allowance Heaven." This could be the opportunity you've been waiting for, to involve your child in an assessment of his spending habits. You have discovered that your son has the niftiest and most expensive collection of baseball cards in the neighborhood. You find out that he is spending lunch money, which is included in his weekly allowance allotment, to expand this collection. You decide that it's definitely time to call a halt to *this* spending practice.

If your child is using his lunch money to buy baseball cards, he's still a hungry guy at lunchtime with no money to ease the hunger pangs. His friends are probably sick and tired of his attempts to mooch their lunches, and he too may soon be so sick and tired that his attention in afternoon classes will be nil. A solution to this problem could be to call the school and see if you can prepay for his lunches. Or send the money with him each day if prepayment is not possible. And, of course, reduce the allowance paid to him by the amount allocated weekly for lunches. If he persists in redirecting his lunch moneys and refuses the cafeteria route, tell him to be creative and pack his own lunch.

It's a rare parent who hasn't been approached with "I lost it and I can't find it" or "Someone must have taken my money; it isn't where I left it." What to do? Do you sympathize? Do you join the hunt? Or do you say, "Tough"? Trust me, there will be a time, and perhaps many, when your son will approach you for an advance. The skill is mastered early.

He may have simply overspent and payday is several days out, or there could be a legitimate event coming up that requires prepayment. In either case, you will have to trust your son—that he is giving you the complete scoop—then put on your judge's robe.

In the case of a legitimate need to prepay for an event without much prior notice, advance the money against next week's allowance, no strings attached. If you find that the child has known about the event for quite a while and failed to do some prior budget planning, take the time to work on this concept and deal with the advance as outlined for lost money and over-spending:

Lost money: If this becomes a frequent occurrence, some detective work is required. Does your child use good methods for carrying and storing his money? Help him develop these skills.

Overspending: Help your child develop budgeting skills.

Now, do you pay or not? Sure, but with the understanding that the "extra" money is an advance on next week's paycheck/allowance. Try not to advance against more than one week's allowance.

And, if you really want to try a sophisticated lesson, add interest to the advance. He will have to learn about loans someday. Use the example of your mortgage or car loan. If you borrowed a portion of the amount to complete the purchase, explain that you didn't have enough in savings to pay all cash. You were able to arrange a loan at the bank, but that loan had strings attached—interest.

Explain that interest is the price you pay to get money that you don't have but want or need. I suggest that you keep your interest low, at about 5 percent. Calculate how much per day your child's loan will cost him by multiplying the loan amount by the interest rate and then dividing by 365 days. If your child hasn't learned multiplication and division, avoid confusing him with your calculations. Or, you could charge from five cents to a dollar, depending on the amount of the child's advance.

I know, I'm talking pennies, but there's a lesson in life here. This might be a good time to introduce Proverbs 22:7—"The rich rule over the poor, and the borrower is servant to the lender." Be up front with your kids. Loans to kids should only be for a week or two. A child will understand that money isn't free and that there is a price to pay when his allowance is reduced by the amount borrowed *plus* interest.

Money-Wise Tip

Kids learn early that "The Bank of Mom and Dad" can be open twenty-four hours a day. Set *your* banking hours and stick with them.

If your child runs short of money week after week, it's time to get out paper and pencil. Remember Frankie's Spending Plan from the preceding chapter? Have your son or daughter keep track of each expenditure on a daily basis—give the child a pad of Post-it Notes and have him or her detail each transaction. Next, provide a piece of poster board with a line drawn down the middle from top to bottom and label the right side *Needs* and the left side *Wants*. Have him put his notes on the board each day, each in its proper category.

At the end of the week, evaluate the board to see what is gobbling up your child's cash. You both will probably see that Post-its in the Needs column are few and those under Wants are many.

Here's the $64,000 question. Ask your child if he thinks he might be bypassing needs and spending too much for wants. Have him carefully evaluate his wants Post-its to identify which things he really wants most, and help him find ways to trim back. At some point, a candle of understanding has to be lit in your child's mind. You can gently guide him to the revelation that *needs must be met before wants can be addressed.*

The middle years kids will probably see that their wants list has grown longer and longer and that the cost per want is more expensive—Rollerblades and CD players come to mind. If this is the case, you can consider some additional household jobs. Or consider suggesting that he create income from odd jobs done for friends, relatives, and neighbors or possibly the old favorite—the paper route.

GRADES: THE GOOD, THE BAD, AND THE UGLY

If there ever was a "hot potato" in parental money guidance, paying for good grades is it. Should you pay for good grades? Most psychologists say no, that parents are far better off to reward good performance at school with sincere and detailed praise or a noncash treat such as stickers for a young child or a CD for a teen.

Some parents will do anything to get their kids' grades up. Others are appalled at the idea of money for grades. Before you give a black-and-white "no" to either side of this issue, consider a compromise.

When a child is young and it is improbable that he or she will be looking for after-school work, paying for grades doesn't make a lot of sense. There is an exception. If your child shows vast improvement in a particular subject, a reward might be appropriate. It could be a coveted treat or a special movie or outing. When your kids stretch and achieve beyond their normal capabilities, applause is in order.

If your older child is doing some heavy-duty studying in lieu of picking up the extra-income lawn-mowing job, consider giving him a "Bravo" by increasing his allowance. After all, some adults get paid for using their brains; others are paid for using their brawn.

Cutbacks and Bonuses

When your kids are lagging in their responsibilities, don't fully meet their commitments, or call an out-and-out strike—don't ignore it. If you have more than one child, your reaction or lack of same will not escape the sibling's ever watchful eye. If you don't react promptly and definitively, you have sent a clear message that dereliction of duty is OK. Your first statement, loud and clear, needs to be "Everyone in this family is expected to chip in and do his or her fair share of the work. You are no exception." If you are ignored or get a response like "Billy [the brother or friend] doesn't have to work as hard as I do; why do I have to?" your classic parental response could be, "Because I said so."

In reality, taking that position has far greater impact with the preschoolers and the early middle years child. When kids are in their teens, they are most likely exercising every bit of independence they can muster. My youngest, Sheryl, was a master of the "Evil Eye" when she heard a statement she didn't like or was asked to do something she considered beneath her.

Parents respond out of frustration to this type of rebellion by saying "If you don't do this, you won't get that." "That" could be an eagerly anticipated outing with friends (even family), shopping, movies, a slumber party, you name it—all kids have a long laundry list of events that they would hate to miss out on.

The bottom line is that if you draw such a line, you need to commit to the announced action/reaction scenario. If the lawn isn't mowed and the dog isn't walked, the shopping trip is history. For teens, withdrawing driving privileges inflicts exquisite pain. Wonder of wonders, your wish becomes their command.

When kids repeatedly shirk their job responsibilities, some parents reduce the allowance accordingly. That may work, but look before you leap and be sure you reduce the allowance fairly. One way is to determine how many chores your child is required to do for his or her allowance. Divide the weekly allowance by this number to determine the pay rate for each job. Don't be tempted to evaluate the job by the length of time each job takes or its degree of difficulty, or you will be quickly drawn into an esoteric debate that will result in a no-win situation for you and your child.

With the pay rate determined, you could then simply add up the jobs not done, multiply by the rate, and deduct from the next allowance due. Usually, after a few deductions, your child will find that his newly adjusted economic status is no fun at all. If you have an eager beaver on the sidelines, you could offer this (these) job(s) and their pay to him or her for a given period. Your "partially" employed child may actually seek other jobs to make up for the hole in his pocket . . . even his pride.

What if his refusal to work also includes the basic tasks for which you do not pay an allowance? It's time to look at which privileges your kid would rather not live without: snacks, TV in the evenings, even a family outing.

Every parent wants his or her kids to do well—to stretch and succeed at their tasks. When they do a *great* job, reward them. When your kids understand the "no-work, no-pay" ethic, they will also understand a "superior-work, better-pay" ethic.

PITCH THE PENNY WHEEL REWARD GAME

When a task is done in an above-average manner, bonuses can be treats, events out, money, etc. The reward selection can be a fun event too. Make a *Pitch the Penny Wheel Reward Game.* All you need is paper, a pencil, and a penny. Make a wheel of prizes—perhaps like the one on "Wheel of Fortune." You may have to censor some of the prize choices your child presents for the wheel—his zeal could overwhelm your pocketbook. When the wheel is satisfactory to both of you, lay it on a table or the floor. The prize winner stands back and tosses a penny at the circle. Wherever it lands indicates the reward. A wheel for each child in your home might be appropriate. Here's what Frankie had on his wheel:

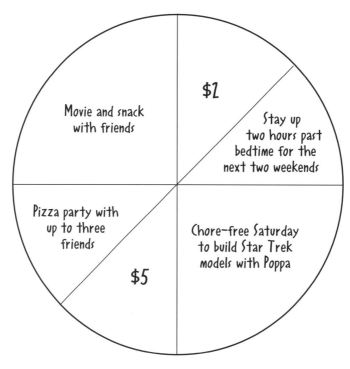

PITCH THE PENNY WHEEL

Your Emerging Teen

When most kids hit their teens, they begin to actively pursue income opportunities outside their homes. They soon recognize that their allowance is not meeting their financial needs/wants. An outside job could mean that the teen won't have time to fulfill his allowance job commitment. If you don't want the teen to take on an outside job, you may want to increase his or her allowance base. Or encourage and cheer him on but with this string attached—require that a large portion of the new income go into a college fund savings account. Extra income for your teen should not be kiss-off money.

Besides a car, the most coveted teen possession is a phone line of their own. A second phone line may make a big difference in your life, too—your friends and business contacts can actually reach you. A friend used the "kid" phone line as a dinner bell. Instead of hollering up the stairs, she dialed her teen's number. If the line wasn't busy, she knew the call would be answered.

Before adding a kids' phone line, it's important for you to lay out the ground rules. Specifically, you need to decide what hours the phone can be used (we had a 10 P.M. curfew) and who pays for what. Charges must be paid for by the teen. In our house, we paid the flat monthly rate for the additional line. We were so relieved to have "our" phone back that the extra six dollars a month was worth it. Do not pay for anything that you didn't agree to pay. Believe me, one disconnect, plus the cost to reactivate the line, does wonders for teen financial responsibility.

It is not uncommon for a teen to have a checking account. You may want to introduce checking accounts in some form of trial run. A good choice could be *Child's Checkmaster*, by Bill Corbitt, which was created initially for his youngest daughter. It involves a home banking type of system where the parents act as the bank (what else is new?). Check vouchers and registers are included for "The Bank of Mom and Dad."

It works like this: If your daughter gets an allowance of $4 per week, it is multiplied by 52, yielding an annual allowance of $208. This amount is entered into her register to open her account. When she needs money, a check (remember this is a pretend check) is written and also entered in the register. At this point, the balance is reduced in her account. The check is given to the parent, who "cashes" it for what she wants in actual cash. The *Child's Checkmaster* system includes a checkbook with register and a sheet of suggestions for parents. You can order it by writing Child's Checkmaster, c/o Bill Corbitt, 55 Cedar Hills Dr., Pocatello, ID 83204. The cost will be approximately $10, plus shipping and handling.

No matter what amount of allowance you decide upon, your child will learn a variety of positive lessons that he or she will carry throughout the money maze of life. By setting a good example with what you spend, budget, save, give, and tithe, you will instill a deep-rooted value system in each child—your legacy to the next generation.

Chapter Eight

SAVINGS: CREATING A DEMAND

Most people will agree that saving money is not a genetic trait; it is a learned habit. There are several primary reasons for saving. Three of the reasons can be categorized as *"Needs"*: *retirement* (a "non-word" for young adults and kids); *presently unaffordable needs*, including education, medical expenses, housing, and cars; and *backup funds* for tough times and emergencies. An additional reason for saving is to accumulate funds for the presently unaffordable *"Wants."*

Kids' emergency needs are usually covered by parent funding. Retirement? Kids are still in that immortal stage of life where they won't waste a moment of thought on this need. But wants are something kids know well. How do you spark your child's interest in saving? Tie saving money into something your kid really, really wants.

Money-Wise Tip

Kids confuse *needs* and *wants*. A parent's job is to "un-confuse" them.

JUMP START FOR SAVINGS

Here's a three-step program to get your child up and running with a regular savings plan that should work.

- *Sources of Money for Savings: Identify*
  Birthday and holiday gifts of money are good sources, but erratic in their timing and amount. An ongoing and routine source for your kid's savings program is most desirable. Allowances are the #1 candidate.
- *Safe Storage for Money: Create*
  Possibilities for storage range from the plain and simple—shoe box, jar, bottle—to the ornate—piggy bank or toy safe. Kids must have a "bank" of their very own; they will need to make deposits and withdrawals, and they really enjoy viewing and counting their growing hoard.
- *Empowerment Through Goal Setting: Cheer Their Efforts*
  Talk with your child about her goals for saving. Are these goals within her grasp: Is the time line reasonable, and is the dollar amount feasible? At first you may need to direct her interests. As the program works for her, acknowledge her efforts and lavish her with praise.

Money-Wise Tip

Keep savings goals *very simple* for young kids.

Simplicity is the byword for kids under the age of five. Savings is a process. When Frankie was saving for his Ninja Turtle Action Figures, we made sure that saving for each targeted treasure would take him no longer than two weeks—a reasonable time line. Prior to the age of five, Frankie kept his money in a colorful crayon-shaped bank. It was easy for him to open for his periodic counting of the coinage of his progress. Like all kids, he liked to look at and feel the money he had saved.

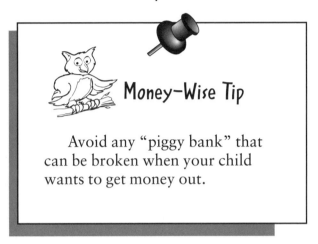

Money-Wise Tip

Avoid any "piggy bank" that can be broken when your child wants to get money out.

By the time they have reached the ages of five to eight, children will benefit from having different containers for their *Spending* money and for their *Saving* money. You and your kid can decide what type of container is desirable. Make it accessible and, preferably, nonbreakable. The emphasis should not be focused on the container, however, but on the regularity of the deposits.

Money-Wise Tip

Keep some savings visible. When the savings jars are full, take them and their owner to the bank.

Frankie's savings are kept in three places. He has an account at the Young Americans Bank and money in banks at his home and our home. He also has his own coin purse for spending money. When he gets his weekly allowance, he portions out his money to the home bank and to the coin purse. We set a goal for Frankie. When his home bank contains more than $10 he can go to the bank and make a deposit in his savings account. This bank savings account gives him the real-world view of counting his money.

The nine to twelve year old is ready to move beyond the shoe box or piggy bank phase of saving. If a "real" savings account at a bank hasn't yet been opened, make haste. A new source of funds for savings—interest compounding—will most likely trigger a big "Wow" from your kid. Do some investigating of the kinds of accounts offered. Some banks charge maintenance or administration fees for their accounts, and some require minimum opening balances. Some fee structures could discourage your child; fees can sometimes exceed the interest paid on the balance. If your bank charges fees, ask if it offers a special account for minors.

Kids like the old-fashioned passbook savings books—each deposit or withdrawal is noted in ink and date stamped. This book provides a very pleasing—big people—alternative to the visual satisfaction the child experienced in looking at his money from his piggy bank. Many banks have eliminated the use of passbooks and have substituted a monthly or quarterly statement. If your bank doesn't offer a passbook you can create your own. Get a small notebook and a date stamp (small change items) at a discount office supply store near you.

Proverbs says, "The simple [naive] inherit folly, but the prudent are crowned with knowledge." As you teach your kids about the merits of savings, the knowledge you will pass on will come back countless times over.

THE IMPORTANCE OF GOALS

Some parents miss the boat when they don't provide their child with the tactile and visual reinforcements needed to keep the savings habit going. But worse yet, they deny their kids much of their enthusiasm for saving when they outlaw "touching the money" in the savings account.

There is a compromise (a magic word for growing the *Money-Wise* kid). If you are adamant that the savings account should be for a long-term goal such as college funds, be fair with your child. Give him reinforcement and access to his account by allowing him to have his own short-term savings goals.

Frankie just got a new pair of Rollerblades. Frankie and his mom had set a goal and they met it. Half the money came from his diligent deposits to his savings account; the other half came from Mom. Frankie's interest in attaining this goal was sustained by posting a picture of the skates on the refrigerator. Very few days passed that he didn't look at the picture and focus on what he wanted to do with his hard-earned money. He had a definite—and visible—goal.

A Month of Pennies

The first surge of hormones hits your child at approximately age twelve. Do these hormones go directly to the brain and suddenly increase a child's wealth of experience and knowledge? Kids at this age are not shy about telling you that they know more than you do about all topics. Here's a great question you can throw at your kids when they hit the *I know it all* stage. Ask them: how many days will it take for you to become a millionaire if a penny doubles each day? The answer: twenty-eight days. Beginning with one cent on the first day and doubling it, you would have two cents the second day, four cents the third day, and so on. On the twenty-eighth day you would have $1,342,177.28!

The calendar on the following page denotes a twenty-eight-day month. Beginning on the first day with a deposit of one cent, the penny is doubled every day. Your kid will think that the end result is *Awesome,* and it is. For the Month of Pennies exercise, have your child draw a matrix with twenty-eight squares. Or use the month of February from a wall calendar.

Have him start at the upper left corner with 1¢ and double the amount in each square until he fills all the squares and gets to the lower right corner. You can test his math skills and require that he use pencil and paper. Have fun! This can be a great wake-up call that illustrates what can happen with a consistent savings plan.

A MONTH OF PENNIES

1) .01	2) .02	3) .04	4) .08	5) .16	6) .32	7) .64
8) 1.28	9) 2.56	10) 5.12	11) 10.24	12) 20.48	13) 40.96	14) 81.92
15) 163.84	16) 327.68	17) 655.36	18) 1,310.72	19) 2,621.44	20) 5,242.88	21) 10,485.76
22) 20,971.52	23) 41,943.04	24) 83,886.08	25) 167,772.16	26) 335,544.32	27) 671,088.64	28) 1,342,177.28

From 1¢ to $1,342,177.28 in 28 days!

One day, I had to go to the grocery store, and I took Frankie with me. The distance from my house to the store is exactly one mile. As we drove off, I asked Frankie, "How many miles high would a stack of one million pennies have to be?" He didn't have a clue. The answer: 95. I had figured this out from a "What If . . ." column I got at my bank.

Then I asked him how many pennies, stacked one on top of each other, it would take to cover the distance from our house to the store. He said, "Oh, Grandma, it would take a lot. Maybe hundreds." "Hundreds," I said. "How about thousands—several thousands?" We calculated that it would take 10,526 pennies to cover the distance from my house to the store. The math lesson for Frankie was dividing 1,000,000 pennies by 95 miles, which equals 10,526 pennies per mile.

IT'S OF INTEREST TO ALL

All of the previous questions and illustrations provide ways to introduce the "magic" of compounding (i.e., interest on their savings accounts) to your older children. The compounding elements are rate, dollars, and time. Money can grow in two ways: deposits and interest deposits from the bank. Children will ask why the bank pays this interest. Explain that the bank has their money and uses it while it's there, and the bank has to pay for this privilege.

Here's a real-life example of the way interest works to grow the savings account over a period of time. Let's say that you have a daughter who is twelve years old. She has two burning interests now—music and clothes. She is a very talented musician and hasn't met a musical instrument that she hasn't loved. She has confided in you that she wants to be the first female conductor for the symphony in your city. She is also a clothes hound.

Astute parent that you are, you know that the potential dollars needed to fund your daughter's goals in education and clothing have to come from somewhere. The unexpected source? Grandma has decided to give each of her grandchildren $1,000 for Christmas. Your goal as a parent is to convince her to bank the money Grandma gives her and try to restrain her from blowing it all on clothes.

The table on the next page shows specific savings balances and the growth rate for each using different rates of compounding interest. Here's how it works. Today your daughter is twelve, and she will enter college when she's nineteen—seven years from now. You have checked with the local bank and found out that her $1,000 can earn 6 percent interest over the next seven years if she puts it in a CD. First find the column labeled 6 percent and run your finger down to the number 7 (for the number of years) and you will see the figure 1.50. Multiply her $1,000 by 1.50, which yields an increase of $500.

THE MAGIC OF COMPOUNDING

This compound-growth table tells you what any sum of money will rise to in any year in the future if it compounds at a given rate. Look down the left-hand column for the number of years into the future you want to project. Read across to the rate of increase you expect. Where those lines intersect, you will find a compounding factor. Multiply the factor by the sum you started with to see what it will rise to in the years ahead.

125

COMPOUNDING SAVINGS
Sum accumulated at

Number of years	4%	5%	6%	7%	8%	9%	10%	11%	12%
1	1.04	1.05	1.06	1.07	1.08	1.09	1.10	1.11	1.12
2	1.08	1.10	1.12	1.14	1.17	1.19	1.21	1.23	1.25
3	1.12	1.16	1.19	1.23	1.26	1.30	1.33	1.37	1.40
4	1.17	1.22	1.26	1.31	1.36	1.41	1.46	1.52	1.57
5	1.22	1.28	1.34	1.40	1.47	1.54	1.61	1.69	1.76
6	1.27	1.34	1.42	1.50	1.59	1.68	1.77	1.87	1.97
7	1.32	1.41	1.50	1.61	1.71	1.83	1.95	2.08	2.21
8	1.37	1.48	1.59	1.72	1.85	1.99	2.14	2.30	2.48
9	1.42	1.55	1.69	1.84	2.00	2.17	2.36	2.56	2.77
10	1.48	1.63	1.79	1.97	2.16	2.37	2.59	2.84	3.11
11	1.54	1.71	1.90	2.10	2.33	2.58	2.85	3.15	3.48
12	1.60	1.80	2.01	2.25	2.52	2.81	3.14	3.50	3.90
13	1.67	1.89	2.13	2.41	2.72	3.07	3.45	3.88	4.36
14	1.73	1.98	2.26	2.58	2.94	3.34	3.80	4.31	4.89
15	1.80	2.08	2.40	2.76	3.17	3.64	4.18	4.78	5.47
16	1.87	2.18	2.54	2.95	3.43	3.97	4.59	5.31	6.13
17	1.95	2.29	2.69	3.16	3.70	4.33	5.05	5.90	6.87
18	2.03	2.41	2.85	3.38	4.00	4.72	5.56	6.54	7.69
19	2.11	2.53	3.03	3.62	4.32	5.14	6.12	7.26	8.61
20	2.19	2.66	3.20	3.87	4.66	5.60	6.72	8.06	9.64

LONG-TERM VERSUS SHORT-TERM: IS IT WORTH IT?

Your goal now is to convince your daughter that saving the $1,000 and growing it to $1,500 for her future education is a better choice than spending it. This will introduce the concept of long-term goals versus short-term goals. Big satisfaction later versus instant gratification now.

You can also teach your kids the Rule of 72. This rule states that if you divide the number 72 by a given interest rate, you will know how many years it will take for your money to double. For example: If you can earn 9 percent per annum, it will take eight years to double your $1,000 (72 ÷ 9 = 8).

Money-Wise Tip

One week a month, do without:
no movie rentals, comics, meals out,
treats at the grocery store. Tally up
the savings—how much could you
save in twelve months?

GETTING STARTED

Getting your kids started on a savings plan or system is often an evolutionary process. Usually it starts with the jar or the piggy bank talked about in an earlier section of this book. If your child's school has an active PTA, your child can participate in the Save for America campaign. PTA volunteers collect your kids' money once a week. It is quite similar to the Bank Day from my childhood.

Save for America volunteers record the deposits on a computer. After all the deposits for the week are recorded, the computer disk and the money collected are taken to the sponsoring bank. Fifty percent of the states in the U.S. participate in the program. To get your child's school involved in Save for America, call (206) 746-0331 or write to 4095 173rd Place SE, Bellevue, WA 98008 for information. Talking to your local bank could also reveal some local school savings programs.

By now your kids should be very involved in their budgeting for spending, savings, charity, and church. It is likely that your child has saved enough so that it makes sense to open an interest-bearing savings account for him or her. Emphasize that no effort is required to earn these "free" additions to their accounts, other than making deposits regularly. You will probably soon find that your kids' druthers become growth. As their savings accounts grow, other options become available. One example is investing, which will be covered in a later chapter.

DEALING WITH THE RELUCTANT SAVER

What if one (or all) of your children can't seem to hold on to a single dime? Not to worry, we are dealing with learned behavior, not genetics. If money "burns" a hole in your kid's pockets, and if this kid is fast becoming your biggest accounts receivable (advances against future allowance), find out where the money is going.

There could be some legitimate cash drains operating on your child's funds, such as friends' or relatives' birthday presents or an increase in the cost of school lunches (or his appetite). If your child is dipping into his savings to meet "unexpected" expenses, however, you should investigate. Your kid could be having trouble with his budget, and some fine-tuning may be in order. Or he may need to find some additional income sources.

If your kid is still operating his spending program out of jars or envelopes or piggy banks, temptation may be the real problem. Consider being his personal (in house) banker until the savings ethic is ingrained and money starts accumulating again. Then a less accessible bank account can be opened.

Your kid (and you too) may be well aware of where all the money is going. All efforts to divert money to savings and out of this spendthrift's hands have failed. You can force the issue with one of these two solution/incentive programs.

- *Payroll deduction* could be a solution that would work for all of you. On payday you withhold an agreed-upon percentage from the allowance and bank it. Once the "pot" begins to grow, your son or daughter will usually see the merit of "out of sight, out of mind (and circulation)."
- *Your child's 401(k) plan* is a creative incentive plan for the truly reluctant saver. If you aren't familiar with 401(k) plans (or pension plans), here's what to do. You withhold an agreed-upon amount of any income received and match it or a percentage of it. This may help your child get on the savings bandwagon at long last.

OPENING A SAVINGS ACCOUNT

Be sure you find a bank that caters to children's savings account—fees, balance requirements, etc., may be prohibitive if your child hasn't saved substantial dollars.

No matter what bank you select, be sure you understand its rules.

• *Minimum Balance Requirements:* A certain amount is required to open the account, and the future balance may not fall below this amount without severe penalty.

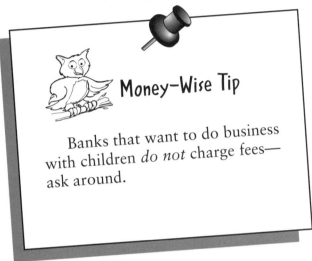

Money-Wise Tip

Banks that want to do business with children *do not* charge fees—ask around.

• *Bank Fees:* A monthly or annual service fee deducted from the child's account could exceed the earnings on a small-balance account.
• *Bank Policy:* State banking policies for children's accounts vary from state to state. Signatory regulations can be a problem. As long as the child can sign his name, he will usually be allowed to make deposits and withdrawals. You will probably be required to be a cosigner for the account (the Young Americans Bank is no exception). Additionally, withdrawals could require both signatures (this prevents parents from withdrawing their kids' money without permission) but in some cases, kids can withdraw without their parent's signature.
• *Forms and Statements:* Make sure you and your child sit down together to go over the deposit and withdrawal forms so he or she knows what do with each one. Review carefully the statements and the copies of all the monthly transactions when they arrive in the mail. Some accounts are called something like "Safe Keeping"—the statements/copies don't physically get sent. Rather, the bank keeps them. This may not satisfy you and your child.

THE KIDDY TAX

Once your child is one year old, apply for his or her Social Security number. So mandateth the IRS, and we parents comply. Any interest on savings or gains on investment accounts in your child's name will be reported to the IRS and will be treated as income for tax purposes. Today, the law (subject to change—congressional whims) reads that your child can earn up to $650 in interest/investment income without incurring a tax liability.

This amount does *not* include the amount you originally deposited or invested. The only tax consideration is the interest earned or dividends or gain on sale from investments (stocks, bonds, mutual funds, etc.). An example: your daughter's savings account earns 4 percent interest annually. In order for her account to incur sufficient interest income to be taxable, she would have to have a balance of $15,000 on deposit to exceed the $650 investment income floor.

If your daughter earned in excess of $650, but less than $1,300, she would be taxed at the kid's tax rate of 15 percent (federal only; check on your state tax rates). If she is under age fourteen and her income exceeds $1,300, you will have to pay the taxes at *your* applicable rate on any amount over $1,300. After the age of fourteen, until she is no longer a dependent or turns twenty-one, whichever comes first, all income a child earns is taxable at the 15 percent rate. The Kiddy Tax came into being because some parents were hiding their own assets in custodial accounts with their children's names on them to avoid taxation at their normal tax rate.

You can give yourself a major pat on the back when you succeed in getting your kids going with a regular savings program. You probably are a parent who has seen to it that saving is fun, exciting, and rewarding for your child. Success calls for celebration. You can celebrate your success in instilling goals and demonstrating the "how to's" in meeting life's material needs. Your kids can celebrate their disciplined efforts to save more and spend less—they aren't sending so many dollars to "cash heaven" these days.

Chapter Nine

MONEY TALKS WITHIN THE FAMILY

When my kids were in the eleven- to fifteen-year-old age range, I did something that made a significant impression on them. It all started when my son told me that his best friend's parents had said that I made a lot of money. At the time I was a stockbroker with E. F. Hutton. And yes, there were months when I did make a lot of money. There were also months when I didn't make enough to pay the mortgage.

I tapped into the kids' visual resources to make the impression I wanted. Every month that summer, I cashed my paychecks instead of depositing them. I told the cashier to give me nothing larger than a hundred-dollar bill and that I wanted plenty of smaller bills too. When I got home with the cash, I gathered up all the bills that needed to be paid that month.

In June my husband and I called a family powwow. We told them that I had cashed my paycheck so they could see what "a lot of money" looked like. They were impressed with the size of the stack of currency that was my paycheck. "Wow" was their reaction to the first $100 bill they had ever seen. Then we got down to business. I laid out the mortgage and car payment coupon books. Bills were laid out for utilities, phone, auto and life insurance, department stores, gasoline—you get the idea.

Next, I dealt out the bills from my "cashed check" like a deck of cards. Each bill was covered with the requisite amount of cash—$1,000 to the mortgage, $150 to gas and electricity, $200 for various insurances, $100 for auto insurance, $300 for health insurance, $150 for gasoline (we lived in California at the time). I laid out money for church offering, savings, groceries, and the kids' allowances. My kids' eyes were wide with amazement when I finished. I said, "Well, there's my paycheck. And, yes, I do make a lot of money." They learned a valuable lesson. I had brought a lot of money *in* the door that day, but it would go *out* the door just as quickly.

Most kids have no idea how much just the basics cost their parents each month. My kids couldn't believe that I had laid out several thousand dollars for the *needed* monthly expenses. And we hadn't yet allocated anything for "fun" things.

I told the kids that my employer had deducted what I owed for some of my tax "bills" before I got my pay. Their mouths dropped open when I told them that state, federal, and Social Security taxes had eaten up almost 50 percent of my gross pay. One of the kids quickly picked up on the fact that not all taxes were deducted from my pay. "What other taxes do you have to pay, Mom?" I told them about real estate taxes, sales taxes, and special city and county assessments—some other items for the needs list.

July has always been an interesting month when it comes to income. With few exceptions, it is our lowest income month. That July, there was not enough money to cover the basic needs. My kids learned *why* a savings program was critical to us—we drew from savings that month so we could eat and keep our house. For the first time they understood what I meant when I said, "We can't afford it this month"—that this was, and always had been, a valid statement.

Remember, kids are very visual. Let them see where your money goes by piling it up on each bill you owe or making a card for each bill (don't forget savings, charity, and church). This exercise will put your kids light-years ahead in their understanding of why spending plans and savings are critical to the successful *Money-Wise* family. Of course, you will probably want to warn them that adults consider discussions about money to be private; the amount of your mortgage, for instance, is not to be discussed outside your family.

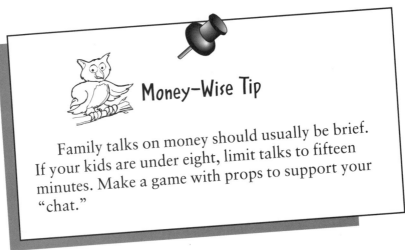

Money-Wise Tip

Family talks on money should usually be brief. If your kids are under eight, limit talks to fifteen minutes. Make a game with props to support your "chat."

Frankie's Spending Plan, in chapter 6, is a pattern you could follow to set up your child's spending plan. When you set up the kids' plans, you might want to show them how they fit in to the family spending plan—what they cost you for all their needs, their allowance, family entertainment, and so on.

Spending plans should not be set in concrete or etched in stone. They are simply guides for using your money. There will be times when you will overspend and others when you won't spend in certain areas at all.

CREDIT CARDS: FRIENDS AND FOES

In 1995 Americans owed more than $700 billion in consumer debt. Two hundred and fifty billion of this amount was owed on credit cards alone. The question always comes up—should a person use credit cards? I believe that credit cards are a valuable tool, but consumers need to learn how to use them responsibly.

An exercise to use for your kids (especially teens) is to review your credit rating. Make this an annual ritual. Get a copy of your credit report. This report will show what you have been doing with your various credit accounts, and it will let you know if your credit habits have been reported correctly. Mistakes are not uncommon. Any mistake can cause a potential creditor to turn you down.

A few years ago, TRW—the largest credit reporting agency—made a settlement with the federal government. The company agreed to the annual issuance of free credit report copies to every person in their files. Write for yours:

TRW
P.O. Box 749-029
Dallas, TX 75374
or call (800) 392-1122.

There are two more major credit reporting agencies you can contact. A fee is charged for these credit reports. Currently the price is $8 for each. They are: TransUnion (800) 922-5490 and EquiFax (800) 685-1111. Your credit report should show the following information for *each* account:

- The name of every credit account you have used and the date the account was opened.

- The type of account and its terms. Past accounts (paid in full and closed) are shown.
- The date of your last payment.
- The credit limit or highest credit balance established.
- The current balance owed.
- Status of your payments—current or past due (past due amounts will be shown as will the number of days overdue—i.e., thirty days, sixty days, and so forth) and it will show how many times an account has been paid late.
- Special problems with your account—collection agency involvement, repossession of goods.
- Public records: legal or court actions such as liens, judgments, bankruptcies, or foreclosures.
- Your legal relationship to the account: Are you individually or jointly responsible or a cosigner?
- Any statements from you regarding your credit report, such as a disputed balance for faulty goods that have been returned but not taken off your record.

Do credit reporting agencies make mistakes and get things mixed up? You bet. Years ago, my younger daughter was denied a car loan based on her credit report. The bank told her that she couldn't afford to make the new car payment because she didn't have enough income to cover all the payments she already had plus a new one. In fact, they told her that she had not included all of her credit obligations on her credit application. The industry term for this analysis is *debt ratio*—you won't get credit if the creditor concludes that your credit obligations are too high compared to your income.

Initially, Sheryl was puzzled; then she became angry. She knew she had filled out the application correctly and had listed all her credit obligations. Later she obtained a copy of her credit report and found that her older sister's credit file had been mixed up (merged) with hers. Even some of my accounts showed on her report. The bank was right—of course she couldn't handle the credit of two other people besides herself. It took us six months to unravel the mess so she could get her car loan.

When each of our kids turned sixteen, we introduced them to credit. We selected a MasterCard account that wasn't used frequently. On their sixteenth birthday we notified the company that we wanted to add our child to the account as a valid signer on the account. I have to confess that we experienced mixed results. Shelley was our "clean credit" teenager. Her responsible attitudes about money, which were evident from childhood, continued. She never charged anything she couldn't pay for from her allowance or earnings within thirty days. My son Frank took a pass on using the credit card; he said he just didn't trust himself. My daughter Sheryl could hardly wait to get her own card. And when she did, she ran amok. Within a very few months, her card was confiscated, cut in half, and thrown away.

The payment responsibility for the account always remained in my name, so I got the bills each month. This enabled me to monitor what the kids were spending and how they were paying.

If I were to go through this exercise today, here are the steps I would take:

1. Have the kids build up savings accounts.
2. Depending on the child's maturity level, somewhere between the ages of fourteen and sixteen, I would introduce her to a secured credit card, *using her savings as collateral.*
3. If she is responsible and grasps the concept of credit—you get to use someone else's money for a time and pay it back—then I would get her an unsecured card either at eighteen or when she goes to college. This card needs some guidelines attached—such as what it can or cannot be used for. You set the rules before handing it over.

Another way to introduce your kids to credit is to open a debit account tied to a savings account. Here's how this works. You deposit money with the bank or credit card company, and this amount is the maximum amount that can be spent by the child using it. The unused money earns interest. You have the option of having the charges deducted immediately from the account, or a statement can be issued for payment. If payment is not made within the specified time limit, the money owed is deducted from the deposited funds.

Money-Wise Tip

Kids rarely think of credit card usage as a "loan." Teach them that loans must be paid back—the sooner, the better.

DO'S AND DON'TS OF CREDIT

Stress to your child early and often that credit card use is real money, as real as the money in their wallet or purse right now. This concept seems to pass over their heads and is not a lesson that is retained for long periods of time. Here are some credit card rules you may want to institute for both you and your kids:

- Don't run the credit card to the limit. Many kids think they are doing just fine financially if they still have credit left on their card.
- Don't charge what you can't pay for in the next thirty days. Discourage the habit of paying the minimum payment shown on the statement. If they don't understand why, when the card company has offered this privilege, explain about the interest charged on the unpaid balance.
- Keep all your receipts in an envelope or box to reconcile with the monthly statement. (You may want to deduct the amount of any item not covered by a sales receipt from allowance.) Have your child verify that the receipt amount matches the statement—mistakes do happen.
- Check your credit report once a year. Reporting errors need to be corrected promptly. In addition, some employers run a credit check on job applicants and refuse to hire if credit problems are evident.
- *Never, never* let anyone other than named cardholders use the card. Not even if it's your best friend. And don't let anyone talk you into using the card for something you wouldn't ordinarily buy.

- Use the card sparingly for gasoline and food—emergencies only.
- Use the card for *Needs*, not for *Wants* (parental permission or at least discussion required).
- Don't use the card for cash advances. Reconciliation with the statement is hard to do because you rarely have a clue where the money went. And cash advances quickly become a habit. Also, interest rates are usually higher, and repayment does not include a twenty-five day grace period.

Another point that must be emphasized with your card-carrying youngster is that your credit is on the line *with* them. Kids under eighteen aren't issued credit cards without a guarantee from a creditworthy adult. If your child isn't a "clean credit," you won't be either.

MAKING MONEY

There are plenty of ways for your kids to make money—whether it is a few dollars for a weekend movie or a major addition to a play set, computer game, clothes, or sports. Why not make earning a little extra money a family event?

Think about the seasons. Winter brings Christmas. Christmas usually brings gifts. In our house, receiving gifts was a privilege, not a right. We always encouraged our kids to plan on a major clean-out of closets, toy boxes, and anything that had not been used or played with for the last six months. The clean-out also included us. My husband is a pack rat—it is almost painful for him to part with anything, even when he hasn't used or worn it in ten years!

With our clean-out efforts, twice a year we had a family garage sale—in the spring and early fall. Our kids were told that any new toys (and, as they got older, clothes, records, tapes, and sports equipment) would not be added if we did not see a need—or, for that matter, if items that were in use were either ignored, misused, or abused.

Proceeds from the sale went into the family pot. One year, we all decided that we wanted a new television. We knew our current one was on its last legs and that any day it could fail to respond when the "on" button was pushed. As a family, the five of us went shopping. We checked out a *Consumer Reports* issue on the latest models available. The one we wanted would cost $450.

As a group, we decided that this would be the ultimate prize for our clean-out efforts and weekend work of all of us manning the driveway sales. Because we talked openly about the cost of the proposed new TV, and the kids knew it was expensive, the kids seemed to put more energy into finding items that would add value to the garage sale. They eagerly participated in the event—even turning it into a party.

Our outgrown skis, coats, games, toys, bikes, skates, unused rugs, appliances, etc., became someone else's treasures. We made almost $500 and celebrated the next weekend with our new TV set and pizza. The TV still works quite well fourteen years later.

We had one other rule. Anything that was not sold would not be brought back into the house. It was donated to a favorite charity the day after the sale.

Other ways to make money include selling crafts, if someone in your family is talented. Whether your skill is flower arranging, sewing, knitting, crocheting, baking, or making dolls, fly hooks for fishing, or something else, there is someone who would appreciate your work. Teaching kids that many people cherish homemade items and are willing to pay for them could create a family project fund. Great places to gather ideas for future projects are charity and church bazaars and many summer and Christmas craft shows that are open to the public.

Here's one other idea. One way you can teach and model helping others is to do any of the above and donate the proceeds to a charity chosen by the family. Every December, I participate in the Santa Claus Shop sponsored by the YWCA. All year we gather items from our households and from merchants. All items are new.

The purpose of the Santa Claus Shop is to reach out to children who live in housing projects. Each child was invited to our "shop," where he or she could select any one gift for each adult in his or her household. Their chosen gift was then wrapped and tagged. Each child left the shop with a treat for himself and a nice gift for Mom, Dad, Grandma, and/or Grandpa.

One of my favorite times was when a little boy decided that the "perfect" gift for his mom was the earrings I was wearing. I took them off and wrapped them. He was thrilled, and so was I.

When Frankie was six, I took him with me to the Santa Claus Shop. He was a little intimidated—some of these kids looked rough, and some were filthy. Soon he was in the swing of things. He learned to enjoy helping kids, especially the little ones, find the perfect gift for their mommy or daddy. He learned an important lesson: Not everyone has a clean bed of his own or gets pizza on Friday nights. Frankie now saves duplicate toys that he receives for the kids who have less than he does.

KEEPING BIRTHDAYS AND HOLIDAYS IN PERSPECTIVE

The "gimmes" is a viral disease that most kids catch during the holidays. This should be no surprise. The commercial barrage blitzes your kids for months prior to the event. The competition for your kids' attention is fierce and myriad. Kids have a terrible time deciding what treasure(s) they really want.

The big day arrives and you hear something like this: "Why did Grandma get me this? I don't want it (or like it)." It's not always easy to return unwanted gifts. There can be hurt feelings (the giver's). The supplying store may not be accessible. The gift may have been bought on sale or is otherwise not returnable.

A few years ago, everyone in our family signed up on the family "Wish Lists." All could review the list for an affordable choice to give to each of the other family members. Did we get every item we wanted? Of course not, but at least a few wishes came true for each of us. Family members would check with each other so there would be no duplication.

JB'S CHRISTMAS WISH LIST

Measuring cups	Stockings	A "Basics" Cookbook
Camera	Barbra Streisand CD	Table Napkins
Slippers	Soup Ladle	Sweater

Catalogs present another technique—they are abundant in the months prior to the holidays. Don't trash them; pile them up for a while and let each family member select one or two. Kids can circle the items they are interested in, or they can cut them out and paste them on a poster board. Guaranteed, there will be a lot of circling or cutting. If the child can read the prices, have him select several items from different price ranges. The purpose is to give you—and Grandma too—some idea of what will really please the kids and also meet your spending plan requirements. Gifts purchased via catalog order are generally returnable—no questions asked.

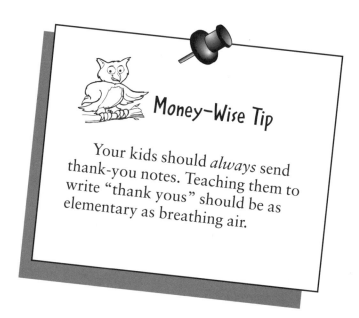

Money-Wise Tip

Your kids should *always* send thank-you notes. Teaching them to write "thank yous" should be as elementary as breathing air.

As kids get a little older, they are more discriminating about gifts. Preschoolers want everything they see, and they see something new nearly every day. Older kids are blessedly more specific. That's the upside. The downside is that their taste is almost always more expensive.

We have all heard Jesus' saying that "It is better to give than to receive." Unfortunately, the focus for giving during the holidays is often on family and friends and not on those less fortunate. My friend John was soon to pass the big fiftieth birthday. He and his family were happily planning a big "to-do" to celebrate the event.

Just before invitations were to be issued for the party, a local family with four young children was burned out of their home, and everything was destroyed. So invitations to John's party included a copy of a newspaper story that detailed this family's plight. A note was attached requesting that attendees bring a gift for one of this family's members. No birthday gifts for John would be allowed.

What a party it was! Mounds of gifts arrived for every member of the needy family. Toys, clothing, housewares—many brought more than one gift. The biggest thrill for John, however, was his own children's enthusiastic response to a giving, rather than receiving, event. John believes that he reinforced the giving philosophy in his children and that he introduced it to many at the party.

WHEN GIFTS ARE CASH

Gifts to children of cash or checks are becoming more and more common. Many wise parents set up a college fund savings account for their children, and they encourage the primary cash givers, usually Grandma and Grandpa, to designate that at least a portion be put in this account. Your child may feel that he should get to use all of his gift as he pleases. If he's over ten, here's your opportunity to talk to him about the cost of college.

Money-Wise Tip

It makes sense to let your child enjoy some of the gift money he receives so he can get in the habit of sending a thank-you note *with feeling*.

What happens if your kids are blessed with two sets of grandparents, and one set gifts the kids beyond all common sense and the other does not? Granted, kids can be materialistic little animals at times. They may be confused by the apparent financial limitations of the one set of grandparents. You must step in to make sure they don't confuse love with money. Help them recall the quality time spent with each set of grandparents.

THE WRONG GIFT

When your child receives gifts that you don't approve of, you must speak up. Try to anticipate the possibility of this problem with family and close friends by offering suggestions when asked. But should you be surprised by a gift that is on your "outlawed" list, let the giver know your feelings. It's probably best to have your child present and to offer some alternatives to the giver and the receiver. You might say something like this: "We appreciate your generous gift, but we don't allow guns in our home. We can take it to the store and exchange it, or you can. Billy, what would you like to exchange the gun for?"

What do you do with the gifts that are the wrong fit for your child? This happens more and more often after your child is age ten. The quickest and easiest answer is to try to prompt the giver of such a gift. Encourage dialogue with friends and relatives on the subject. Sometimes, givers simply don't have a clue what will satisfy a maturing child. A gift certificate could fit to a tee.

DOWNSIZING IS BAD NEWS

The nineties made two words household terms: downsizing and reengineering. If you have been caught in this, or expect to be, the family belt will have to be tightened. It's rare that a layoff or firing comes out of the blue. There is usually at least one warning bell that rings in your ear. The question is not, Do you let your family know that financial problems will be coming to live with you? It is, rather, *How* do you let them know? Tell them the truth to the degree that each child can understand at his age. And do it sooner, not later; your child will sense your tension and know that something is going on. Perhaps you can draw on the story recounted earlier of how I communicated to my kids my family's experience with bad news.

Money-Wise Tip

Kids are almost psychic—they can "feel" when there is bad news in the air. It's Family Meeting Time.

When cutbacks in spending are the inevitable choice, revisit the *Wants* and *Needs* lists.

Kids need to know at this time that they won't be destitute, but the *Wants* list will definitely be a non-dietary item in the family menu for a while. Reassure your child that the *needs will be addressed.* Your kids will be provided with food, shelter, warmth, and clothing. The quantity and quality may downsize, but you *will* weather the storm together.

Two books are suggested: Barbara Hazen's *Tight Times* (Puffin Books) and Beverly Cleary's *Ramona and Her Father.* Both books are about a father who loses his job. Age range for either is six to ten years. Scout your local library for new books that address this subject.

DIVORCE: PUTTING THE GLOVES DOWN

Divorce brings unique financial challenges to a home. Obviously, we don't have room to go into details here, so if you need more information, there are a variety of books about divorce and the children of divorce. One of the classics is *Mom's House, Dad's House: Making Shared Custody Work,* by Isolina Ricci (Simon & Schuster). Add this one to your bookshelf. *Surveying the Breakup: How Parents and Children Cope with the Divorce,* by Judith Wallerstein and Joan Berlin Kelly (Ticknor & Fields) offers excellent advice. Two other books that can be helpful are *A Guide to Divorce Mediation,* by Gary Friedman (Workman), an excellent resource that will reduce the costs and get communication back on track; and mine, *The Dollars and Sense of Divorce* (MasterMedia, Ltd.), which looks at the reality of divorce and outlines the planning that needs to occur.

Decisions that are not covered in a legal agreement are covered by defining which parent has the ongoing decision-making rights and responsibilities (sometimes this will be joint) for such areas as: communication between parents—when, where, and how; who will pay for and choose lessons, vacations, health care, transportation, and education; and how undefined visitation periods will be handled. Other decisions include:

- Who will care for the children when the custodial parent has to be away and if the "other" parent is to be advised of this temporary change in custodial care.
- Generally speaking, a child's illness and injury require that the other parent receive prompt notice.

- Information flow between parents regarding school: grades, special events, teachers' conferences.
- Arbitration of differences in opinion that the parents are either unwilling or unable to resolve on their own. Often other professionals are identified that can be called upon for assistance in resolving such disagreements.

AVOID GOOD GUY/BAD GUY

Children love *and* need both of their parents and have fierce loyalties to both. Do not, do not, do not "bad-mouth" your ex—bite your tongue.

Children will, and can, make their own decisions in time about who is the "good guy" and who is the "bad guy." Most parents (this includes your ex) do the best they can with the resources they have available at the time. Avoid appointing yourself judge and jury. And if you are caught in the middle of a "buying the child's love" scenario, don't join in.

Granted, children's loyalties can be swayed at times by gifts and special outings. But remember, you are after long-term results. The "Disneyland" parent is usually a short-term situation. Grin and bear it, and tell the child that he is lucky that his other parent is so generous.

REVISIT YOUR SPENDING PLAN

The financial demands on the divorced/custodial parent are tough. And they are often made more difficult when support payments don't come on a regular basis. Remedies for late payment of support through legal action will not be covered here. What is covered is the need for straightforward talks with your child about this new financial environment that has resulted from the divorce.

Carefully go over the new spending plan with your kids. They need to know why things can't be like they used to be, and further, that you are really doing the best you can under the circumstances. Invite them to brainstorm with you. Do they have ideas that can make the new spending plan more livable for all; can they be more helpful to you in making it a success? It's amazing how kids can pitch in—they have to be included, up front, for enhanced success.

Try very hard to establish good communication with your ex. Unfortunately, children master the art of manipulation quickly, and divorce brings this talent out in a big way. They play on the guilt of both parents and use it to get things that are definitely *Wants* and not *Needs*. Talking to the other parent will reveal their little plots and put an end to efforts to get you on the materialistic bandwagon. Quality time spent with the kids is the answer. Talk with your ex and establish routine allocations of this quality time that work for both of you.

BLENDED FAMILIES: PLAY NO FAVORITES

Remarried parents have to guard against the "Cinderella" syndrome. Put simply, this is playing favorites with your children, to the detriment of newly acquired stepchildren. First, you have to be sure that you are not afflicted with this child-damaging illness. Then you have to deal with the relatives and friends on both sides. Let them know how important the new stepchildren are to both you and your new spouse. This means that if Grandma comes loaded with gifts for "her" grandkids and nothing for the other kids, tell her the others may feel left out and you'd love it if she'd consider bringing something for them as well. Gifts are voluntary, but this is a new family unit and should be treated as such.

CUTTING THE PURSE STRINGS

Nicole is one of my closest friends. Her daughter is a junior at a West Coast university. One day, a message was left at my friend's office. It was from her daughter. "Mom, can you fax me some food?" My friend's first reaction was amusement—this kid has a sense of humor. Then, the mother in her became alarmed. She called for the details behind the message. Her daughter said she had *no money for food*. This didn't make sense to Nicole. They had spent a lot of time on the daughter's college budget, and there was more than enough in it to cover her basic needs. Truth will out: Jessica had been downtown shopping, and she just couldn't resist a sweater she found. The price tag—$100.

Like mother, like daughter—they both had expensive taste in clothes, so Nicole understood the enticement of a beautiful sweater. On the other hand, Nicole was angry. The sweater was not a budget item. Wise mother that she is, she offered two choices: "Take the sweater back for a refund, or eat it."

Jessica responded creatively. She took the sweater back and put it on lay-away. She got a partial refund, ate that month, and got the sweater two

145

months later. A case of you can have your sweater and eat it too!

Nicole took a big step by saying no and cutting the purse strings. Kids often think that their parents have a bottomless pit of money, and in some cases they are right. And, like Jessica, they have lapses of memory on the definition of *Needs* and *Wants*.

Save yourself some headaches and heartaches, and make sure that you have equipped your teen with experience in: checking and savings accounts, record keeping and balancing, credit cards, and spending plans. And, if you will soon have a college-age youngster, take the time to go over new spending items: dorm or apartment rental, furnishings for the new residential situation, how phone calls home will be handled (obtaining a calling card or an 800 number or participating in the special teen billing programs with one of the many phone companies are good solutions), how often you can afford the cost of travel home, etc.

When you begin to cut the purse strings, your child will be on the path to adulthood. Good for them and Bravo for you.

Chapter Ten

COLLECTING: JUNK, JUNK, AND MORE JUNK

Is your daughter's room jammed with Barbie dolls and your son's with comic books and baseball cards? Are they unable to part with the toys of their infancy and toddler years? Yes? Welcome, then, like it or not, to the collectible club.

There's an old adage that if you keep something long enough it will come back in style. Childhood toys are sought-after items because Americans are in love with nostalgia. When the nostalgia bug bites, collecting begins with those loved things from childhood. What's hot today will most likely be hot collectibles thirty to forty years from now.

When you absolutely can't stand the overpopulated condition of your kid's room and you are tempted to tell him that *a lot has to go* (to the trash or Goodwill), think again. He may be hoarding the beginning of a collection that will appreciate in value over the years if he keeps it. My parents did everything they could to discourage me from collecting. At the age of six, I discovered comic books; you name it, I had it. Hundreds of comics filled every corner of my bedroom; Superman, Super Boy, Archie, Casper, Little LuLu and Nancy, to name a few.

I had three brothers and was therefore more of a rough-and-tumble little girl; dolls were never a priority. But an aunt gave me a Madame Alexander storybook doll, and I was enchanted. These dolls had a wonderful porcelain quality to them, perfectly coiffed hair, and exquisite period and ethnic clothing. They didn't talk, cry, or wet; they weren't meant for cuddling or taking to bed. They were meant to be looked at and collected. My aunt gave me more, one for each birthday and each Christmas. Over the years, my collection of these dolls became quite extensive.

When I married, my mother cleaned out my room. My collections of comic books and Madame Alexander dolls were discarded. Those comic books that originally cost ten cents and the dolls that cost ten dollars would be worth thousands of dollars in today's collectible marketplace.

An important caveat needs to be added. Even though someone may say your (or your child's) favorite things are worth a lot of money, beware. Almost always, there is a deep discount taken on resales.

Prices quoted on collectibles by a dealer are not what you will get when you wish to sell your treasures. When selling collectibles, from comic books to fine antique furniture, it's a buyer's market.

BE A DISCRIMINATING COLLECTOR

If you have a child who has shown signs of being a pack rat and seems to have potential as a collector, help him develop good collection skills. For example, if you have a sports enthusiast under your roof, one of the many types of sports figure cards could be the choice. Is there money to be made here? You bet! The most valuable baseball card is the 1910 Honus Wagner trading card from Sweet Caporal cigarette packages. Wagner demanded that his photo be removed from trading cards because he was a nonsmoker and didn't want to support the tobacco companies. A man truly ahead of his time! Today, if you can find a mint condition Honus Wagner card, expect to fork over $300,000 to buy it.

What about cards depicting some of the more contemporary sports figures like Michael Jordan, Joe Montana, and Mickey Mantle? They all have value. In 1995, Mickey Mantle died. Before his death, a 1952 Topp #311 card in mint condition was valued at $30,000! Expect this one to jump up in value. If you have one of his cards, especially if it has been personally autographed, you have a valuable possession in your hands.

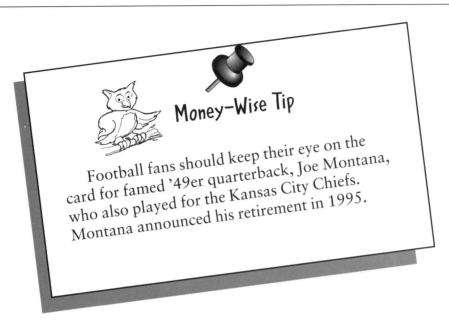

Money-Wise Tip

Football fans should keep their eye on the card for famed '49er quarterback, Joe Montana, who also played for the Kansas City Chiefs. Montana announced his retirement in 1995.

In 1995, Orioles baseball player Cal Ripken broke Lou Gehrig's streak of 2130 consecutive games. Wheaties cereal featured the new legend on its boxes. They became the hottest new collector item that fall. Why? Because General Mills, the maker of Wheaties, forgot to get a license from Major League Baseball, a major league boo-boo. Ah, but collectors swarmed in. Within days, the value of their $3 box of Wheaties climbed to $75. The question becomes, Do you eat the stuff?

MARVEL'S OVERKILL

A few years ago, Marvel Comics decided that they were going to "kill" Superman. There was a lot of press concerning his impending death. Collectors/investors lined up at comic book outlets to get the final issue that would recount the dastardly deed. The demand was so intense that Marvel comics went back to press seven times. As a result, the anticipated appreciation in value of this issue is not going to be great because too many copies were distributed.

Collectible pricing responds first to buyer interest and then to availability. Buyer interest in Superman's death declined and will remain depressed, due to the great quantity printed. The first printing has some added value, but subsequent issues can be purchased today at the original newsstand price.

MOVIES AND MUSIC YIELD MORE THAN ENTERTAINMENT

When the movie industry and fast-food chains found each other, it was love at first sight. It was a marriage made in heaven. Kids' meals at fast-food operations come with a toy in the sack or box that today is usually tied in to a recently released kid movie. Those toys and the box, if applicable, are collector's items. Might as well tuck away the decorated plastic cup the soda comes in too.

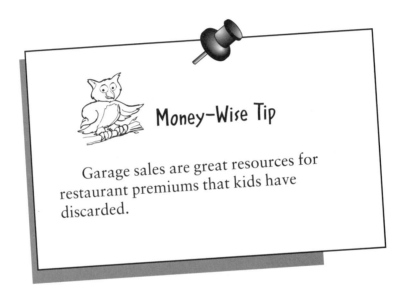

Money-Wise Tip

Garage sales are great resources for restaurant premiums that kids have discarded.

Do your kids love music? CDs and audio tapes they all know, but they won't recognize an LP or 33⅓ or 78 record. Those old records gathering dust in your (or your mom's) attic could fund a nice vacation. A kid who is a music buff could embark on a terrific collection. Truly a groovy way to make a buck. A Beatles recording sold originally in 1960 for a dollar now is worth a few hundred dollars—it's worth even more with the sleeve or jacket it came in.

In 1956, country and western singer Jim Reeves made his first album under the Abbott label, and it sold for three dollars. Its value today is $1,000, if you can find a copy of it. Then there are those demo records that were never released to the stores. They have more value than those that were released.

Have your music buff/collector keep his eagle eye out for special release or promotional CDs, audio tapes, and records that are usually distributed only to DJs. These are worth far more than the subsequent public releases. Movie sound tracks are also popular choices: The track for Humphrey Bogart's movie *The Caine Mutiny* is worth more than $10,000.

ACTION FIGURES ARE WHERE THE ACTION IS

The first action figures for boys were the G. I. Joe series. Today, these figures are so popular that there is a G.I. Joe guide to the value for each figure that has come out over the many years they have been around. Other action figures, primarily made to interest boys, have taken the throne from old Joe—Batman, The X-Men, Power Rangers, Ninja Turtles, Aliens, and Star Wars and Star Trek and the like. Figures from "Star Trek: The Next Generation" disappeared overnight from store shelves when they were first introduced. Each figure is imprinted with its own serial number denoting the date of manufacture.

Grandson Frankie is a devotee of Ryker, known to Captain Picard as No. 1 in the "Star Trek: The Next Generation" series. Within a few months, this figure's value increased from a few dollars to more than $100. The most popular Ninja Turtle figure was not one of the four Turtles, but the lone female of the series, non-turtle reporter April O'Neil.

The most famous female collectible is, of course, Barbie. Barbie is fifty years old now. Collectors prefer that these toys remain in their original packaging—to your kids this means hands off. Barbie dolls sell for six to thirty dollars each, today. Remember the brouhaha about Barbie and math a few years ago? Mattel created the Teen Talk Barbie series. What she spoke about upset a lot of parents. The "math-is-hard" line of dolls was immediately yanked from toy store shelves when parents (and the media) complained. This boo-boo in a popular line became a collectible overnight.

Encourage your collector kids to look for toy lines that are popular and for a line that has figures that are slightly different. In the Barbie line, most of the dolls are blondes. The Barbie with hair other than blonde will be worth more as a collectible.

151

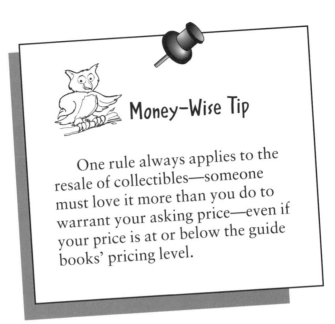

Money-Wise Tip

One rule always applies to the resale of collectibles—someone must love it more than you do to warrant your asking price—even if your price is at or below the guide books' pricing level.

IDENTIFYING TRENDS FOR THE FUTURE

- *Nostalgia counts.* Adult collectors of toys usually focus (because of their nostalgic value), on toys from their childhood years, and especially target ages seven to ten. Collectors say that a benchmark for a collectible is that it must be at least twenty years old. So pay sharp attention to what your seven to ten year old likes the most and help him or her focus on that toy line. And then, get the boxes and attic space ready for the twenty-year wait.

- *Your collector kids will have to treat their toys carefully* if they want to realize the best value from them later as collectibles. If your kids have zero to minimal interest in collecting, forget about what usage the toys undergo. After all, they are their toys. But if collecting is an objective, care needs to be given. And keep the boxes these toys come in. Grandson Frankie sold his six Power Ranger figures a year later, garnering a lot more for them than they originally cost, even though he had played with them. He had kept the boxes. For Frankie, Power Rangers were passé, but the new bills in his pocket weren't.

- *Movies and TV count.* Consider Walt Disney for a partner to your collector kid. Megamillions are put into commercial tie-ins. Millions of these toys and figurines are produced, but they seem to just disappear. So have your kid pick up one or two of each promotional series that comes out. Let the child play with one of each, and put the others away as a nest egg for him. He can, of course, review his collection at any time, but back in the box they go when he's through.

- *Collect what they love.* Collecting should be fun and not laborious for your child. Have her tell you what she really would like to collect and then help her to get a complete set if what she loves has different models and types in a series. Once the collecting bug bites, you will have a struggle at times convincing her that not all toys are collectibles. Some definitely should make a trip to the flea market or the trash when she outgrows the desire to play with them.

Hobby and comic book stores often carry published guides that serve as a starting point for you and your kids to determine the value of their collectibles. Another source is the public library.

Money $ense Resource Center

- Tomart Publications created a series of guides. The range of collectible types referenced is vast. Some of their published titles include:
  Tomart's Price Guide to Action Figure Collectibles, by Carol Markowski, Bill Sikora, and T. N. Tumbusch. The guide covers most action figures. In addition, there are separate guides dedicated to specific figures, such as G.I. Joe.
  Tomart's Price Guide to Golden Book Collectibles, by Rebecca Greason. Did you know that those little books from your childhood are worth money now? Learn and earn more by reading.
  Tomart's Price Guide to Hot Wheels Collectibles, by Michael Strauss. Hot Wheels are still hot—this guide lets you know just how hot they are.
  Tomart's Price Guide to Character and Promotional Glasses, by Carol and Gene Markowski. Tells you all you need to know about all the glasses from the fast food/movie tie-in promotions that are multiplying in your cupboard.
- *The Collector's Guide to Baseball Cards*, by Troy Kirk (Wallace-Homestead Book Company) tells baseball card collectors everything they need to know.

- *The Collector's Guide to Autographs*, by George Sanders, Helen Sanders, and Ralph Roberts (Wallace-Homestead Book Company) is the perfect guide for autograph seekers of the famous and not so famous.
- *The World of Barbie Dolls: An Illustrated Value Guide*, by Ferris and Susan Manos (Collectors Books) belongs on the bookshelf of the Barbie devotee.
- *Comics Values Monthly* (Attic Books, Ltd.) is the perfect partner for the comic book aficionado.
- *Kovels' Know Your Collectibles Price List* (Crown Publishers) is ideal to tell you what your treasures are worth.

Part Three

TEENAGERS

Chapter Eleven

CAUTION: TEENS AT WORK

Unless you are a rarity, your years of parenting a teenager are likely to be played out in the survival-of-the-fittest mode. Teens have youth and the resultant, boundless energy in their corner. Often it seems that they are certainly more fit for the match than their parents. If the foundations laid in the previous years have been effective, you can, with faith and a humorous outlook, survive the teen years and win at least a Pyrrhic victory or two.

A major concern as a parent is to rear your children in a way that assures you that they will be self-reliant adults one day. Strange as it may seem, teens have the same goal. So, in the teen years, their efforts to break the ties that bind them to the big "Ps" (that's you) are seen every day. Ah, but here's the rub. The other recurring theme of the teen years is *money*. Teens truly believe they need, rather than simply want, money. Your pockets may not be deep enough to meet their needs, but what parent's are?

Teenage Research Unlimited annually surveys teens and their parents regarding data on the employment of teens. In the nineties, one-third of teens (the twelve- to nineteen-year-old group) worked at jobs outside the home on a year-round basis, not just summer vacation employment. The amount of money earned by the teenage workforce is staggering. In 1995, teens' wages were almost $90 billion. Gross pay per week: twelve to fifteen year olds—$25, sixteen to seventeen year olds—$57, and eighteen to nineteen year olds—$123. It is, therefore, critical that your teen have broadly based financial management skills.

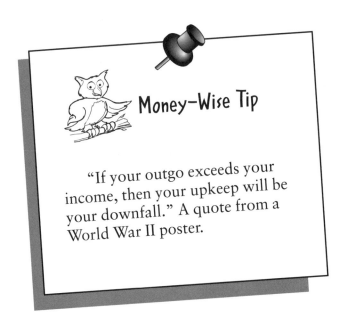

Money-Wise Tip

"If your outgo exceeds your income, then your upkeep will be your downfall." A quote from a World War II poster.

To find out what your teen knows about money management, duplicate the test on pages 271–72 and have them take it. But first, take the test yourself, giving the responses you think they are likely to give. Then you will have some idea about the degree of penetration your money counseling has had in their minds.

THE PROS AND CONS OF AFTER-SCHOOL JOBS

High school seniors who have jobs (after school and on weekends) average more than twenty hours of work in a week. These kids are really holding down two jobs: schoolwork and paid work. Four negative factors can affect your child's success in these two endeavors.

The Pros: An after-school job will help kids mature and prepare for the real adult world. They become more self-reliant. The income from their jobs gives them the opportunity to learn and put into practice a viable spending plan. As the newest member of the tax-paying population, they come to appreciate how much of your money goes to areas that you can't directly control. (Just who is FICA, and why is he taking my money?) With specific goals, they can sock away money for college or, most likely, a car.

The data show that both girls and boys enhance their self-esteem and gain confidence through outside work. Confidence comes from successful interaction in the real world of business, and self-esteem comes from the realization of earning power—they are (at least in part) taking care of themselves.

THE CONS INCLUDE:

Grades often decline: Every once in a while you hear or read a wonderful story telling of a student who excels at school, at home, and at work. The reason this is news is that it is the exception and not the rule. When kids begin to work, usually late in their high school careers, grades often decline. Many teachers accommodate these kids by reducing their load of homework and the number of long-term assignments, which includes outside reading. It might be said that teachers take the attitude, if you can't lick them, join them. What a mistake!

Materialism increases: America has evolved into a society of instant gratification. Too many Americans want it all and they want it now. Microwave cooking presents a good analogy—you've got a meal with a few zaps compared to hours of simmering to savory goodness in the oven.

Teens *work and spend* and get up the next day and do it again. It is a rare day when they *work and save*. They see the "gadget" they want to buy and, as soon as possible, they buy it. Then, the cycle repeats itself until they reach the pinnacle of teen materialistic endeavor—their own car.

Did they sit back and enjoy the fruits of their labors? Probably not. Do they experience the savory taste of success? They don't have time. What is alarming is that many American teens have become addicted to money.

This addiction results in an artificial standard of living that teens are loathe to sacrifice for long-term goals. Their educational aspirations become more oriented to the income the education will produce than to that which will satisfy the heart and soul in the adult employment world. They have watched many adults. They begin to feel that they too must have a new car at least every two to three years.

Alcohol and drug use increases: Researchers have compared teens whose primary income source is allowance from their parents to teens whose income is from outside the home. The results show that teens with outside jobs use more alcohol and drugs. The reasons for this are not totally clear, thus the remedy is not. The first possibility is that these kids have more money to spend. And perhaps accountability for the dollars they spend is not a part of their family lexicon.

Additionally, these kids are exposed to older teens, and they may take part in drug and alcohol use to appear "cool" and/or to enhance their ability move up in the ranks of "fitting in." Another possibility is that they may have seen their parents or others use alcohol and drugs to relieve stress, and they follow suit. After all, it's hard to hold down two jobs and cover the home front too.

Parental authority declines: According to recent studies, one-on-one interaction between parent and child totals only fifteen minutes per day. Teens have to leave early for their school job, and they sometimes have only a minute or two to bolt down food that hopefully resembles a balanced breakfast. Then they hit rush hour to commute to school by bus, car, or foot power. School is usually over for them by 2 to 3 P.M., and they can opt to socialize with friends, study, or go directly to their second job.

Dinner at home with the family is a thing of the past for these teens. Fast food after school or during a work-hours break is the usual fare, though penurious teens come home to eat a "delicious and nutritious" bowl of cereal or piece of cold pizza scrounged from the fridge. Study? They study on the run when they get home if they didn't study earlier.

Lights out, and a new but identical day begins in just a few hours. When do you, the parent, get your fifteen minutes with your teen whose existence is frenetic? Rarely.

WHAT TO DO:

- *Place a limit on time dedicated to outside employment.* Make sure that you haven't portrayed that you think that working outside the home is either the greatest thing they do or the worst. Your parenting efforts to create a sense of independence in your child should be positive for both of you. If your kids are going to work for pay, infuse in them a sense of moderation.

- *Help them dispel the philosophy of "more is better,"* and substitute a philosophy of balance. Work together for this balanced philosophy through efficient allocation of their time spent with school (studying and activities), outside work, family activities, recreation with friends, church, etc. Emphasize the pitfall of overcommitment—poor performance will result in one or several areas. Teens need to learn to budget time as well as money. Very soon in their future, time will be money.

Here is what federal law says about child labor limitations. For fourteen to fifteen year olds, the law says they can work a maximum of three hours on a school day or eighteen hours within a school week. Forty hours of work are permitted during nonschool weeks, with no more than eight hours per day. Summertime is not treated in the same manner with regard to the hours they can work. Between June 1 and Labor Day, these fourteen and fifteen year olds can work from 7 A.M. until 9 P.M. For teens over sixteen, there are no restrictions on the number of hours they can work and none on the time of day they can work.

- *Keep an eye on homework:* I believe that the biggest job you have in helping your child fine-tune his time budget is in the area of homework. If grades slip, a family powwow is in order, immediately. Something has got to go. Cut it now, and make the cut as painless as possible for all.
- *Monitor automobile usage:* The automobile is the big news at age sixteen. Before you hand them the keys for the first time, lay out the ground rules. Responsibility for additional insurance and gasoline costs have to be, at least in part, the teen's obligation. Discuss what hours, days, destinations, passengers, etc., are allowable. In my opinion, teens should pay for all gasoline they use, and they should pay for the better part of the insurance premium increase that resulted from adding them to your policy.

Some parents have found that the new teenage driver develops a case of grade dropsy. No errand is rejected when you have a new teenage driver in the house—he is having a good time. Driving is fun! I strongly advise that you nip this attention to RPMs, mag wheels, etc.—and quickly. It would be wise to suspend at least a portion of the teen's driving privileges if grades are suffering. Moderation of the suspension can be considered if grades improve or return to normal. Remember, driving is a privilege, not a right. Some driver's license test papers give teens this message for you—perhaps you could get a copy and post it.

FINDING THE PERFECT JOB

Some people never find the perfect job. Teens don't have the range of choices and pay that adults do, for some very obvious reasons. Teens first of all rarely put in a forty-hour work week year-round, nor do they stay on a job long enough to make extensive training cost-effective for an employer. Plus, they don't usually have the qualifications, skills, and experience that adults have. But, like adults, teens prefer work that is interesting and not stressful.

Where Do Kids Usually Start Out?

- *Flipping burgers.* The affair with hamburger heaven lasts for a relatively short time with the teen. The glamour is short-lived, but the work is excellent training for future jobs: Many people who landed their first job this way consider it the hardest work they have ever done. The learning curve for new employees is not at all steep. In a few months, they have mastered being on time, working within the team, filling orders under pressure at noon and dinnertime, and being pleasant to customers.

  Most hamburger joints pay minimum wage. Don't expect bonuses or benefits. A plus is that drive time to work is usually minimal—just about everyone can get to a fast food stand within five to ten minutes from home or school. Many stores, such as McDonald's, applaud kids who maintain good grades while in their employ by paying an extra ten to twenty cents per hour.

  If your teen waits tables or gets on a pizza delivery route, he can pick up tips. He needs to check with management to find out how tips are reported for taxes. Many restaurants assume a percentage and add it to the base pay when year-end income is reported to the IRS. The true figure will then need to be reported by your teen on his tax forms.

- *Retail sales.* My first job, in 1961, was as a sales clerk for the May Company department stores. The big pay was $1 an hour. Many teens start their real-world job experience in department stores, working at minimum wage. Kids can learn about merchandising and hands-on customer service. Working for a small retail operation does have additional advantages. In some cases the teen can work directly with the owner. Duties can include cashiering, setting and discounting prices, merchandise ordering and display, and taking inventory. A fringe benefit is that merchandise can be purchased at a discount.

- *Baby-sitting.* Most girls and some boys take their first for-pay job baby-sitting. This job has a lot of responsibility because the care of young children requires decision-making skills, and some decisions require great maturity. Baby-sitters don't usually make the money that teens make in retail and fast food. They do, however, have the flexibility to decide the hours that they work, the days they work, and who they will work for. Pay will vary depending on location, number of kids to care for, even the time of day or night. Most likely they will receive $2 to $4 dollars an hour.

  Unfortunately, an occasional parent will return at the end of the evening with an excuse for being unable to pay and a promise to pay sometime in the future. If your daughter has previously baby-sat for them and been paid, the reason sounds legitimate, and the arrangement for payment is satisfactory, no problem. But some parents have no intention to pay; they use one baby-sitter for free as many times as they can get away with it, then find a new one. Talk to your teen about such a possibility before it occurs so she will know what to say. If your teen wants to continue baby-sitting for the parent, she will need to set some ground rules. The teen may want to state that she will not baby-sit again for the family until *after* she receives payment and that in the future she must receive part or all of her pay at the beginning of the evening.

- *Community volunteer.* There are advantages to working and not getting paid. The pay comes in the form of experience in social work, medical careers, etc. In addition, your teen may meet some prominent people who could be excellent contacts for the more permanent jobs of the future.
- *Small businesses.* Many small businesses are willing to take on a teen as an intern. Pay ranges from zero (with the concept being that experience is invaluable) to minimum wage. This could be a "look-see" way to find out if the business is interesting enough to pursue.

In our office, Meghan works eight to ten hours a week. She has gotten a few bonuses. She got her birthday afternoon off with pay. Her work includes assembling press kits, inputting computer data, and working on the newsletter. She also prepares the mailing of thank-you gifts for our speaking

163

engagement clients. Meghan can specify what days and hours she works. This flexibility for busy teens is often possible for small businesses.

GETTING A JOB

One of the first things your teen can do is to look for "help wanted" signs in the windows of shops and businesses nearby. The teen will fill out an application and will either interview on the spot or wait for a call. Encourage your teen to look for a job that is different from the usual jobs teens have—take the contrarian approach. Some interesting opportunities could come up. Also tell him to put his application in at places that have not posted "help wanted" signs. If a business has an opening but has not yet put up a sign, your teen may be hired for it without facing the numerous job-hunting competitors that signs bring in.

Meghan is a neighbor's child, and my first inkling that she could be a good employee came when we were at dinner in her home early one summer. We were shown around the house, and I was very impressed with the immaculate condition of her bedroom. Later that evening I told her mother that I planned to contact the nearby high school and talk to their teen placement counselor concerning a part-timer. Meghan's mother said I should first talk to Meghan, because she was going the same route for a job when school started. Neither Meghan nor I expected that our job hunt would be filled in our own backyard and with such flexibility.

If transportation is not a problem, have your teen check the classified ads. Many professionals now have evening and weekend hours for their businesses and practices.

Money-Wise Tip

Lee Ellis has put together The Career Exploration Kit—a basic package for kids in grades eight to ten. It contains a career guidance booklet, an audiotape explaining the career development process, and a career-interest inventory survey. Call (800) 722-1976 for information.

Your Teen's Résumé

Encourage your teen to put his or her accomplishments in writing. Include scholastics, extracurricular activities, and community activities, and highlight the ones where kudos have been given. Your daughter, who is a master negotiator, might have a résumé that looks like this:

1993 TO PRESENT
BABY-SITTING AND CHILD CARE

- Skilled in negotiating with children ages 2 to 10

- Skilled in creating new games to offset possible addiction to TV

- Expert in assisting children ages 4 to 10 in identifying their needs versus their wants

- Baby-sitting started in 1993 with one family, increased to 10 families from referrals based on highly satisfactory performance of duties.

The majority of employees of teenagers do not need a résumé; many will refuse to look at one and want only to see a completed application. But office jobs will often ask for a résumé, and the process is valuable anyway. Have your teen write down: (1) what his objective is (what type of job he wants); (2) his experience, especially if it is related to the objective; (3) his hours of availability; and (4) references.

When your teen first shows interest in looking for a job, assign him the task of bringing home two or three applications. You will then be available to answer the inevitable questions, and you can look over the applications with him after he has completed them. Did he miss a question or misunderstand what the employer wanted? Did he answer a question in such a way that his application would automatically be rejected? In the future, he might find it easier to fill out a batch of applications without bringing them home, but he should take along an index card filled out with data he will need and might forget: his Social Security number; former employers, dates worked, and a phone number for each; names, addresses, and phone numbers of two or three references (who usually cannot be family members).

Clothes *Do* Make the Teen

No grubbies allowed, nor is formal dress appropriate, unless your teen has his eye on the maître d' position. Conservative is the best choice—for girls a simple dress, blouse and skirt, or stylish pants outfit; and for boys, dressy shirt and slacks (with or without a jacket) and possibly a suit. Tailor the clothing choice to the dress mode of employees where the interview is taking place. How do you find out? Check the dress of employees by observing from the outside or visiting the reception area and observing "housekeeping" as well as the receptionist. Or, just ask.

Money-Wise Tip

Do not, do not, do not wear clothes with holes in them. And take out the nose-ring!

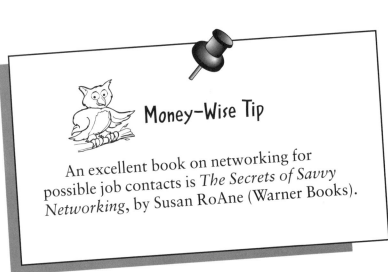

Money-Wise Tip

An excellent book on networking for possible job contacts is *The Secrets of Savvy Networking*, by Susan RoAne (Warner Books).

BE POLITE AND PERSONABLE

Teach your kids how to shake hands. Boys are generally more skilled. It is important for the young person to learn to make eye contact, repeat the person's name out loud, and say "It's nice to meet you, Mr. (or Mrs.) Smith." Practice does make perfect, and it's amazing how many people miss the boat by not knowing how to shake hands.

If your son or daughter is required to attend a function where name tags will be used, have him or her place the tag on the upper right shoulder. Why? When people shake hands with them, they have eye contact with the name tag.

THE TAX MAN COMETH

The real world of business really impacts your teen when he gets his first paycheck. Federal, FICA, state—all these withholding taxes are your kid's partners in work for pay every payday. Employees who earn less than $2,500 annually (the current floor at this writing) are not liable for federal income tax.

Make sure that your child's employer is withholding the correct amount from each paycheck, if you feel that the child will exceed the floor. Kids are not tax wise, and if their withholdings aren't correct and they owe tax to Uncle Sam, their tax bill could require a loan out of your pocket if they haven't saved any money—an amount Uncle Sam doesn't credit you for!

Payroll stub formats vary. Have your teen contact the payroll department if there is any question about the information detailed on the stub. And tell your teen to check it carefully each payday—mistakes happen. Make sure your teen gets a W-2 Wage and Tax Statement from any employers he had during the previous calendar year by January 31 each year so taxes can be filed correctly and on time.

When your kids start working outside the home, one important form they will have to fill out is Form W-4, Employees Withholding Allowance Certificate. If you are very sure that your child will earn less than $2,500 from all his or her jobs for the calendar year, he or she can claim an exemption from withholding. To be exempt an individual must meet one of the three following conditions:

Money-Wise Tip

When your son or daughter works outside the home, he or she has to start paying Social Security withholding tax. There is one interesting exception—if the child works at the college in which he is enrolled as a full-time student, he is exempt from this tax.

- No tax liability is anticipated for the upcoming calendar year.
- If her income exceeds $650 and her parents plan to claim her as a dependent, she has no non-wage income (dividends or interest from savings).
- No taxes were owed in the preceding year.

In the 1990s, Take Your Daughter to Work Day was birthed. For the first time, daughters were welcomed in the workplace by both fathers and mothers. I think this was a grand idea, but what about Take Your Son to Work Day?

Many high schools have "Career Day" types of programs that have been going on for at least twenty-five years in some locations. They provide older teens with an opportunity to check out job markets and ask questions about the pros and cons of a specific job, the risks and rewards, and the myths and realities. They may see demonstrations of product development, manufacturing, and marketing from wholesale to retail. And they may see why some products succeed and some products bomb. If your teen's school isn't hosting such a program, see what can be done to get one going. Nothing teaches so well as "Life 101."

RETIRING YOUR TEENS

Teens think they are invincible and immortal. They don't have a clue yet as to how quickly the years pass. For teens, retirement is not yet in the list of events for their future.

Anyone who makes money is eligible to open an individual retirement account—IRA. The primary reason for introducing teens to this investment opportunity, is to get long-range planning in their minds. Teens can, like you, invest up to $2,000 per year of their earnings in an IRA.

Go back to the Magic of Compounding Table on page 126. Let's say your daughter, age nineteen, has accumulated $2,000 in an IRA account, and you want to see what she can expect the account to be worth at age thirty-nine. The average rate of return for twenty years is 10 percent. At the end of twenty years, her $2,000 has grown to $13,440. No taxes have had to be paid during the deferral period of time. Any subsequent deposits would, of course, up the ante of the gains in value. Add another twenty years at 10 percent, and the account would be worth $90,316.80. If this appeals to your daughter, show her what she would have at age sixty-five— $145,410.48. All seeded with only $2,000 at age nineteen, with an annual rate of growth at 10 percent.

By starting your kids thinking about retirement when it is a foreign word, you not only reinforce a savings habit, but you introduce them to the concepts of profit sharing, pensions, deferred compensation, and 401(k) programs—lifelong habits that will pay back many times over.

Money $ense Resource Center

Some excellent books on jobs are teen specific, and others require an "adult-minded" teen for readability. Here are a few suggested titles for the mature teen (and yourself).

The Pathfinder: A Guide to Career Decision Making
By Lee Ellis. Covers making good and bad career decisions, résumé writing, vo-tech schools, college, and overall career decisions. Available through CFC (800) 722-1976, or write: P.O. Box 1476, Gainesville, GA 30503-1476.

Your Career in Changing Times and *Finding the Career That Fits You*
Both by Lee Ellis and Larry Burkett. Both books look at conducting job searches and successful interviewing techniques. Both are available through Moody Press.

Lifetime Employability: How to Become Indispensable
By Carole Hyatt. A guide to the mysteries of the business universe that will help you evaluate your attitudes, skills, and goals. One of the objectives of the book is to increase your staying power and to be alert to changing opportunities. Available through Master Media, Ltd. (800) 334-8232.

The Career Coach
By Carol Kleiman. Kleiman has three columns that are nationally syndicated: "Women at Work," "Jobs," and "Your Job." This book will serve as a navigator for the ups and downs of the workplace. Available through Dearborn Financial Publishing, 155 Wacker Drive, Chicago, IL 60606-1719.

Chapter Twelve
ENTREPRENEURING: THE ABCs

Quick. What do lemonade stands, garage cleaning, gift wrapping, bike repairs, and pet walking have in common? Answer: They are five of more than 150 project and business ideas that kids of all ages can get involved in that were culled from a few books on the subject. When kids express a desire to start their own business, the first ideas that come to their minds are the old standbys from your childhood and mine—lemonade stands, lawn mowing, and baby-sitting.

Encourage your young businessperson (and yourself too) to stretch beyond tradition for fresh opportunities to make some money. Find ideas that fit their interests and abilities. That's what Daryl Bernstein did. In his book, *Better Than a Lemonade Stand* (Beyond Words Publishing), he describes fifty businesses. His book isn't just another idea book. He describes the "start-up" parameters for each, lists of needed supplies, the allotted time needed for setup and eventual operation, and even advertising ideas that are specific to the particular venture. Bernstein has "walked his talk." He tried, and was successful in, all fifty of the businesses he describes—all before he was sixteen.

He offered maid service for the homes of caged pets. His house-sitting services included picking up mail; watering plants; feeding, watering, and walking pets. And for real fun, he was a birthday party director for hire. Like a lot of kids, he started with a lemonade stand. The success of this venture quickly led him to seek something more profitable. Bernstein succeeded, where many kids don't, because he observed a need and found a way to fill it. He began lots of innovative niche businesses this way.

The grand opening of a lemonade stand during the winter months in my home state of Colorado would fail miserably. Instead of taking the well-worn trails to entrepreneurship, open your kids' eyes to less conventional possibilities.

Newspapers are delivered even on the worst of our winter days and are left on driveways sometimes thigh-deep with snow. A service a Colorado kid could provide would be to *re*deliver the newspapers to the front steps of his neighbors' homes. People flock to our state to enjoy the winter sports, but I suspect residents would pay to avoid skating or skiing down their driveways to get their paper. In fact, one way to initiate the service is to give it a free run. Your child might redeliver the papers, then later in the day call on the neighbors to see if they liked the convenience of getting their paper on the porch.

Most will respond quite positively. Then the child can let them know what his terms are for continuing the service. Your kid could charge $1 per week or $3 per month if paid in advance. Get ten subscribers—an easy $30 per month that an eight year old would be glad to have. A chat about responsibilities should be delivered *before* anyone prepays or makes a commitment to become your child's customer. What if he collects in advance, spends his money, then decides he doesn't like his job? If your child drops out, who replaces the service or repays the money—you?

You might want to forestall this problem—and allow him to continue to work toward a *future* payday, rather than doing drudgery to earn money he has already spent—by collecting his earnings from him and then distributing them on a weekly "payday." (If taxes will be owed, withhold them.) If the child collects tips, he can keep them, but he needs to report the amount to you.

Getting Started

On my last visit to the Young Americans Bank in Denver, I picked up a brochure entitled "How to Prepare a Business Plan." This brochure outlines the information a bank wants to see when reviewing a venture in advance of lending money to the business (Young Americans *really does* make loans to kids for their businesses).

A business plan or proforma includes: the product or service; who will run the business; what is the overhead (supplies, equipment, etc.); what income can be expected. And, most important to the bank: how much loan money is needed, how it is to be spent, and the repayment terms possible from revenues of the business. The brochure points out that a business plan helps define the issues a youngster will face in starting a business.

Money-Wise Tip

There are four major areas of any kid's business venture that your entrepreneur should outline *on paper*:

- A basic description of the idea(s)
- Where did the idea come from?
- What is the product or service?
- Who is the customer?

In advance of the preparation of a formal business plan (which few kids will do without help and encouragement), *Money-Wise* kids need to ask themselves a series of questions.

Included are:

- What am I going to do?
- When will my business be in operation (seasonal or year-round)?
- Who will my customers be?
- Can I do this in my neighborhood, or will transportation be necessary?
- What will I call my business? (Will the name tell prospective customers what I do?)
- Is there competition for my product or service? (If there is: Are people satisfied with what they are getting? Can I do it better or differently? How much are they paying?)
- What should I charge, and how do I expect to be paid (at the time of service or in advance, or after the service is rendered)?

- How much of my time will I have to devote to the business, and what time of the day and day of the week is appropriate?
- Is any special equipment necessary? What supplies are needed to start, and what is needed for continuing operation?
- How much money will I need to get the business started, and where or how will I get it? If I borrow money, how will I pay it back if my business isn't successful?
- How will I advertise to let potential customers know about my business?

And most important of all,

- Is there a need for my product or service?

A few resources supportive parents can obtain to help their budding entrepreneurs get up and running include the following.

The Busine$$ Kit—how to own your own business, for ages ten to eighteen.

The cost is $49.95, plus $8.95 for postage and handling. The kit includes: manuals, tapes, stationery, and other tools. It show kids how to start and run a business, with support via an 800 hotline phone number kids (or you) can call for advice as the business progresses. This kit is expensive, but use of its toll-free number could save you dollars and time down the road. To purchase or get further information call: (800) 282-5437.

A Lemonade Stand: A Guide to Encouraging the Entrepreneur in Your Child—for supportive parents. This book written by Emmanuel Modu (Bob Adams, Inc.) includes information on tax considerations for the kid business, legal issues, and various concepts your child should know. For example: If your kid's business will earn more than $400, self-employment tax (Social Security) is assessed.

The next two books work well for you and your child, when used together:

Fast Cash for Kids—for kids under age sixteen
Written by Bonnie and Noel Drews (Career Press), this book identifies

more than one hundred money-making projects. Projects are grouped according to the most appropriate season of the year.

The Teenage Entrepreneur's Guide—for kids sixteen and up.

Written by Sarah L. Riehm (Surrey Books), this book includes information on business plans, bookkeeping, and paying taxes.

Another valuable resource is:

The Teen's Guide to Business, by Linda Menzies, Oren Jenkins, and Rick Fisher, presents excellent role models from all ethnic, economic, and geographic backgrounds. This is solid information on how to succeed in a user-friendly, illustrated format. Available through MasterMedia, Ltd. (800) 334-8232.

The Drews, authors of *Fast Cash for Kids*, make some important points that even adults need to be reminded of. When kids are trying to pitch their ideas or services to adults, they should:

- Tell all the reasons why they think the potential customers should buy the product or services and how they will benefit.
- Tell why it is important for them to purchase or subscribe right away.
- Not give up if told "No" (if the prospect isn't interested, ask if he knows of someone who might be).
- If the potential customer says "Yes," provide the product or service promptly, courteously, and thoroughly each time ("Thank yous" are important too).

MISTAKES HAPPEN: PARENT ALERT

What if your kid bites off more than he can chew? Kids, like adults, often overextend themselves when they are excited about something new. Step in and help them focus on what they really can do with their resources of time and ability. If you see they are heading the wrong way, don't just criticize, but also offer a solution or two for their dilemma. Praise them when they succeed, and pick them up, with love, when they fall. Also, ask your child if he is having any fun being a businessperson. If he responds negatively, go back to the drawing board for a new venture. Adults may have the discipline to keep working at a job that they don't like, but kids usually don't.

When starting up a business, kids will make some of the same mistakes that adults do. Undercapitalization is the most common; they don't properly identify what they need to buy in supplies, equipment, etc. And they may not have figured correctly what the costs will be down the road to sustain the business—the cash flow concept. Cash flow means getting enough customers to pay for the goods or services you offer that you can replenish your inventory or supplies.

With the first blush of success, the young entrepreneur may be blinded by dollar signs in his mind's eye. It is very likely that, if you don't monitor him, he will oversell his product or service and thus be unable to supply his customers on a timely basis.

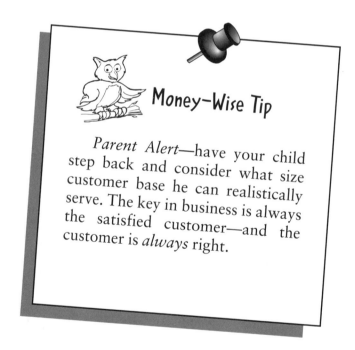

Money-Wise Tip

Parent Alert—have your child step back and consider what size customer base he can realistically serve. The key in business is always the satisfied customer—and the customer is *always* right.

THE IMPOSSIBLE-TO-SATISFY CUSTOMER

OK, in the real world, the customer is not always right. That's only a slogan. Will the kid have the freedom to drop an annoying customer? If he can't, he may begin dreading his job. Sticking with it can, of course, be a learning experience, but, depending on his age and the situation, the experience might be too overwhelming.

If one customer is causing your child apparently needless headaches, it may be time for you and him to talk to the customer. Ask the customer how the service could be done to his or her satisfaction. As an adult, you will probably have a better "feel" for the situation than your child does (although the customer might well be nicer to your child in front of you). The customer's complaint may be legitimate. Or you might agree with your child that, yes, this customer seems impossible to satisfy. If the arrangement is still not satisfactory (to everyone involved) in two weeks, your child can drop the customer. (If you are unsure of your child's physical safety, or if he is afraid of the customer, dropping the account immediately would be a wiser alternative. Children's instincts are sometimes better than adults' here.)

KIDS, INC.: BOARD MEETING IN SESSION

You might want to encourage regular board meetings (parents attend these) to review your youngster's business progress. A review of the pricing for your kid's product or service is important. He may be losing customers to the competition if the price is too high—regular review of the competition's services and pricing is a must. Or he may not be charging enough.

Let's say your son has a lawn mowing and general yard maintenance service. One customer contracted to have her front yard mowed and the front flower beds weeded once a week for a price of $20. This customer now wants him to weed the backyard at no extra cost. Time for review—your kid needs to ask for more money. He won't do the extra work if the answer is no. Point out that if he takes too long on one job doing "extras," he may not get another customer's yard done correctly and on time.

The second regular item to be reviewed at your board meetings is the income/profit picture of the child's business. Is the business making a profit after expenses are paid? If not, identify the reasons and find ways to get the business in the "black." Or encourage him to consider other new ventures that can be profitable.

If the business is humming right along and your kid is making a bundle, what is he doing with the money he makes? Is he reinvesting his profits and/or spending every dime on himself? Encourage a savings plan that puts away close to 50 percent of his net profits (income less expenses). Encourage him to salt away as much as possible.

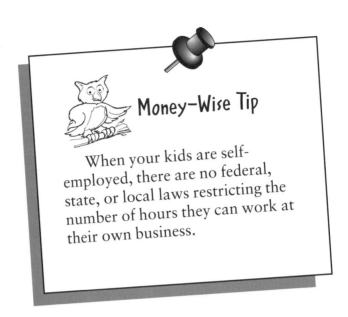

Money-Wise Tip

When your kids are self-employed, there are no federal, state, or local laws restricting the number of hours they can work at their own business.

HERE COME THE FEDS: FORMS AND TAXES

Whenever there is money to be made, there is usually some red tape attached—taxes. If your kid's business has one employee—the young entrepreneur—and doesn't have any other paid "gophers," there are no restrictions on the number of hours your child works or when, during the day, he can choose to work. Under federal law, fourteen is the minimum age for most nonfarm work. But the federal law applies only to employer/employee relationships.

So, to avoid this issue, both you and your kid need to think twice about hiring other kids to man the expanding business. It might make more sense to take in another kid for a partner than to hire work done. But if he does want to hire other kids to help with the work of cleaning garages or repairing bicycles, say hello to the world of government forms. A free publication, *The Handy Reference Guide to the Fair Labor Standards Act,* can be obtained by calling the U.S. Dept. of Labor at (202) 209-4907. This booklet will, hopefully, clarify the do's and don'ts of the issue of employees.

If kids decide to operate their business under any name other than their own, they are required to register the business name with the county clerk's office in the county of their business operation. Most kid ventures start as a sole proprietorship. If your child's endeavors pan out to be a major gold strike, seek tax and legal advice. It's amazing how many businesses that started out headquartered in garages and backyards have produced young millionaires!

They may also need to get a business license. Check with your local authorities for the requirements on new businesses in your locale—*before* your kid gets under way. Some penalties for noncompliance are severe. Also, before your kid starts plying his trade in nearby neighborhoods, have him check the targeted business areas for street signs that prohibit any solicitation. Some subdivisions or complexes have these signs only at the main entrances.

Check out the local tax situation. Your kid's goods or services may be subject to taxation, by one or all of the local tax authorities. Find out now. Unpaid taxes, and the penalties and interest assessed on them, could come out of your pocket.

For further assistance in helping your entrepreneur learn about the responsibilities of having his own business, there are two national organizations that offer ongoing assistance and resources.

Junior Achievement coordinates interaction between schools and businesses. They offer hands-on experience to students regarding business organizations, management and marketing techniques, and production procedures. For information, write to Junior Achievement, 45 E. Clubhouse Drive, Colorado Springs, CO 80906, or call (709) 540-8000.

The Center for Entrepreneurship is an organization that offers comprehensive, one-stop resources in educational opportunities for your young businessperson. Adults and students are welcomed. For information, write to The Center for Entrepreneurship, Wichita State University, 1845 N. Fairmount, Wichita, KS 67260, or call (316) 689-3000 and ask for the center.

Your local Chamber of Commerce can be a good source for programs for aspiring entrepreneurs. In addition, The National Association of Women Business Owners; Girls, Inc.; and the Girl Scouts of America all have programs designed to reach out to young people. Don't forget your local library as another fine source for resources on entrepreneurship. Cassettes, videos, and books galore are available upon presentation of your library card. And the price is right—free.

Chapter Thirteen

CREATING A WALL STREET WIZARD

Picking stocks can be likened to playing a game of darts. Like the dart player, aim and fire at your targeted stock and you can have a complete miss, a bull's-eye, or something in between. Even the best of professional advisors will admit there is some luck involved in picking stocks. However, although a logical, rational, and educated approach to selecting stocks for investment might miss a few of the "shooting star" stocks, it will produce a portfolio of solid stocks with consistent earnings and growth. Over the years, I have become convinced that there are ways that any novice investor (adult or child) can "play" the stock market. And with some homework, the novice can outperform the vast majority of the professionals, sans the dart board.

In the eighties I taught a weekend seminar for forty women at a local university. On the first day, I presented the basics of the stock market, highlighting a few of the simple rules for evaluating the information available to the investor who is considering a stock purchase. That kind of information is readily available in publications such as *Business Week*, *U.S. News & World Report*, *Money* magazine, and *Kiplinger's Personal Finance Magazine*.

I showed the group how to determine book values; percentage increases; price/earnings ratios; and ratios of profits and dividend distributions to growth, sales, and earnings, etc. For the companies that were presented, the corresponding *Value Line Investment Survey* was included. *Value Line* is one of the top-rated stock advisories and is available at no cost at most stock brokerage offices. If you do not have a stockbroker, the local library is a source (free!), or you could subscribe on your own. It's expensive—more than $200 per year.

The seminar participants were taught how to read the *Value Line*. Homework was assigned for the first evening. They were asked to evaluate stocks of companies in the fast-food industry. Their evaluation was to be based on historical information such as annual percentage increases (or decreases) for gross sales, profits, and dividend distribution. The challenge was to identify the company they would invest in if the money were available to them, based on the new knowledge they had gained from their evaluation.

The following morning the results were presented. The majority of the class had chosen a stock that few of them had ever heard about. That unknown stock of the eighties is a stock whose shares are held today by major institutions all over the world.

The following year this stock gained significantly. The company displayed an aggressive and forward-looking approach to business. Investors seemed to appreciate the vision of the company's management. This was no surprise to the stock market neophytes who had attended my seminar. What was the stock? Wendy's, named after the daughter of owner and founder Dave Thomas. You may be thinking, *You were teaching adults, what can you teach to children?* Plenty.

KIDS ARE CAPITALISTS

Ten percent of kids age eleven and over put savings into stocks and mutual funds. In 1972, I became a stockbroker. Four years later, I was in front of my daughter's eighth grade class to present what I knew about the stock market. Together, the class and I developed a typewriter company (on paper only) and named it after their teacher. As we took the company through production and sales of typewriters, the students learned about profit and loss statements and balance sheets. They learned about the different kinds of stock, common and preferred.

We also covered bond issues. We floated an issue called Grandma's Bond with 7 percent interest, maturing in 1977, to obtain operating capital to fund our projected growth. When we finished, each student—with an average age of thirteen—could dissect an annual report and put together a business plan that would be admired by any banker.

Ten years later, my younger daughter's school asked me if I would develop a stock market seminar for their senior class. I fine-tuned what I had done earlier for the eighth grade and took on the seniors. These kids developed a soda company, learned the ways to capitalize their venture, and dug into the elements of a balance sheet (do we really need to inventory that many bottle caps?). On paper, we developed The Mid-Peninsula Beverage

Company. We took it into the production and marketing of products, and we eventually sold the venture.

Then we went on to learn about trading on the stock market. They devoured the Apple Computer annual reports I had supplied. Each kid was given a theoretical $100,000 investment account, with the challenge to increase the account through "trading" on the real stock market. I was their broker, and they had to call me at a prearranged time each day with any trades (buying or selling) for stocks in their portfolios.

The kids were not allowed to just sit on their portfolios. They were told they would flunk the class if they didn't position their moneys in some type of investment. Like the real world, brokerage fees and commissions were charged against their accounts for each trade they made. By the time the class ended, most students had more in-depth knowledge of the stock market than their parents did.

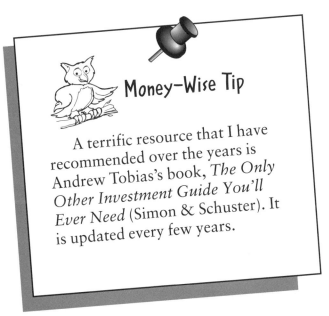

Money-Wise Tip

A terrific resource that I have recommended over the years is Andrew Tobias's book, *The Only Other Investment Guide You'll Ever Need* (Simon & Schuster). It is updated every few years.

Historically, no single investment has outperformed the consistency of the stock market. It is true that there are people who have become millionaires overnight, some from the invention of some gadget, but they are in the minority. The majority of successful investors use segments of Wall Street. If you are a novice to stock investments, you will learn a lot from this chapter, and so will your kids.

How to Select Stocks and Eat (or Play) Them Too

One of the best ways to get your kids involved in the stock market is to step up and purchase some shares. When you buy one or two shares of stock, you will be a bit dismayed when you see the value of your investment immediately decrease via the deduction of brokerage fees and commissions. However, the lessons you and your child will learn are priceless.

When Frankie was in his Mighty Morphin Power Ranger period, his adoring grandmother (me) checked out the local Toys R Us to see what toys had resulted from the love affair kids had with this series of programs. I learned a lot. The general manager of the store told me that the shelf life of a Power-Ranger related item was seven hours—a merchant's dream—and that waiting lists for many items were routine.

He also told me that a general manager of an auto parts store (an adoring parent) offered to give a deep discount on the prices of all his merchandise—but only if the toy store manager would give him advance warning of the arrival of any shipment of Power Ranger toys. A person doesn't need a Ph.D. to know someone was making money—a lot of money—and very quickly.

Notice what kids are spending money on. There's Nintendo, Sega Genesis, Sony, and Marvel comic books. And, don't forget what kids like to eat—why not a comparison of Pepsi and Coke for your first exercise in stock watching? Or compare the performance of Wendy's versus McDonald's and other fast-food outlets.

When considering stocks for your child's investment program, make your selection from a market segment he understands. You will have his interest immediately, and you will keep it. If your kids are into sports, consider companies that make sport shoes, clothing, and equipment. How about movies and music? Let your kids check out the companies that produce and/or distribute their favorites. If parents and kids keep their eyes and ears open, the opportunities for interesting investments are limitless.

Pay close attention to TV commercials as the holidays approach, or take a walk in a big toy outlet to scan the huge array of toys and games. Which ones beckon to your pocketbook? The old standby toy lines, Tonka Toys and PlaySkool, are produced by one company, Hasbro; Mattel produces both Hot Wheels and Barbie.

SOME PERKS COME WITH OWNERSHIP

Unless your kid is a child prodigy, he or she may not be very enthusiastic about receiving stock shares for a gifting occasion. At least not initially. There are some ways to get their attention. Try food, electronics, and entertainment companies for starters, because many of these companies offer a goodie bag or perks to shareholders.

For example, the William Wrigley, Jr. Company sends each stockholder a hundred-stick box of gum at Christmas. Tandy Corp. routinely gives shareholders a 10 percent discount off a purchase at Radio Shack. This can add up quickly. In fact, Tandy allows the 10 percent discount on purchases of up to $10,000, as long as the purchases are all made at the same time. Ho-ho-ho.

If you like Disney, you may love the Big Red Boat and its "family fun" cruise package, combining Disney World and Big Red Boat cruises. Disney's Magic Kingdom Club offers its shareholders the opportunity to purchase the Club Gold Card. For $39, shareholders get a variety of discounts, ranging from 10 to 30 percent, at different theme parks and resorts. There are discounts for the Big Red Boat and rental cars.

TRENDS AND FADS

At a garage sale, Frankie and I came across something that was hot in the eighties. Pet Rocks cost five dollars new, but this one could be purchased for five cents. Do you remember Cabbage Patch dolls? Parents spent many hours in lines to pay $100 or more for such a doll, but in a very few years, the price of them plummeted and the producing company went into bankruptcy.

Pet Rocks and Cabbage Patch Dolls are categorized as fads and not trends. The only time that fortunes or empires are made as a result of a fad is when an investor gets his money in the pot early when the stock price is low and out before the fad dies and the stock price and/or the company dies. Obviously, it's a risky investment.

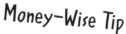

Money-Wise Tip

Before going any further, get a copy of *Ump's Fwat: An Annual Report for Young People*. The cost is $3 from The Academy for Economic Education, 125 NationsBank Center, Richmond, VA 23277, or call (804) 643-0071. Ump is the original caveman capitalist. The book will help kids learn and understand the basic terminology used in the stock market and capitalism. A teacher's guide is also available for $3.

Money-Wise Tip

Remember that children need a Social Security number when they reach the age of one. Your child needs one before any custodial accounts can be set up. The appropriate forms are available from your local post office or Social Security office.

LET THE BRAINSTORMING BEGIN

When you make *any* kind of investment that will be held in your minor child's name, an adult's name will have to be included as custodian.

First, set aside time for a monthly family investment meeting. Since the stock market can "move" a lot in a month, you can choose to meet more often. Let your kids know that this will be a time for brainstorming investment ideas and strategies. With your copy of *Ump's Fwat* in hand (you and your kids can each afford to have one at the low price of three dollars), roll up your investment sleeves.

- Whenever I taught a stock market class to young people, the classics of Disney and McDonald's were on most kids' investment wish list. Their choices expanded after they were more familiar with the methodology of investing and their awareness level of opportunities was heightened.

- A lot of information is free, so start with your library. Most have a terrific investment section, and they should also carry the *Value Line Investment Survey*. In *Value Line*, you will find, on one page, all you want to know about a targeted company. Its past, present, and analysts' projections for the future are included. A sample from *Value Line* for Mattel, Inc. and how to read it can be found on page 197.

- When your kids have narrowed their investment opportunity target list down to a few companies, write or call for their annual reports. The mailing addresses can be found in *Value Line*. Review the annual reports, and select one company that you are comfortable with *and* excited about. Then take the plunge and purchase one or more shares. If a mutual fund is your selection, a minimum investment will be required. Review the *Money $ense Resource Center* at the end of this chapter for a list of groups that can minimize commission costs.

When buying just a few shares of stock, making a profit is minimized. Commissions for buying and selling can gobble up what is gained, but the lessons and experience are valuable. Don't be afraid of approaching a broker for assistance. When I was a broker, it was routine for parents to open an account for their kids. And many transactions were for less than $100.

If you don't have a broker, I recommend you contact your local office of Charles Schwab & Company. Their customer service is excellent, and they are dedicated to education—no matter what the age! There are many young companies (and distressed old ones) whose shares sell for a few dollars; a few years later, they often sell for many times the lower price. See my discussion on Mattel, on pages 198–99.

- Teach your kids how to read the stock prices quoted in the newspaper for the various stock exchanges, particularly those in the *Wall Street Journal*. Your local paper also carries quotations, but they aren't as extensive as in the *Wall Street Journal*.

PRE-INVESTMENT QUESTIONS

Before you spend one dime on any stock or mutual fund (or any other investment), you and your kids should address the risks involved.

1. Can you afford the risk of the investment—the possibility of losing part or all of your money? If the answer is no to part, don't do it. If the answer is no to all, you should reevaluate your timing in the investment. When you invest in stocks, it is rare that they become worthless overnight. Regular checkups on the underlying company's progress are important. If bad news starts to hit, it is very likely that the company's stock price will decline.

The Call? If you can't afford to lose $1 (mentally or financially), you have no business investing. Stay with a passbook savings account, and don't invest in anything else.

2. When you invest, determine your upside objective and your downside. Most view investing with "the sky is the limit" approach. Don't. When you invest, set percentage increase and decrease goals. If your upside or downside goals are reached, sell and take your profit or your loss. And if the investment stays flat for a long period, consider moving the funds along to another investment.

The Call? Here's another way to determine your buys, holds, and sells. If you had more money to invest, would you use it to buy more of this investment? If your answer is *Yes*, maintain your position; if your answer is *Maybe,* consider selling a portion; if your answer is *No,* sell (there's always something else you can put your money in).

3. What if someone tries to get you to invest in a stock or investment and your "gut" reaction is negative?

The Call? Don't invest. Trust your intuition.

Money-Wise Tip

Do yourself a favor. Identify the downside in any investment you make. Twenty percent works for me. If a stock or fund declines that much, I cash out.

CREATING A FAMILY INVESTMENT CLUB

Money-Wise Tip

A collective group is a great place to find out who spends money on what—and who no longer buys what, and why.

Investment clubs are regaining their past popularity. Start your own with your family, and ask any and all members of your extended family to join in—aunts, uncles, and grandparents, etc. And make sure everyone includes their kids too. Actual funding for the club will come primarily from the adults and working members of the club. The kids are the beneficiaries, inheriting their proportional shares. When they reach working status or adulthood, they too can become bona fide financial partners in the club. Prior to becoming a legitimate partner, they can't vote on specific investments. But their input can be insightful. Remember, kids are a big consumer group.

In an investment club, money is pooled, and research and information on investments (both existing or future) is discussed. Some clubs are very small and some are quite large. The rationale is that two or more heads are better than one. All age ranges can bring their "hot" issues up for discussion.

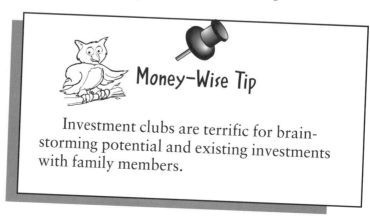

Money-Wise Tip

Investment clubs are terrific for brainstorming potential and existing investments with family members.

How do clubs get the pool of money for investing? There is usually a monthly requirement each voting member pays into the pool. New clubs will either have to start with a large initial investment ($100 to $500 each) or wait until the smaller monthly requirements ($25 or more) add up to enough to begin buying stocks or other investment vehicles. The voting members bring copies of information on investments to the meeting for discussion. Investment choices to buy or hold are made by popular vote. Sometimes clubs have local financial advisors and stockbrokers speak at their meetings.

If you are interested in starting a club, you can contact: The National Association of Investors Corp. (NAIC), P.O. Box 220, Royal Oak, MI 48068, or call (810) 583-6242 for their information packet. Their $32 annual membership fee (for a club) includes a subscription to *Better Investing* magazine. NAIC also charges $10 per individual member per year, and this includes a copy of the magazine. The information packet includes a club partnership agreement form and general information on how to set up accounting procedures.

Investment clubs are an easy and fun way to put your toe in the stock market waters. There are some wonderful success stories. Most of the members had little or no knowledge of the stock market when they started.

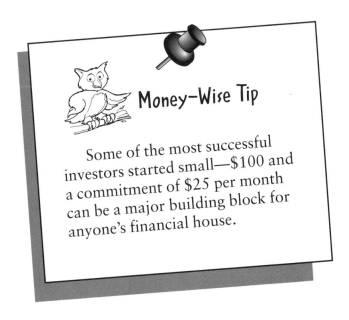

Money-Wise Tip

Some of the most successful investors started small—$100 and a commitment of $25 per month can be a major building block for anyone's financial house.

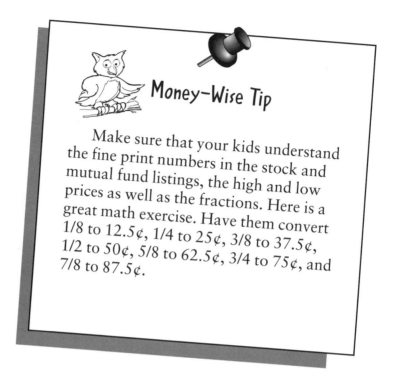

Money-Wise Tip

Make sure that your kids understand the fine print numbers in the stock and mutual fund listings, the high and low prices as well as the fractions. Here is a great math exercise. Have them convert 1/8 to 12.5¢, 1/4 to 25¢, 3/8 to 37.5¢, 1/2 to 50¢, 5/8 to 62.5¢, 3/4 to 75¢, and 7/8 to 87.5¢.

MUTUAL FUNDS ... LET SOMEONE ELSE DO THE DRIVING

After you decide which mutual fund you want and you buy in, the fund managers make all the investment decisions for you. The shareholders—you and the kids—don't get as involved in evaluating individual companies because a single mutual fund investment is comprised of hundreds of companies—and who has this kind of time? Perhaps you think that mutual funds are boring; that they don't have as much pizzazz (and no Christmas presents from William Wrigley Co.), but mutuals do have some advantages.

Mutual funds offer diversification (your risk is spread over many companies—all your eggs aren't in one basket). Each mutual has a professional management team who watches the stocks in the fund and makes daily decisions regarding them by watching the market carefully. Your fund is probably watched more carefully than you ever would or could. In the sixties, when I first started in the stock market, there were only a handful of mutual funds—a few hundred. Today, there are many thousands.

Funds have a variety of objectives, and most of the objectives hinge on growth and income. You, as a parent, probably will be interested in funds with objectives of growth or aggressive growth. In other words, you want your investment to appreciate in value. Income-producing mutuals that pay periodic cash payments to the shareholder are not the usual strategy for families with young children.

Any time you see growth as a descriptor for an investment or a fund, there is going to be some risk. But there is always some level of risk in any investment. Growth funds have a higher level of risk than income funds. But growth-type mutual funds make the most sense for kids' investments. Here's why:

- When you have kids, you have time to let the market "do its thing" and make you some money as a result of the fund's good management team, who watch and react to the ups and downs that are inevitable in the stock market. Mutual fund performance, beginning in the 1920s, shows that: Funds that are made up of the stock of large companies have had an average return of 10 percent annually, and funds that concentrate on a portfolio of smaller companies have averaged 12 percent. Either one has had a better rate of return than a savings account at your local bank.

- Mutual funds enable the small investor to get into the same pond where the big fish swim. Mutual funds can buy shares more cost efficiently than a small investor can because they buy volume. No, they don't get a discount on the share price, but they do pay less in commissions and brokerage fees. The small investor always pays a disproportionate amount in fees for his stock transactions.

- All funds have buy-ins (entry dollars). Some can be as low as $100 if you agree to set up a monthly addition (as low as $25 per month) to the fund that is automatically withdrawn from your checking or savings account. I do this with my IRA moneys and regular fund investments. You can consider this a tithe to your family's future financial security.

Some mutual fund companies are now directing their products toward families. AIG Capital Management Corporation created the AIG Children's World Fund 2005. The prospectus is presented in multicolors using cartoon characters—Green$treet$ Kids—created by Neale S. Godfrey. The fund's goal is to build for college. Information on the fund can be obtained

193

through any stockbroker. Stein Roe has a no-load fund that consists of kid-oriented stocks—i.e., Disney, Coca-Cola, McDonald's, Hershey, etc. For more information, call (800) 774-2104. The Young Americans Bank has a special arrangement with Invesco Funds where kids can invest as little as $25 a month. For information, call (303) 321-2265.

MONEY MARKET MUTUAL FUNDS

Once saving has become part of your life, money market mutual funds need to be explored. This type of mutual fund is comprised strictly of investments in money instruments. T-Bills, bonds, notes, CDs, commercial paper, and banker's acceptances are the most common investment in a money market mutual fund.

The value doesn't fluctuate; it holds at $1. The interest rate does change daily. These funds are not covered by FDIC insurance the way CDs and money market savings accounts are covered at your bank or savings and loan. But—and it's a big but—if the fund is investing primarily in U.S. Treasury obligations and CDs issued by major banks, the lack of FDIC insurance should not be a hindrance to your participation. But if these are its major investments, the interest rates it pays will be lower.

Minimum balances will vary. You can get your money back by merely writing a check. As a rule, money market mutual funds will pay anywhere from 1 to 1½ percent higher than what a bank or savings and loan will pay on their money market savings accounts. Don't invest in a mutual fund unless it has a money market fund within it. With a phone call, you can transfer your funds to the money market until you are ready to continue investing on the stock side.

The godfather of money market funds is William Donoghue. His classic, *The Complete Money Market Guide,* is available through Bantam Books and includes 800 numbers, mailing addresses, objectives, and minimum requirements for each of the funds contained in the guide. Originally published in 1981, it has been updated many times. It is available in paperback form, and it belongs on your bookshelf.

DIVIDEND REINVESTMENT PROGRAMS

Once you have bought shares in a company that pays dividends, you may be able to participate in a dividend reinvestment plan. These are also known as DRIPs. This means that when future dividends are paid, you can automatically take your dividends and purchase additional shares instead of taking cash. The plus is there is no commission cost for purchases of new shares.

Some companies will allow you to add additional cash for stock purchases from your pocket without incurring commission costs. Ask if this option is available to you when you purchase your original shares. Approximately eight hundred companies offer such plans, including companies like Coca-Cola and McDonald's.

Money-Wise Tip

The Directory of Companies Offering Dividend Reinvestment Plans is an ideal resource for getting more shares of stock without paying a commission. Contact Evergreen Enterprises, P.O. Box 763, Laurel, MD 20725. The cost is $28.95 plus $2 for shipping.

REDUCING THE COSTS OF INVESTING

At some point, discount brokerage houses and ways to save commissions will crop up. If you are investing with teenagers, they will know all about discount shopping. Banks and many brokerage firms set up special fee schedules for custodial accounts. Don't forget to check out the discount brokers, including Charles Schwab, the largest discount broker in the country, at (800) 266-5623; Kennedy, Cabot & Company at (800) 252-0090; and Securities Brokerage Services at (800) 421-8395.

Money-Wise Tip

Charles Schwab has written an excellent book on saving big bucks in commissions. Add *How to Be Your Own Stockbroker* (MacMillan) to your personal library.

Some sources totally bypass brokers. First Share at (800) 683-0743 offers a unique strategy where they link members of their co-op and match up transactions. The cost is a $12 membership fee which includes a handbook with all necessary details. After you join, you will be charged the market price of the stock, plus a transaction fee of $11.50 any time a transaction is completed. Low Cost Investment Plan of the National Association of Investors Corp. at (800) 583-6242 charges a one-time fee of $5 for the initial purchase of a company's stock, plus the actual price of the stock share(s). For any NAIC member who buys shares in the more than one hundred firms that participate in their plan, there is an additional charge of $5 per company, plus the actual share cost. NAIC also charges a $32 annual membership fee.

VALUE LINE INVESTMENT SURVEY

It makes sense to compare a company whose stock you are considering for investment to companies that are similar or in the same field. To determine what its specific averages are, including increases and decreases in several areas, there's help at your fingertips. The following is the *Value Line Investment Survey* of a company that will be familiar to you and your kids—Mattel, Inc. Mattel is the largest U.S. maker of toys—most notably, Hot Wheels and Barbie. Note the key areas I have highlighted for you.

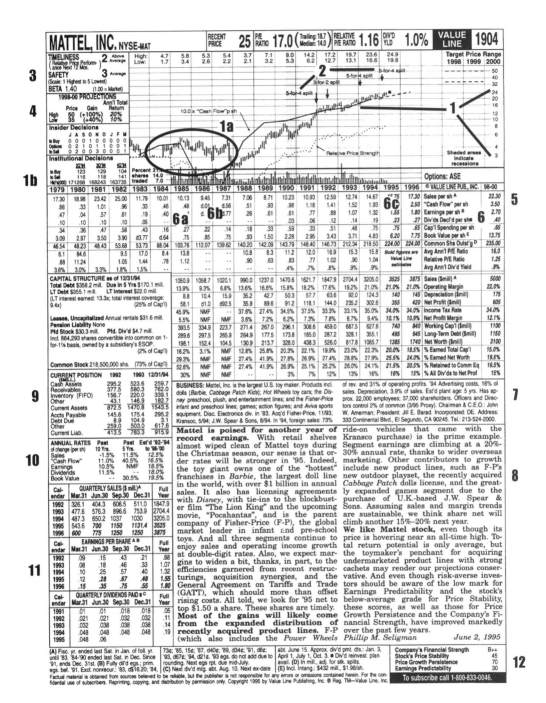

Mattel, Inc. Value Line Investment Survey

Mattel, Inc. *Value Line Investment Survey*

1. This chart illustrates that Mattel has fluctuated in price, beginning in 1983 with a trading range of less than $3 per share to a high of $25 per share. As you can see, this stock has had some price swings.

1a. You will note that there was not much action in the price before 1988. Certainly this is not one that would have made you a fortune during the five years between 1983 and 1989, but if you owned one hundred shares or more, during this period you could have doubled your money. The stock oscillated between $3 and $6 per share, and thus the profit picture would have been attractive. But with just a few shares, such as ten or less, commissions would have gobbled up your profits.

1b. Mattel's stock is owned by many banks and mutual funds.

2. Note that Mattel has had four stock splits: 1991, 1992, 1994, 1995.

3. Be aware of the timeliness and safety ranking. Both of these are based on a 1 to 5 scale, with 1 being the best and 5 being the worst. Mattel is ranked 2 in timeliness. This means that it is above average and its market value is increasing ahead of the overall Dow Jones Industrial Average. Its safety is 3 and is based on the financial condition of the company as well as the oscillation of the stock. In other words, you shouldn't lose much sleep if you own it.

4. Take projections with a grain of salt. They are not guarantees of stock movement, price increase, or profit.

5. The actual financial reports are important. Note the increased sales per share, earnings per share, book value per share, capital spending (if a company is planning for growth, there should always be funds allocated for capital spending), average annual PE (price/earnings) ratio, and net profit margin.

6. If you desire income from your investment, note the kind of dividends per share. Mattel doesn't pay much in dividends. Its yield is approximately one percent (25¢ on $25). Therefore if you need income, this is not a stock that will meet your criteria. You may be thinking, Why would I want this stock if I don't get an ongoing return on my financial investment? The answer is that returns are not always measured in dividends. Companies that are growing and

expanding like Mattel is need cash to grow. Growth usually enhances the stock's overall market price.

6a.   Note that Mattel chose to interrupt the dividend payments in 1984 and did not pay dividends again until 1990.

6b.   Also note that Mattel went into a tailspin in earnings per share in 1986 and 1987.

6c.   In 1995, a 23 cent per share dividend was paid.

7.   The center section is important. It tells who the company is, what their major products are, who the CEO (chief executive officer) is, and the company address and phone number. It often states percentage splits of the revenues that are generated from major product lines. Here's an interesting side note. When you address complaint letters to the CEO, action usually results.

8.   Major information is noted, as well as changes in the directions of the company and how the investment community feels or projects. For those of you interested in career changes or job repositioning, this is an ideal section to read. Knowing about future products could put you or your child one up in an interview.

9.   Current position represents the last two years as well as the current year, with a break-out of assets and liabilities.

10.   Annual rates represents the last five and ten years on percentage increases for sales, cash flow, dividends, earnings, and book value. If all the assets were liquidated and all the liabilities paid off, the remaining moneys would be divided by the number of outstanding shares, and you would arrive at the book value. Another term is net worth. These annual rates include estimates in increases and decreases for the next year.

11.   Current financial data are provided on dividends paid, quarterly sales, and earnings for the preceding four years, as well as estimates for the current year.

12.   The company's financial strength is important. If you are conservative, then it makes sense to go with an "A" or better rating. If you are willing to take a little risk and look at companies that may be growth oriented (such as Mattel), then a rating of less than "A" may be perfectly all right.

Investing in the stock market can be an enriching educational experience. And fun to boot. By selecting stocks that your kids are actively interested in, you are steps ahead of the crowd.

If your stock market wizard had purchased one hundred shares of Mattel, Inc. back in 1988 for $200, his investment would have grown to $7,525 by 1995, a 3537 percent increase. Not bad for a few Hot Wheels and Barbies!

Money $ense Resource Center

Books

The Only Other Investment Guide You'll Ever Need
By Andrew Tobias (Simon & Schuster). A terrific resource that I have recommended many times over the years.

Sound Mind Investing
By Austin Pryor (Moody Press). A step-by-step guide to buying mutual funds. Moody has also created a "mini-book" series from Pryor's work. Choose from: *Debt-Free Investing, Money Markets and Bonds, Mutual Funds, Stocks, Investments That Fit You, IRAs and Annuities*, and *Investing Lessons I Learned the Hard Way*.

The Directory of Companies Offering Dividend Reinvestment Plans
An ideal resource for buying shares of stock without paying a commission. Contact Evergreen Enterprises, P.O. Box 763, Laurel, MD 20725. The cost is $28.95 plus $2 for shipping.

Buying Stocks Without a Broker
By Charles Carlson. Available through McGraw-Hill for less than $20.

How to Be Your Own Stockbroker
By Charles Schwab (MacMillan). An excellent book on saving big bucks in commissions.

Donoghue's Mutual Fund Almanac
Updated annually and sells for $42.95, which includes shipping and handling. Call (800) 343-5413 for information.

Magazines and Periodicals

Taking Stock of the Future

Offered free by the New York Stock Exchange's Educational Services Dept. And while you are at it, send $6 and get a copy of their guide, *The Investor's Information Kit*. Write: 11 Wall Street, 17th Floor, New York, NY 10005.

Spare Change and Square One

Two excellent resources for investors. *Spare Change* is designed for young investors and includes contests, investment advice, and money games. *Square One* is for adults. To get sample copies, send $3 for each to the Amy Rauch-Bank, 259 Peninsula Lake Drive, Holland, MI 48357-2854. Annual subscription for each is $29.95, and each publication is published bimonthly.

Investor's Guide to Low-Cost Mutual Funds

Available through the Association of No Load Mutual Funds, this is one of the best resources for detailed information on mutual funds. It is updated twice a year, and the cost is $5. Contact The Mutual Fund Educational Alliance, 1900 Erie Street, Suite 120, Kansas City, MO 64116.

Games

The Reward Game

A hands-on stock market game. Players learn to buy and sell stock, bonds, real estate, and gold. Inflation is a factor, and it does fluctuate. Players are allowed to borrow to buy assets, but they have to pay it back. The player who accumulates $10 million, free of debt, is the winner. The cost is $35 plus $5 for shipping and handling. Contact the National Center for Financial Education, P.O. Box 34070, San Diego, CA 92163, or call (619) 232-8811.

The Stock Market Game

An excellent aid for teaching about the stock market. It covers research, portfolio analysis, and current events and their impact on the market. It also sharpens math skills. Contact the Securities Industry Foundation, 120 Broadway, New York, NY 10271, or call (212) 608-1500 for information on using it at your kids' schools. The game is not available for individual purchase, but is designed to be played by teams in the classroom. The cost will vary.

Chapter Fourteen

LOOK OUT: MY KID WANTS WHEELS

As teens march through their fifteenth year, they remind their parents that they will be driving soon. Some expect to have unlimited access to the family car, some expect to have some access to the family car, and some expect to have a car of their own. Do yourself and your kids a favor and give them the lowdown on buying cars before the magic sixteenth birthday.

As soon as you hear rumblings, it's time to feed information in. Kids rarely grasp the concept of what it means financially to own their own set of wheels. Before yours begin to salivate over the classified listings for cars, send to them to the local library. *Consumer Reports* puts together guides on both new and used cars. These cannot be checked out, but your teen can take notes. They need to start their research early if they intend to own a car of their own.

THE STOCKPILE BUILDS

One of the most important things that you can do while you strategize what car is appropriate and how it will be paid for is to encourage your kid to stockpile every penny possible. If owning a car is the goal, then the majority, if not all, of gifts, after-school and weekend earnings, and any other moneys that come his or her way should be placed in a savings account. Being prepared should become your teen's credo.

Until he or she has saved up enough money to either augment what you're going to contribute (if anything) or pay all of it, be prepared to lend out your car and to chauffeur him or her around. Often teenagers would rather hitch rides with their cronies.

A critical factor is to remind them what the bottom line of car ownership is. It's not just putting $5 in the gas tank. It's all the other goodies that are attached. From the cost of insurance, maintenance, and repairs, to their time. Maybe a "bottom-line" reminder about responsibility, maturity, and independence is also in order. Just about every parent will tell you that when their kids get wheels, time dedicated to schoolwork declines.

THE PLANNING BEGINS

When it comes to buying a car, you and your teen's bottom-line objective should be fairly simple: You want the best possible deal that you can get on the car that is selected.

Having said that, keep in mind that the seller, whether a dealer or a private party, also has a bottom-line objective: He wants to make the highest profit on the car you will buy.

In other words, you are on opposite ends of the pole. The commonality is that you both want a good deal. The way you and your teen will get the good deal is to plan. Planning means that there are steps involved. And there are several in buying a car.

Your teen (and you) need to:

- Assess your needs
- Establish a car budget
- Understand the seller's objectives
- Shop for the car
- Determine the real value of the car
- Test-drive the car
- Negotiate the best deal
- Complete the paperwork
- Finally, take delivery

When my daughter Shelley graduated from college, my husband and I rewarded her with a Ford Maverick, the car of her choice at the time. She had worked hard the past four years—getting good grades and living on her own. While she was in college we paid tuition; she covered all other living expenses 100 percent. Prior to its delivery, she had owned two other vehicles. The first was an old jalopy—a truck that she had fallen in love with. It only cost a few hundred dollars back in 1979, and it wasn't worth much more than a few hundred dollars. Within a few months, we knew that she had not bought wisely. She moved from the pickup truck to a more modest Subaru. Again, it was used, but far more practical.

For purposes of this chapter, I am going to assume that the car your teen will own will be a used car. Few teens have the thousands of dollars required for a new car. And I think parents are nuts when a brand-new, shiny car is delivered to their brand-new sixteen year old. Why? Let's start with statistics.

Teens have accidents. Boy teens have more accidents than girl teens. An insurance agent friend of mine confided that he has never represented an insured family where the newly licensed teenage boy has not had an accident within the first year. Granted there are times when it is not the teen's fault. But as you know, insurance companies don't pay a lot of attention to that. All they know is that money is going out and rates get raised to offset it.

When you sit down with your teen, the car budget needs to be probed and analyzed. Exactly how much money is expected to be paid for the purchase? In addition, how much will license fees and any taxes that may be required with the initial purchase be? How about car insurance and any emission and safety repairs that are often required with used cars? And finally, what about normal maintenance and any non-warranty repairs? It can add up to a hefty amount of money.

SEPARATING THE *WANTS* FROM THE *NEEDS*

What you *need* from a car is often different from what you *want*. Car wants can carry a potential car owner into la-la land. These are the dreams and fantasies with all the bells and whistles you'd like your car to have. The needs are more down-to-earth. Are the tires in good condition? Is the engine well-maintained? Is the car reliable in foul weather? All are necessary components for a safe automobile.

Unfortunately, a lot of people drive cars—the age of the driver is not the only factor here—that they feel define their self-image. Let's face it: If people bought cars only for basic transportation needs, getting from point A to point B, Porsches and Maseratis would probably disappear. When you sit down with your teens to evaluate what their needs are, not only is it time for you to roll up your sleeves, so must they.

There are a variety of factors you must consider. Ask, are they going to be driving on highways and freeways a lot? Or, are they going to be doing short stops and hauls? Will passengers be many or few? Are you going to need their assistance in taxiing siblings to events? What's the climate like? Do you have the four seasons, or do you come from one of the sunshine states where driving conditions are more optimal? Is your teen a hard or an easy driver; i.e., does he make quick stops; does he ride the brakes? Keep in mind that just because your teen drives conservatively when you are in the car, that does not mean his style is the same when you are out of it.

Impress upon your teen the seriousness of selecting, evaluating, and purchasing a car. On the opposite page is a car condition checklist. It covers the exterior, interior, engine, and even the trunk of a proposed car. You have my permission to duplicate it because you will need several copies as you go through the car evaluation process.

Each item is rated 1, 2, or 3, with 1 being terrific or excellent condition, 2 being average, and 3 poor. After you and your teen have gone through each section for each car being considered, total the number of 1s, 2s, and 3s. Some of the items (such as air conditioning) may not be available on all cars. These items are noted with parentheses ( ). Mark them with an X if the feature is available on a particular car. Then rate that feature, if the rating is relevant.

CAR CONDITION CHECKLIST

Make _____ Model _____ Year _____

Vehicle ID Number _____

Seller's Name and Phone Number _____

Body Style:

2 Door _____ 4 Door _____ Convertible _____ Station Wagon _____ Van _____

Pickup _____ Hatchback _____

Drive Traction:

2 Wheel _____ 4 Wheel _____ None _____ Engine Size _____

Engine Type _____ Transmission Type _____

Interior Ratings: 1-Excellent 2–Average 3–Poor

Air bags: Driver ( )_____ Passenger ( )_____ Air Cond. ( )_____

Heater/Ventilators _____ Defrosters: Front ( )_____ Rear ( )_____

Adj. Steering Wheel ( )_____ Arm Rests ( )_____ Cruise Control ( )_____

Carpeting _____ Dashboard _____ Door Panels _____ Door Locks _____

Floor Mats ( )_____ Glove Box _____ Headrest _____ Horn _____

Mirrors: Rearview _____ Side _____ Radio ( )_____ Speakers _____

Seat Adjusters: Manual _____ Power _____ Tape Player ( )_____

Seat Belts: Front—functions & releases _____ Back—functions & releases _____

Folding Seats _____ Side-Impact Beams ( )_____ Sun Roof ( )_____ Upholstery _____

Visors _____ All Gauges on Dashboard Working _____ Windshield Washers _____

Windows: Glass _____ Cranks _____ Headlights _____ Dome Lights _____

Emergency Flashers _____ Turn Signals _____ Interior Lights/Other _____

Other _____ Other _____ Other _____ Other _____

Driving Condition:

Ease of Starting: Engine Cold _____ Engine Hot _____ Idle Speed: Engine Cold _____

Engine Hot _____ Steering Wheel Vibration: Idle _____ Low Speed _____

High Speed _____ Turns _____ Engine Revs Up or Down Smoothly _____

Exhaust System _____ Manual Transmission—Clutch Release: From Stop _____

While Moving _____ Manual Transmission—Gear Shift 1st _____ 2nd _____ 3rd _____

4th _____ Reverse _____ Park _____ Automatic Transmission: Shifting P to D _____

Acceleration _____ Underway _____ Reverse _____

Brakes: ABS (Anti-Lock Brakes) ( )_____ Squeal _____ Pull _____ Pedal Adj. _____

Noise _____ Stopping Distance _____

Engine Compartment:

Cleanliness _____ Fluid Levels _____ Battery Tie-Downs _____ Battery Cables _____

Air Filter _____ Radiator & Hoses _____ Heater Hoses _____ Vacuum Belts _____

Fan Belts _____ Smog Equip. _____ Washer Reservoir _____ Oil Gauge _____

Spark Plug Wires _____

Trunk Compartment:

Carpeting ( )_____ Spare Tire ( )_____ Jack ( )_____ Lug Wrench ( )_____

Exterior Condition:

Dents in Body _____ Paint _____ Signs of Previous Accidents _____ Top _____

Trim _____ Bumpers _____ Hub Caps _____ Antennae _____ Side Mirrors _____

Brake Light Covers _____ Head Lamps _____ Fog Lights _____ Gas Cap _____

Gaskets: Window _____ Doors _____ Wiper Blades _____ Door Handles _____

Locks _____ Windshield & Windows _____ Parking & Taillights _____ Tires _____

Wheel Rims _____ Oil Spots Under the Car _____ Front Suspension _____

Exhaust System _____ Rust: Rocker Panels _____ Undercarriage _____ Body _____

Overall Appearance _____

Total #1 _____   #2 _____   #3 _____

If you have majority of #1s, the proposed car is in excellent condition.
If you have majority of #2s, it's average.
If you have majority of #3s, avoid this car like the plague.

Remember, this checklist will only work if you let your emotional side take a backseat to your keen eye.

To Market, to Market

There several markets to look into for used cars. There are, of course, friends—yours or your teen's—who may be replacing their present model with a new one. You have a lot of other possibilities. Consider:

- Independent used car lots
- Used car lots located at new car dealer locations
- Rental car company resale lots
- Bank and leasing company repossessed cars
- Public auctions
- Company fleet sales
- IRS and government sales and auctions
- Private parties

Let's look at each of these possibilities.

The Independent Used Car Lot

Prices are usually higher in independent used car lots. The only way the owner makes money is by selling cars. They don't have new cars as "deal makers." What they have is what they got . . . somebody's rejects. And what they got is what they hope you buy. As a rule, used car lot dealers should be avoided. They are places individuals often go to when their credit is poor, they need wheels, and they basically have no other alternative.

New Car Dealers' Used Car Departments

The new car dealer's used car department is many steps higher than the independent used car lot. As a rule, a new car dealer will maintain only the better used car in its inventory. And because of the dealer's reputation in the community, it doesn't want to be known as a junk dealer. Expect to get some type of warranty from this dealer.

RENTAL CAR RESALE LOT

As a frequent traveler, I rent a lot of cars. My company maintains accounts with Hertz, Avis, and National. In every city we travel to, we are fairly confident that available cars will be in excellent condition. Rental car companies buy their fleet of cars directly from the manufacturer, and they save big bucks. Believe it or not, they may pay less for a car than a dealer would for a comparably equipped model. The rationale is really quite logical. Auto manufacturers are confident that if individuals rent their cars enough times it will influence their future buying attitude. A subtle marketing strategy!

Rental companies keep their cars in operation for 12,000–15,000 miles. After that, they go to the resale lot. During the rental life, cars are maintained in top performance. When it is time to go to the resale lot, many agencies sell their vehicles for less than a dealer can. Why? Because they bought it for less.

It's not surprising that some dealers will attempt to discredit rental car resale lots by telling people that renters usually abuse the cars during the rental period because they don't own them. The reality is that the opposite is true. Rental companies maintain their fleet better than private parties maintain personal cars. Their care of a rental vehicle is, as a rule, exceptional.

There are a few drawbacks. Not every make and model is available, as most rental companies build their fleets with just a few models and brands. In the old days, a problem was lack of a warranty. New cars today carry such an extensive mileage or multiyear warranty that that usually isn't a problem. The warranty passes to the new owner.

If you are considering the rental resale market, know that there will not be any manufacturer rebates, nor will they offer to service your car. But then, when you buy a used car, rarely is "service" a consideration. You go to the local mechanic, or your teen rolls up his/her sleeves and changes the oil. To track these folks down, look in the Yellow Pages under used automobiles or call Hertz, Avis, National, or other rental agencies directly and ask where their cars are available for resale.

REPOSSESSED CARS

Many times when people get into financial trouble, cars that they bought on time or put up as collateral get repossessed. Banks, finance companies, and leasing companies have picked them up because the owners/buyers couldn't make the payments.

The graveyard for repossessed cars usually is a dealer auction. But there are times when a bank or a financial institution will advertise that they have cars available to the general public. Call a large bank in your community and ask if they have repossessed cars available for resale. If they do, ask if you can view them before the auction.

As a rule, the financial institution is trying to cover its debt. Your objective is to pay the least amount possible—a deal. If the repossessed buyer owned the car for less than two years, the "deal" that you are trying to make may be too rich; the bank doesn't want to take a loss. But if the former owner had it for more than two years, the "fat" of the loan/interest has been covered to a great deal. In other words, the remaining balance is the car value. Deal away!

Another way a lender can sell a repossessed car is on a "sealed-bid and quote" basis. This means that the public is allowed to look at the car and write an offer, place it in a sealed envelope, and give it to the dealer. At a specified future date the envelopes are opened, and the car goes to the highest bidder. In this case, don't be surprised if the lending institution sets a minimum bid.

If you are considering looking at financial repossessions, ask for permission to have the car thoroughly checked by a qualified mechanic. If the lender says no, then pass. You don't need someone else's headache/nightmare. When people are in financial trouble, they often redirect their energies and commitments away from the things they are going to lose. And they could actually abuse the car with the attitude, "Who cares what I do or what it looks like? I'm going to lose it anyway."

PUBLIC AUTO AUCTIONS

There are two types of auctions, "dealer-only" and "public." Only licensed auto dealers are able to participate in the "dealer-only" auction. "Public" auctions are open to all comers. There is a myth that if you attend a public auction, you will get a great deal. Most cars that are at public auctions are ones that dealers can't get rid of. In other words, they are passing their problems on to you. If you are considering going to an auto auction, make sure that you have a qualified mechanic/technician to give you input. It is going to cost you a few dollars, but in the end it could save thousands.

COMPANY FLEET SALES

It's not unusual for large corporations and governmental offices to buy a fleet of cars for business use. As with the rental companies, they resell them after so many miles and replace them with newer vehicles. These types of sales will be advertised in your local newspaper under the "legal notice" section and in used car ads.

As a rule, cars are available for a look-see, and sales are often conducted either by open-auction or by sealed bid, with the highest bidder taking the car home. Use caution here too. If you can't determine the condition of the car and you don't have immediate access to a qualified mechanic or technician, pass. These cars are not as well-maintained as car rental agency vehicles.

IRS AND GOVERNMENT SALES

When the IRS and the government decide to conduct a sale, they usually advertise quite heavily. It's also not unusual for a local police department to hold an auction. The police will tell you if one is in the works. As a rule, none of these agencies conducts auctions more than twice a year. I wouldn't suggest this for the average buyer, because it is almost impossible to fully evaluate the cars, much less take a test run.

My editor says that for some people an auction is the right choice. She bought her first car this way and found it to be exactly what she needed. She had $1,500 in savings, including money for insurance and any up-front repairs, so she needed a *cheap* car. Her brother was at an auto auction picking up a car he had bid on when he found an AMC Concord he thought she might be interested in. It had been owned by the motor vehicle division of the state and was thus well-maintained. The person who had bid $500 had changed his mind, so it was available for purchase at that price. It had 113,000 miles on it, but she drove it for two years and never had a repair that cost more than $300. She sold the car for $450 when she went to college. An auction is a gamble. You can't test-drive. But you can look at the cars, you do know whether or not they've been maintained, and it can be a *cheap* gamble.

PRIVATE PARTIES

These sales usually occur by word of mouth (someone knows someone who's going to sell a car) or through the local classifieds. Most likely, private parties are your best source for a used car purchase. Most private sellers have an incentive to sell their car fast. They are moving, or they have replaced the car already or are on the verge of replacing it with a newer model. They believe that they can get more money from a private resale than from their dealer in a trade-in option.

When looking at a private party purchase, it is important to clarify what the ad means. For example, if the car is advertised as recently tuned-up, does it mean that it has had a major overhaul that cost many hundreds of dollars or just a minor tune-up? Find out exactly what they've done. As in any communication, everyone has different jargon and different interpretations of meanings. Ask if they have copies of receipts for ongoing maintenance work.

If this is the route that you and your teen will most likely take, the best strategy is to look for a "one owner" seller and one who has kept track of his maintenance and service. I have a friend who is a strong believer in checking out the radio stations that have been programmed on the four to six automatic buttons most cars carry today. If they are programmed for rock and roll or heavy metal, the primary user has been a young person who may not have been as kind and gentle as the person who is the classical FM music devotee.

Before you make a commitment to a car, make sure you have it checked out by a mechanic/technician. Visit either your local bank and/or public library and get a clear picture of what the automobile is worth with the help of *The Kelly Blue Book*. It may be your best friend. The typical number of miles a car racks up in an "average" year is considered to be 10,000–12,000. Anything over that means the car has had a lot of use; anything under gives you a bonus.

Buying through a dealer can be more expensive, but it is usually safest because of warranties, as well as the dealer's reputation. And the car will be discounted already. In addition, you are protected by the federal "lemon laws"; not so with a private sale. If your purchase turns out to be a dud, a dealer will eventually have to fix the problem. With a private party, the seller is out of the picture. No lemon law will help you.

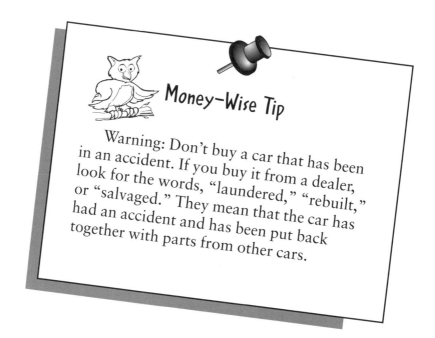

Money-Wise Tip

Warning: Don't buy a car that has been in an accident. If you buy it from a dealer, look for the words, "laundered," "rebuilt," or "salvaged." They mean that the car has had an accident and has been put back together with parts from other cars.

In most cases when teens want a car, they will take just about anything they can get their hands on. Granted, their preferences may be for the sportier models. In many cases, you can get a better deal with a car that was a family vehicle, such as a wagon or van, than that sporty red coupe.

OTHER GUIDES

There are several other resources that you can consider. One of my friends, Gart Sutton, is one of the top trainers of sales personnel of new and used cars within the various automobile associations. He is the author of a book entitled *The Professional's Guide to Selling New & Used Vehicles*. I'm a big believer in trying to find out what the professionals are taught and trained in their strategies to get a buyer to purchase their cars. Sutton's book lets you in on the inside. As of this writing, it's available for $19.95 and can be ordered by calling (714) 675-1333.

There are two other resources that I would encourage you to connect with. One is a book, *Don't Get Taken Every Time* (Penguin Books), by Remar Sutton (no relation to Gart Sutton). This is an excellent guide to negotiating for a car. And the second is, of course, *The Consumer Reports Used Car Buying Guide*, which can be ordered by calling (800) 272-0722. The cost is approximately $10 and worth every penny.

Putting It Together

Because of the track record of most teens and driving skills—or lack of them—I would avoid the temptation of getting anything brand-new. As soon as a new car is driven off the lot, it depreciates by at least 20 percent of the price that you just paid.

For money sense, it makes sense to do everything you can do to head your kids off from borrowing funds for the purchase of the car. After all, if they are under eighteen, which means they are underage, you get to be the cosigner. When they begin talking about buying a car, tell them whether or not you will help financially with the purchase. If you will not cosign, tell them that, because they will need to save a greater amount of cash for the purchase. Most car loans are expensive. By the time the car is paid off, especially in the used car area, the car may have run its useful life and the cycle has to start over.

As my editor bluntly pointed out when we were working on this section, "Few sixteen year olds *need* vehicles, but boys especially seem to think that they do." Sit down with your kids. Is this a *want* or do they truly *need* it? Do they live far away from their school and have no bus to get them there? Do they not have transportation because of circumstances within your family that prevent you from being the taxi, or are they now working after school and on weekends and needing transportation? Do you really need their help in assisting you as a taxi driver for siblings or for running other errands?

Encourage your kids to stockpile every dime they can—from gifts, from weekend jobs, and from whatever their sources are. When it comes to buying a car, it costs a lot of money. It's just not the front-end price; it's the maintenance, repairs, paying for tickets (have you talked about that?), insurance, and gasoline. It's even where it is going to be parked. As a parent, you must show them how to break out the real costs of operating a car.

Finally, I think it is important to lay out consequences. Consequences will happen if they don't pay their share of insurance, maintenance, gasoline — whatever you decide beforehand. Consequences come when there are accidents and tickets. And consequences should be directly tied in to grade point average. It is not uncommon for grades to drop when a car is bought. When our children were teenagers both my husband and I strongly felt that maintaining decent grades (which in our household meant nothing below a B) was a critical element in car ownership. If a C cropped up, the car was grounded.

You may feel that that may be a hard line to take, but after all, our goal was to get them out of the house, independent, and self-reliant. Having a decent education plays a major role. Owning a car is one the first major visible steps that adulthood is right around the corner. Your teen must be ready to accept all the responsibilities and consequences that go with it.

THE TEN-STEP PROGRAM TO BUYING A CAR.

Incorporating all the information that has been given in this chapter, here is a step-by-step plan for both you and your teen.

1. *Know exactly what your teen wants.* Sit down and list his or her needs, preferred model, and equipment requirements. It's important to stick to the list except for a few small items that might have been initially overlooked. Don't make major changes.

2. *Know your budget.* Know exactly how much can be spent. Don't forget to include all the extra charges—insurance, maintenance, gasoline, etc.

3. *Be prepared to shop.* Even though your teen thinks he or she knows it all (what teen doesn't?), it's important for you as a parent to know what constitutes a good deal. Your teen needs your input here.

4. *Use the "Car Condition Checklist"* (pp. 207–8). Inspect the proposed merchandise, not one that is similar. Be methodical and thorough, going over every inch inside, outside, and underneath the hood.

5. *Negotiate wisely.* It's a great time to teach your kids a lesson about negotiating. Eighty percent of successful negotiation is simply being prepared. In other words, they have done their research, they know what the values are, they know what resale is—classifieds as well as the *Kelly Blue Book* will be your guide. One of the traits of the skilled negotiator is the ability to walk away. If the seller is not willing to meet what you feel is a fair and realistic price, be willing to walk away.

6. *Know exactly what the going price range is for the style and model you are considering.* Use the *Kelly Blue Book* and *Consumer Reports.*

7. *Don't exceed your preset budget limits.* A valuable lesson can be taught here. After all, why set out what the maximum is beforehand in your research mode—what you can afford and what it's worth—and then exceed it?

8. *Put everything in writing.* Don't leave any loose ends dangling. If the seller makes promises, have him or her put them in writing, especially if this is a private transaction. Remember, private transactions, as in non-dealers, are not covered by the "lemon laws."

9. *Have a qualified mechanic check the car out.* This is not an option. Unless you or your teen is a car mechanic genius, get input.

10. *Double-check everything.* Make sure all your figures, including taxes and vehicle registration, are in line.

Good luck.

Chapter Fifteen

COLLEGE IS POSSIBLE

Outside of a major health expense, the biggest cash outlay for your children will be college. Proverbs warns, "A sensible man watches for problems ahead and prepares to meet them. The simpleton never looks and suffers the consequences."

Paying for a college education may be the biggest outlay of money you will ever make in such a short period of time. The costs of college tuition are high today and, according to experts in the field, will continue to rise at a rate of 7 percent per year. This means that one year's tuition at a private college could cost as much as $55,000 in the academic year of 2010—a four-year degree program would cost more than a quarter of a million dollars. By that time, Harvard University estimates four years will cost $385,000—disgusting!

Money-Wise Tip

Sometime during your child's junior or senior year, it's heart-to-heart time. Let him or her know exactly what you can afford and what you cannot. Also let him or her know when moneys can be expected while they are at school, if any.

These are sobering figures for any parent to contemplate. With a little planning, you can reduce the future outlay for your child's college education. As costs have continued to rise, college officials and parents have found ways to make college more affordable—without compromising the quality of the education your child will receive.

GUIDELINES FOR THE ROAD

Throughout this chapter, there is an assumption that parents will be footing the majority of the college costs. That, of course, is not always the case. I believe the student should be footing some, if not the majority, of costs. Why? Because there is a lesser probability of goofing off. If you talk to parents from the post-college years, they will tell you that their kids wasted some time—money—during some of those years in school. Time that was directed toward partying, carrying the minimum requirement for full-time status, or just relishing being out on their own. All the newfound freedoms can carry a heavy toll. Some kids are just not ready for the emotional, psychological, and physical stimulation of being independent from Mom and/or Dad as an overseer in everyday life. Many times, only when lower-than-expected grades come in does the student's recommitment to the goal resurface—graduating.

Wait a minute, you are thinking. *You just told me that a top-notch school could cost $250,000 to $385,000 after 2010.* Yes, that is true. But few students/families pay 100 percent of anything today. There are a variety of financial packages put together using student loans, grants, scholarships, work for tuition, etc.

In other words, if your child wants to go to college, he can. It takes work. It should not be viewed as a right or a gift with no strings attached. When a child takes on the responsibility of "student," his or her obligation to you (and the institution) is to do well, not to be frivolous with time (theirs, the school's, and yours) and definitely not to waste money (yours and theirs).

Because of the tremendous increase in the costs of education, I believe it is unrealistic to expect your child to pay all the expenses in today's economic environment. We all know of students who have worked themselves through school, paying every cent along the way. It could have been you.

My parents never planned on their daughter going to college. In our family, those moneys were allocated to my three brothers. If it was going to happen, it was up to me. In my case, I did pay every cent. But I was not nineteen years old. I didn't start college until I was thirty-two; I now hold both master's and doctorate degrees in business. Savings, current earnings, and student loans were the money sources I went to.

Because I was in my thirties and forties when I went for my degrees, I did have an advantage over my younger classmates. I knew what I wanted and where I was going, and I had put together a road map on how to get there. Most likely, your kids are not sure what they "really want to do when they grow up."

If you sense this is where they are, and you want to be money-wise with your education dollars, let me suggest a few options before thousands of dollars are spent in "finding oneself."

- Consider having your child forgo college the first year after graduation from high school. Instead, he can work full-time and bank the majority of money for tuition the next year.

- If your son or daughter thinks he or she knows what to concentrate studies in, encourage him or her to work part-time (approximately ten hours a week) in the chosen field while attending classes. This augments the college fund (at least it will pay for books) and puffs up the résumé when he or she hits the real world.

- Summer vacation will not be a vacation. Either work full-time so that all moneys can be banked for the coming semester; sign on as an intern in the chosen field (knowing that there may be little or no pay given— pay is experience); or donate full-time hours to a worthwhile mission or cause (parents should be in on the decision of what is worthwhile).

- Too many students are stretching the four-year program for a bachelor's degree to five years. Tell your kids four years (in some cases, it can even be squeezed into three) is all that you will underwrite/contribute to. If the incentive is there, they either have to bring in the additional money sources themselves or increase the course load they are carrying.

- A bachelor's degree is a minimal entry card today. Many schools offer combined degree programs: a double bachelor's, such as in business and engineering; or a combined master/bachelor degree program.

- If your child has savings and investments, this is the time to use them. After all, isn't this one of the long-term objectives you have been teaching all these years?

221

- Unless a car is a necessity, skip having one on campus. Having the use of one, especially the freshman year, can easily be a contributing factor in not studying—it's "cool" to cruise.

- If your child lives in the dorm, insist he or she eat the food in the meal plan. Today's kids think eating and fast-food establishments are synonymous—lots of money disappears here.

- College textbooks are overpriced. If you visit the campus before classes start, go to the bookstore and check out the price of used books. Next, ask the clerk in the store what the repurchase policy is for used books. The bottom line is that campus bookstores pay just a fraction of what they resell the used books for. Students can save hundreds of dollars by bypassing the bookstore and checking out message centers in the student union and dorms that offer books by exiting students.

THE COMPETITIVE GRADUATE

Today's workplace market is extremely competitive for anyone, especially those just leaving college. Being unique can give your child a step up. What do I mean by being unique? Most companies are now insisting on "experience." Sounds great, but what if the last four years have been in school—no hands-on work experience in the field of choice?

Encourage your children to get internships between their junior and senior years. By working one year in the workplace, they have both the education and the experience, a definite step ahead of their classmates. If you have the funds to underwrite their independent living while interning, do it. It's an investment, just like tuition. As they complete their senior year, many companies will hold positions for the new grad.

WHERE TO GO

Selecting a school takes a lot of work. For some, because of financial considerations, the local community college will be the starting point. For others, money constraints are minimal, which opens up more choices. During the last year of high school, many families begin to review and visit potential schools. They evaluate everything from the physical layout of the campus, to scholastic ratings, to even what the cafeteria food tastes like.

The Big Day Is Coming

As college admission approaches, it is time to set up a planning session. Does your daughter want to live off campus in her own apartment? How will that be paid for? Is there a possibility of taking a year abroad? How would that be paid for? Will your daughter need a car on campus?

Have your kids work out their goals and how to pay for them. They need to be realistic and realize they may not achieve them all. When making a financial plan for their college years, make sure that reasonable price tags, not guesstimations, are put on costs. If your child does not have a checking account by now, get one set up. If she is attending school away from your local area, a bank should be selected in the new location.

Once your kids enter college, they'll be bombarded by credit card companies. Your kids may end up with more credit offered to them than has ever been offered to you. Does a credit card make sense? Yes. The college years are the easiest time to get a first credit card and establish credit. But there are lots of cautions. Translation: discussion time.

Before she leaves for college, discuss credit cards and get a commitment from her on how she will and will not use one. Tell her that if she gets into trouble with it, it is her problem—you will not bail her out. Perhaps you might get her to agree that if she goes overboard (agree what that means) she will either cut it up or give it to you for safekeeping. There could be financial ramifications if she does not do so. Perhaps if she continues to charge and lag behind in payments, you will discontinue providing spending money and she will need to get a part-time job and come up with her own. Make it clear that non-budgeted splurge items charged on the card are her problem—but that you will take that problem seriously if she refuses to.

You must be very clear what the credit card is to be used for. It's not uncommon for kids to run up charges without a clue what they total. Some, unfortunately, expect the Bank of Mom and Dad to bail them out.

For a credit card that has a reasonable rate, contact the USAA Federal Savings Bank. It has a special program for college students, does not charge any up-front or annual fees, and charges about 12 percent interest. You have a choice of a Visa or a MasterCard.

Reducing the Costs

Most money books forewarn you about the enormous costs of college education. Don't put up a mental block and decide that saving enough to cover college costs is an absolute impossibility. There is a growing number of methods you can use to reduce the total education bill. Most of the time, choice of college is a joint decision between parents and child. Sit down with your child and brainstorm about how to get the desired education while staying within the budget. Options to consider:

- *Start your child's higher education at a community college.* An excellent *Money $ense* strategy would be to select a local community college or a state college for the first two years of your child's college program, and plan for the junior and senior years at a "big name" university for the elite degree.

- *Send your children to a public university.* Many states offer an excellent public university system. Residency status qualifies you for significantly lower tuition costs, which could lower your total outlay by 50 percent. The added bonus: Travel costs for your child to come home for holidays and extended weekends are very low—a lot less than an airline ticket from New York to California. If your child is interested in another state's university, check out the residency status requirements and see if you can work toward meeting them.

- *Encourage your child to finish college in less than four years.* Passing advanced-placement exams when taking college courses in high school can speed your child's progress toward a college degree. Well-known universities, such as Stanford University in California, are proponents of completing college in their system in less than four years. Why? According to their president, advanced education has just gotten too expensive. Amen to that logic.

- *Enroll more than one of your children in the same college.* Many colleges and universities give reduced rates for tuition to families with more than one sibling attending.

- *Send your child to your alma mater.* Most schools offer tuition breaks to the children of alumni.

- *Work for the school your child attends.* One of the perks offered to teaching staff members is reduced or zero-tuition cost for their children. Some offer the same perks to non-teaching employees. Ask.

- *Investigate work/study programs.* Many colleges alternate study with periods of career-related work (sometimes called internships) to reduce the costs of tuition.

- *Prepay tuition.* It has become more and more common for states to have such prepaid tuition programs. You generally pay a sum of money based on current tuition costs and your child's anticipated enrollment date. The plan will guarantee that tuition will be covered when your kids are ready, regardless of tuition cost increases since you began the prepayment program. Some private schools also offer this type of program.

Colleges, both public and private, and even some banks and brokerage firms are offering "guaranteed tuition" programs. The Michigan Educational Trust was the first of its kind. It permitted parents of kids (at any age, including newborns) to pay as little as $3,000 today for four years of tuition in the future, at any one of the state's fifteen public colleges or twenty-nine community colleges.

Your child's anticipated enrollment date determines the full amount you will pay. If you start paying when your child is a newborn, you will pay the smallest amount. Costs go up from there, especially if you wait until your child is in his or her teens. Other states now have similar programs. Before you jump on this bandwagon, you need to probe and ask a few questions. What looks like a good deal always has strings attached.

- If you prepay, what recourse do you have if the school closes down before your child enters college? Will you get your money back? Is prepaid money placed in an escrow (separate and held in trust) account?
- What happens if you are no longer a resident of the state where you prepaid tuition when your child is ready for college? Can you get your money back if you must be a resident and you no longer reside in the state where the college is located?
- What happens if your child doesn't want to go to the school you selected years ago? Can you get your money back? What about interest on the deposit?
- What happens if your college-age child doesn't pass entrance exams and is not accepted for attendance at the college you chose and paid for? If he is turned down for admission, can you get your money back?

Prepayment can offer you some terrific options and cost savings, but, as you can see, there are some strings attached. Investigate the "strings" before you write your first check.

In addition to the innovative Michiganders, many other fine non-Ivy League schools have come up with creative ways to help you get your kids through college. At Hartwick College in New York, students who maintain a B- or better average can convert a percentage of their student loan or student aid to a grant (grants do not have to be repaid).

In Ohio, Antioch College has a special program designed for assistance to middle-income families, who comprise the bulk of America. With it, a student's loans at Antioch will be forgiven if he or she stays and graduates. Tuition plus other related costs usually exceed student loan amounts. But every dollar counts—a few thousand here, a few thousand there.

In Wisconsin, St. Norbert's offers a type of annuity. When your kids begin their freshman year, you can pay an extra $2,000. That extra $2,000 guarantees that tuition and fees will remain fixed for four years. What does this mean? If an $11,000 base increases at 7 percent per year for the next three years, you would see a $2,500 increase. Thus, if you opt to put up the $2,000, your net savings would be $500.

But look before you pounce on this savings opportunity. You might be able to invest the $2,000 somewhere else and get a better rate of return for the period of time the money is tied up in the college's bank account. If you have confidence that you can invest more wisely, don't prepay. On the other hand, what if tuition and fees increase more than 7 percent, say 15 percent? In this case, prepaying becomes more attractive.

The bottom line here is that, in spite of the high cost of a college education, there are ways to get assistance. According to the College Board, anywhere from 45 to 50 percent of undergraduates in recent years received aid. Aid came in the form of student loans, work/study programs, and grants. Their calculations did not include aid that came from grandparents and other relatives.

MONEY $ENSE COLLEGE INVESTMENTS

Many academic advisors say that if you can save up 50 to 60 percent of the cost of your child's college education, you will be in pretty good shape. What if you can't save that much? Any amount will help. The key is to start early and save regularly. If you do this, you will accumulate an investment nest egg. That nest egg can be used for investment opportunities in both mutual funds and stocks. Over a period of time, stocks have increased in value more than traditional savings accounts and bonds have increased.

Keep in mind that a higher rate of return on your investment usually means that a higher degree of risk is involved. No matter what degree of risk you are willing to accept, a variety of saving alternatives are available.

UNCLE SAM AND YOU: EE SAVINGS BONDS

One of the most conservative options is the Series EE savings bond. Earnings from these bonds are exempt from state or local taxes. For families of certain income levels, any EE bonds purchased after 1989 that are cashed in to meet educational expenses are also exempt from federal taxes. Check with your local bank to see if you qualify for the exception. Basically, EE bonds are a no-brainer, and they work.

ZERO-COUPON BONDS

Zero-coupon bonds (zeros) are a popular vehicle for college investment funds, because they pay all interest and principal at maturity. Many parents like to know exactly how much money they will have on the day their child will start college. Having zeros that mature when your child enters school can fill that need. There are two types: taxable and tax-exempt. Tax-exempt zeros will generally produce a lower rate of return, but may be the choice for the higher income family.

Baccalaureate bonds are special municipal zero coupon bonds that are issued by some states. The interest on these bonds is exempt from federal, and, in some cases, state and local taxes. The zero coupon Treasury bond is issued by the U.S. Treasury. In these bonds the accumulated interest is federally taxable but exempt from state and local taxes. Because of the different way these bonds are handled tax-wise, make sure you get tax advice before placing any moneys in the zero family.

CDs

The College Savings Bank (800) 888-2723 sells certificates of deposit (CDs) that are federally insured. Known as the CollegeSure CDs, they have maturities of one to twenty-five years and usually require a minimum investment of $1,000. There is a significant penalty for early withdrawal prior to the maturity date. The rate of one CD is adjusted each July and applies retroactively to all funds held for the year. In a rising interest market, this could be good news. If interest rates are declining, not so good.

STOCKS AND MUTUAL FUNDS

Most financial advisors believe that if you have the time (more than five years to college-age kids), your college kitty should be comprised mainly of stocks and mutual funds. Earnings on stocks and mutual funds have consistently outperformed bonds and other fixed-income investments *since 1926*. Overall, the average return for stocks and mutuals has been 10 percent per year. A portfolio of individual stocks and no-load (no up-front fee) growth mutual funds will allow you to minimize your risk while accumulating college funds. When your kids reach college age, you can gradually shift assets out of this portfolio to cash instruments such as money market savings accounts.

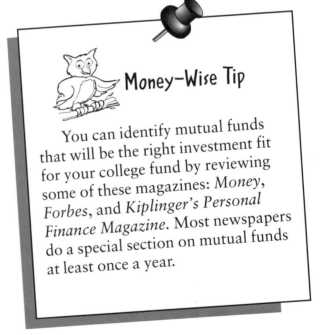

Money-Wise Tip

You can identify mutual funds that will be the right investment fit for your college fund by reviewing some of these magazines: *Money*, *Forbes*, and *Kiplinger's Personal Finance Magazine*. Most newspapers do a special section on mutual funds at least once a year.

A word of caution. When you are in the process of identifying the right place to invest money for your college fund, don't go with the one that had the best rate of return during the previous year. Murphy's Law usually comes into play. Today's star may be tomorrow's joke. Look at the track records of funds over a period of years—how do they compare for a particular period (three, five, ten years, etc.) compared to others? You want to choose from funds that show good performance over a period of time.

Money-Wise Tip

You don't need a zillion dollars to start your mutual fund participation. Many funds allow a minimum beginning investment of $250. Some are lower but require a commitment to continue adding regularly to the fund via automatic withdrawals from one of your bank accounts.

Money $ense Resource Center

Donoghue's Mutual Fund Almanac by William Donoghue ($40). Call (800) 343-5423 to check total cost, including shipping and handling. One of the best overall books for you to sharpen your knowledge of the mutual fund market.

The Handbook for No-Load Fund Investors. To check costs (around $50) call (800) 252-2042, or write: P.O. Box 318, Irvington, NY 10503. Follows more than 1,500 funds and includes all performance data.

The Investor's Guide to Low Cost Mutual Funds, published by the Association of No Load Funds, can be obtained by writing to the Mutual Fund Education Alliance, 1900 Erie Street, Suite 120, Kansas City, MO 64116. Call (816) 471-1454. Cost is $7.

The Individual Investor's Guide to No Load Mutual Funds is published by The American Association of Individual Investors. It is updated annually. Current costs can be obtained by calling (312) 280-0190.

Morningstar Mutual Funds is one of the recognized experts in mutual fund analysis. It is also quite expensive. Current costs are $395 per year, so it makes sense to review this at your public library or a brokerage house before you buy it. (Your break-even point for recouping the cost: You need to earn an extra 2 percent after taxes on a $20,000 investment.) More than 2,500 funds are covered and rated each year.

IF YOU HAVE TO BORROW, THE BEST WAYS TO DO IT . . .

Even if you save or invest regularly during your child's pre-college years, you may still need to borrow to cover expenses. If you are not eligible for any federally subsidized loans, a variety of attractive loan alternatives may still be at your fingertips. Interest expense on second mortgage home equity loans, up to $100,000, generally is fully tax deductible. But such loans offer a serious potential problem: You could lose your home if you lack the means to repay.

Interest on other types of loans, such as consumer loans, cash advances on credit cards, and personal loans from noncommercial sources (such as relatives) are *not* tax deductible. Some financial institutions offer credit lines that feature an interest-only payment option and defer repayment of the principal balance until your child graduates. Hopefully, after graduation time, your overall monthly cash outlays will be reduced significantly.

If you have a 401(k) plan at work, you may be able to borrow against the assets in your plan. Loans against a 401(k) may carry a lower interest rate than other loans do. Current federal guidelines require payment in full on these loans within five years. Before tapping into this source, check out the guidelines with advice from your tax advisor.

The federal government offers loans through commercial lenders that are not based on financial need. Some can be for the parents' use, but usually they are for the students themselves. In addition, college and university loans may be more widely available as schools become more creative with the financial options and payment plans they are willing to offer. Call the school's financial aid office and talk to one of the officers. Ask what is currently available and what new programs they anticipate offering or participating in.

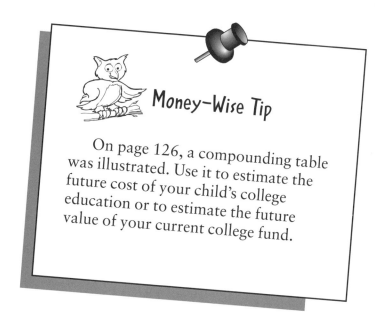

Money-Wise Tip

On page 126, a compounding table was illustrated. Use it to estimate the future cost of your child's college education or to estimate the future value of your current college fund.

Your child's college costs are doable, but you need to start planning now. Talk with financial advisors about sound financial planning techniques and strategies. Make sure that you review the appropriateness of your direction on a periodic basis after you start your plan. Market conditions change, as do your personal needs.

Federal loans, the Perkins and the Stafford loans, are worth investigation. The financial aid officer at your child's chosen college can determine whether you will qualify for either of these loan programs—and can tell you how much money you will be eligible for. Perkins loans carry the lowest interest rate, currently at 5 percent, and are fixed. Stafford loans vary with a cap at 9 percent. The good news is that no interest will be owed on either type of loan while your child is in school. When your child leaves school or graduates, payment begins. You do not have to establish financial need to get a Stafford loan, but there is a twist if you don't. The rate and repayment parameters are the same, but interest accrual begins when the loan is taken out. The Stafford loans allow for loan limit increases each year, an allowance for increased tuition.

Another program that is available is the U.S. government's Government PLUS program. PLUS stands for "parent loans for undergraduate students." PLUSes carry a variable interest rate. At this writing, they range between 6 and 7 percent, have a 10 percent cap, and charge a 5 percent origination fee. If you need to borrow a total of $20,000, this means that there will be a $1,000 origination fee on top of it. In addition, you must begin to make monthly payments immediately. Payment is *not* deferred as in other student-related loans.

FINANCIAL GIFTS FOR COLLEGE

If you have excess money, or if you have a relative who wants to contribute to college for your child in the future, it's time to bring the topic to the table. Federal guidelines allow a $10,000 annual gift tax exclusion that is not taxable for the recipient. Any gifts will be from "after-tax dollars." Any amounts over $10,000 should be discussed with your tax advisor prior to giving same.

HOW TO HOLD TITLE TO KIDS' MONEY FOR COLLEGE

Every state has a Uniform Gifts to Minors Act (UGMA) that allows you to be the custodian for funds given to your child for any purpose. You have the legal authority to hold and manage them on your children's behalf. But don't forget the Kiddy Tax we reviewed in a preceding chapter. If your kids are under fourteen, any gains, dividends, or interest over $650 becomes taxable. Your child will then have to file a tax return at a rate of 15 percent. Any earnings in excess of $1,300 will be taxed at the parents' current taxation rate.

Any money held in a custodial account is still considered legally owned by your children. With UGMA, you must transfer the holdings to them when they reach the age of eighteen. This can be a "Catch-22" if your child is not very responsible. You may fear that money allocated for college will be spent for other (possibly frivolous) choices by the newly wealthy eighteen year old. Your dreams and plans go out the window or down the drain.

Some kids do not turn out to be college material but will be very capable of finding a good job with potential. Others are problem kids. If you have assessed the situation and determine that you prefer not to have the college fund distributed at age eighteen, you have some legally correct options for UGMA funds. Place the funds in an investment, any alternative that restricts your child's access, with a maturity date later than your child's eighteenth birthday—zero coupon bonds, or perhaps a CD. A small amount can be given to the youngster at the time you reinvest, with the promise that the funds will be turned over as they mature. You can hope that your child will always reinvest the greater portion of this fund, but you have to count on your previous good work in instilling the saving habit.

Another option for pushing out the disbursement date beyond the child's eighteenth birthday is to bypass UGMA provisions. You can use the UTMA, which stands for Uniform Transfers to Minors Act. The difference between the two is that disbursements for UTMA occur on the twenty-first birthday, versus the eighteenth for UGMA. (In California, it stretches to twenty-five.) Unfortunately, not all states have passed UTMA, so check with your banker, financial planner, broker, lawyer, or accountant to quickly find out what is available where you live.

There's No Free Lunch

The government does not require that you pay for your child's college education. There are a few states, though, that specifically require that the cost of college be included in calculations of support payments in divorce cases. Since the teenage population sits on a megabillion-dollar-a-year income from all sources, it's not unreasonable to expect your teen to prepare for participation in the funding of her college education. After all, college education is the foundation of her future meal ticket.

In my household, we picked up the tab for all undergraduate education for our kids (all post-graduate degrees were to be their financial responsibility, and so far none have gone on). We drew the line, however, at paying for living expenses if they wanted to go to college and not live at home. How did my kids pay for these expenses? They had part-time jobs during school months and worked full-time in the summer. They also took out student loans which were not paid back by their parents—they paid them back.

Getting College Aid

The amount of money your child can obtain for college assistance from the federal student aid programs will be based primarily on your income, not your assets. Current federal guidelines exclude your assets when determining student aid distributions if your family's adjusted gross income is less than $50,000 and you file a 1040-EZ or 1040-A tax form. And, here's a clincher. Currently, even for those whose income is more than $50,000, parents are only required to use 5.6 percent of their assets to pay for college after various other allowances are taken into consideration. Kids are expected to use 35 percent of their accumulated assets. But then, if that is what they have been saving and investing for all these years, why not?

Money-Wise Tip

Do yourself a favor. Determine your anticipated eligibility for financial aid. Obtain a copy of the *Free Application for Federal Student Aid*. Contact the student aid office at a nearby college or university. You will be able to determine what portion of your income will be required to fund your child's education.

There are no standards for the student aid application forms used by colleges and universities. There are, however, some questions they all will ask. Included are:

- Do you have any cash value available on your life insurance policy(ies)?
- Do you have access to retirement, pension, and 401(k) plans?

Federal student aid calculations don't include these amounts. But schools are looking for ways to reduce the amounts that they would need to spend to supplement your child's educational costs. Some will meet as much as 100 percent of the difference that the "need" formula calculates, based on your current income and assets, if they come into play. That difference is made up of a mixture of work/study programs, student loans, scholarships, and grants.

There are several excellent resources to assist you through the financial aid maze. *Don't Miss Out* by Anna and Robert Leider walks parents through worksheets and formulas so that no stone is unturned. You can obtain this book by contacting Octameron Associates, P.O. Box 2748, Alexandria, VA 22301. Another guide is *The Student Access Guide to Paying for College* by Kalman Chany with Geoff Martz, available through the Princeton Review at your library or bookstore.

These guides offer a variety of strategies to enhance the contributions from federal and state governments and the college of your choice that can help fund your child's total educational costs. Included are strategies for spending all of the money from your child's existing funds first. Remember, the formula says 35 percent of their assets are to be used. If you use them all, then this percentage isn't available.

Let's face it, the money pot is getting smaller in a lot of areas, and that includes student aid. As your kids approach the time when they must make their choice of colleges, you as a parent must be prepared with the questions for the financial aid officers. Ask them how they treat outside scholarships. Some schools will take the value of the scholarship and reduce the amount that they would consider giving in the form of aid. Others exclude any scholarships, allowing you as the parent to adjust your contribution via the scholarship funds.

There are many things included when the college figures the total student aid package you can get. The following are a few of the questions you can ask them:

- How do they determine whether a student and his family can qualify for student aid? If you know that you don't meet any of their criteria, don't waste your time.
- What are the requirements for students to meet the financial aid commitments? Do they have to participate in a work/study program?
- Do they include books and some spending money in their aid package?
- If your student does qualify for aid, will he qualify next year, assuming that your financial picture doesn't change?

The Leiders' book is chock-full of additional questions that you can arm yourself with before you begin your probe.

Never Underestimate the Power of Bargaining

If your kids have a special talent such as golf, music, or sheer brilliance, you have a bargaining tool. Today's colleges are in a competitive marketplace. Don't be afraid to negotiate.

In the chapter on preschoolers, I told you about my niece Crissy when she was age 3½. Since then her athletic talents, which include volleyball and basketball, have made her a star player. In 1996, she will graduate from high school. The preceding year was marked by letters from coaches from all over the country. Crissy had something they wanted—her outstanding athletic abilities. Her parents now have a bargaining chip. If your child has a special talent, make it known to the school of your choice (if they don't already know about it). And check out what other schools might offer to have your talented youngster attend their college. If their offer is better, bring it to the table at the chosen school before you commit to it. And perhaps you can, like Cris and her family, get the school and the college funds you want. It could be a great position to be in.

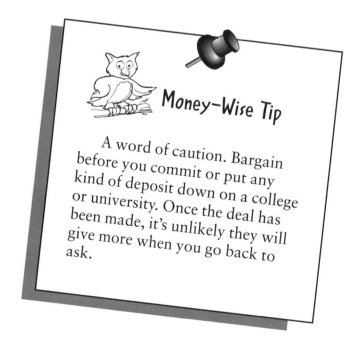

Money-Wise Tip

A word of caution. Bargain before you commit or put any kind of deposit down on a college or university. Once the deal has been made, it's unlikely they will give more when you go back to ask.

WHAT ABOUT SCHOLARSHIPS?

When I was working on my doctorate, I subscribed to a service that proclaimed that it had the inside skinny on all the scholarships that were available. Did it? Not really, but I did part with $90 of my money. Too many times, the lists of moneys and awards are quite narrow in their eligibility. One of the most current services available today is the *College Aid Sources for Higher Education*. The service is available for $30 and can be obtained by calling (301) 258-0717.

If you want to tap into your *Money $ense* savvy, you can reduce the cost to $18. How? By purchasing a copy of the booklet entitled *Need a Lift* for $2 from the American Legion, P.O. Box 1050, Indianapolis, IN, 46206. With proof of purchase, the service from the *College Aid Sources for Higher Education* becomes available to you for $16. For do-it-yourselfers, Octameron Associates also publishes *The A's & B's of Academic Scholarships*. Write P.O. Box 2748, Alexandria, VA 22301 for a list of other publications that can help.

Don't be afraid to ask the financial aid officer, or the equivalent, at the high school that your kids attend. I have also found that local community college financial aid offices can be of assistance. These individuals often know of scholarships and other resources that may not be within the mainstream, but could be a perfect fit for your child.

All in all, higher education—the entry fee for the ability to earn more money as an adult—is going to cost money. A lot of it. Start putting money aside. If you have relatives who are inclined to give gifts in excess of $25 for birthdays and special holidays, you've got partners. Ask them to contribute to your child's college fund through gifts that would go toward investments in a mutual fund or savings account.

WHAT WILL THEY BE WHEN THEY GROW UP?

What happens—gulp—if it looks like your kid is not headed toward college? He has expressed no interest and has excelled at none of the academic pursuits which you feel are important. I believe that some parents need to back off. And—let's face it—there are lots of positions, especially in the blue-collar area, that don't require a college degree. What they require is mechanical, sometimes even technical, skills—skills that can be taught through other trade and internship programs.

Some kids don't have a clue what they want to do as an adult. On one hand, you want them to be open and study different areas. On the other, you don't want to produce a professional student who never graduates. It is probably better for this student to wait a year or two before going to college. The wait will give him or her a chance to explore various career possibilities.

When your kids show some interest in a possible career path, encourage them to seek an internship. They may not get paid one penny for the work they do with a company or a professional in the area of their interest, but recent studies show that companies are routinely hiring former student employees for full-time positions after they complete college. And there's no better time to find out that a career that once looked interesting is a definite mismatch with a young person's personality, interests, or skills.

The only clues I had as a youngster that I would be speaking and writing professionally as an adult were the fact that I was a superb note passer in my middle years and that I always got in trouble for talking too much. Other than that, nothing that I was interested in as a kid pointed me to the vocation I now pursue. If your kids aren't quite sure what they want to be, don't push too hard. I know some terrific doctors who started out majoring in P.E.

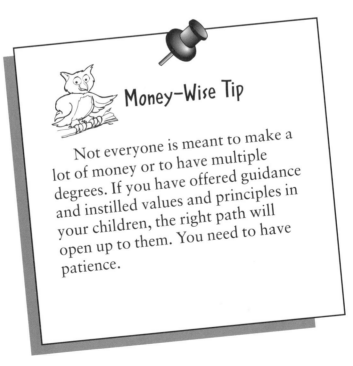

Money-Wise Tip

Not everyone is meant to make a lot of money or to have multiple degrees. If you have offered guidance and instilled values and principles in your children, the right path will open up to them. You need to have patience.

You can lay out all the data about a college education yielding greater earnings—which is usually true—yet there are many, many individuals who have never set foot in an ivory tower and have succeeded handsomely. As a parent, one of the most important things you can do is to help your children identify their talents and skills and nurture them—which takes discipline for any parent. It is so easy and tempting to direct/shape kids where we think they should be. God may have other plans. Your son or daughter has talents and gifts. Whatever direction he or she takes should be based on them, not on your druthers.

Part Four

MOVING INTO
ADULTHOOD

Chapter Sixteen

A WEDDING
TO REMEMBER

Throughout this book I have emphasized financial planning for the events in your child's life. A wedding is certainly an event that will require planning and money. Most parents will eventually be asked to march into the wedding zone with their offspring. You may even get to be old hands at it, if you have more than one child. You and your soon-to-be-married son or daughter want and deserve to have the perfect day you anticipate. You can start by learning about the traditions and new trends for weddings from the myriad books and magazines published about this industry.

Yes, industry. Believe it or not, the average wedding is planned for two hundred guests and costs approximately $15,000. Your first thought—*That's impossible!* But consider the elements: the wedding gown, the flowers, the cake, the photos, the invitations, the music—and then there's the reception and/or catering. That sounds like a lot, but there's another important category called miscellaneous. A miscellaneous cost in decor is the candles to use during the ceremony. Good candles are costly.

Weddings are big bucks, and families have floundered financially when the wedding plan is allowed to grow to monstrous proportions—both in budget and in size. Is a second mortgage on your home necessary to pay for a wedding? I don't think so. Thousands of dollars and countless hours of planning allocated for an event that lasts only a few hours? This wouldn't be my choice. How many can *really* afford a $15,000 party? That amount can cripple whatever savings many families may have.

Many brides and grooms pay for their own weddings today. These couples are usually educated and have their careers in order before marriage. Their attitude is often "It's our bash, no matter what it costs." And today it's not unusual for the groom's family to share expenses or contribute substantially. Why should the entire burden fall on the bride and her family? The days are over when the groom's mother simply hands her guest list to the bride's mother and expects not to pay for anything. The financial situation of each family should also be taken into consideration. If the groom's family is better able to afford to pay for a wedding, *wants* to do it, and does not have to go into debt to do so, then that's the way it should be.

One of the great myths promulgated about weddings is that most are perfect. That's almost impossible. Why? Because of the number of people that are necessarily involved in a wedding. Each one is a variable in the complicated wedding formula. You won't be able to please everyone, and Aunt Matilda (who you haven't seen for twenty-three years) is bound to find something she can criticize. Most weddings are for the bride and groom but paid for by their parents. So these are really the only people who must be truly satisfied with the proceedings.

Another myth is that all wedding consultants and businesses are committed to helping you meet the goals of your well-planned wedding budget. Though many do help the wedding party get the most for their dollars, there are some whose primary game is to make money. Making a profit is the goal of all businesses. However, some of those in the wedding business try too hard to encourage the expensive and unrealistic decisions made by naive brides, grooms, and family participants who are mesmerized by the romance of it all. All merchants and suppliers for your wedding should be checked out through your local Better Business Bureau. And definitely try to check out reputations by word-of-mouth.

Instead of aiming for the *perfect* wedding, when your time comes to be the parents of the bride or the groom, be smart and plan for a *wonderful* wedding. Why not even a *fun* wedding? If your target is the latter, rather than the former, you'll not only survive but you could have some laughs along the way.

In 1986, my younger daughter told me that a wedding was in the works. I had no idea what I was getting into. We started our wedding plans with a notebook. We listed the essentials. Many of my friends had already experienced runaway wedding costs. So I thanked heaven early on that Sheryl didn't want a wedding that would compete with the national debt in total dollars spent. This also pleased my husband (her stepfather). We would be picking up the entire tab for Sheryl's big day.

The first thing that we had to secure was the site and the date. There was never any question about the site; it would be at the church we attended. Since we were members, there was no cost for the church rental. (Non-member families were generally charged $500 for the church alone.) However, additional costs included the organist, the wedding coordinator, and the minister. Since each church varies, check out your preferences before making a commitment.

Sheryl wanted an evening wedding, and the church was available for the date she wanted. With our name on the church calendar, the next item on the agenda was the reception site. Sheryl wanted something different, but fun, that would help keep the costs to a doable level for the hundred people we estimated would attend the wedding and the reception. Both she and her soon-to-be-husband loved Chinese food and thought it would be great to put together a meal of Oriental hors d'oeuvres. They wanted a local and well-known Chinese restaurant to cater and host the reception. Our wedding was to be the restaurant's first wedding party, as well as its first party after reopening. They assured us that their remodeling project would, without a doubt, be completed several weeks before the wedding. So the date would work.

Our next project was The Dress. Sheryl thrilled me with the good news that she did not want to spend a lot of money. She found the *perfect* dress in the J.C. Penney catalog. This sounded good to me, and I loved the price— only $225. Score one for Sheryl.

We still had more to do. The invitations were ordered. A band that she liked had been secured for the evening at reasonable cost. Several members of my church offered to help in the music area. And our favorite bakery would provide a beautiful cake. The photographer had been referred by the vocalist. Videotaping was not as big when Sheryl got married as it is today. Friends who had brought their video recorders taped the wedding. The only expense here was for making copies of the tape.

Our perfect wedding teetered on the brink of disaster less than forty-eight hours before the wedding day. The Chinese restaurant called and said the remodeling hadn't gone as scheduled. In other words, they wouldn't be open, they wouldn't be ready, and we couldn't have the reception there. The owner told me to go to my "backup" plan. *What* backup plan?

Our small evening wedding planned for a hundred guests had now grown to two hundred and fifty. I told those in my office not to tell Sheryl that we had hit a snag. All normal work ceased in my office; everyone's full concentration focused on resolving the problem. In a short period of time, all the major hotels knew about the Briles wedding. And several had suggestions about possible places for us to consider. The day before, one hotel actually had a cancellation of an event on the same evening that we needed. We now had a place for our wedding reception, but our guests didn't know about the last-minute change of venue. So, as the guests left the wedding ceremony, they were handed maps to guide them to the new reception site. The good news was we had a place for our guests to go; the bad news was that it doubled the overall costs of Sheryl's wedding.

One of the most important things I think you need to keep in mind as the underwriter or partial underwriter of a wedding is to be careful to stay with your plan. Be vigilant about the most common problem in all wedding plans—guest list inflation. And don't forget the miscellaneous expense items. For instance, Sheryl made me very happy about her choice of a $225 wedding dress, but she also needed undergarments, shoes, a headpiece, a veil, a petticoat, and the "going away" clothes. Then there are gifts for the bridesmaids and the groomsmen. What about a limo ride for the bride and groom from the wedding to the reception? And last but not least, what is the plan for the honeymoon?

In most cases, the groom or the groom's family foots the bill for the honeymoon with the first-time wedding. I have also seen situations where the bride and groom didn't request wedding gifts—they had everything they needed. Instead, cash was given toward the honeymoon; the bride and groom registered at a travel agency.

Remember, something old, something new, something borrowed, and something blue. The bottom line is that you can spend a lot of money. If a wedding is on your calendar, here are some areas you need to consider:

The Bridal Gown

"The Dress" is, for some daughters, the first and most important step in their wedding plans. And all agree that she should be the most beautiful bride ever. She will spend many dreamy hours with bridal magazines and catalogs. And she will likely fill a folder with clippings of her favorites. When her feet touch the ground again and the budget for the gown and all of the accessories has been decided upon, the place to shop will hopefully be somewhat defined. Be sure to go for an initial tour of various types of stores to see what really is the most flattering style (in your price range, of course) for the bride-to-be. The best thing you or your daughter can do is take along a trusted friend who is willing to say that a dress looks like a potato sack on her.

If you are considering using a bridal shop or the bridal section of a department store, query your friends and encourage your daughter to do the same. What places of business would they avoid like the plague? Where are the bargains and the most reliable service? Keep in mind that some shops add enormous markups to their cost for a gown and also may use false discounting. You may wonder what I mean by "false discounting." Let's say the recommended retail price from the manufacturer for the gown you like is $1,000. The bridal shop tag says $1,200, and the clerk offers a discount of 10 percent. Your net price is $1,080—not such a good deal. You paid $80 more than the suggested retail price.

Some shops will cut the designer/manufacturer tags out of the dress, so you can't do any comparison shopping. Beware of their sales pitch. *Never* buy a gown from which the labels have been removed! There are so many "copies" floating around that one would have no way of telling whether or not she got the "real" thing.

Small bridal shops will often make an excellent deal on a gown, especially if it's a discontinued sample. Bridal manufacturers have style changes *every six months*, but gowns do not "go out of style" for many years. Last year's gown can be an incredible bargain! Because of the tremendous competition, quite often a small bridal shop will give the bride wonderful personal service that she wouldn't find in a department or larger store.

Word-of-mouth will provide seamstresses who work from their homes and create fabulous gowns. One thing to remember is if you have a custom-made gown, you may save several hundred dollars in alteration costs. If your daughter-bride is interested in a seamstress who works from her home, ask to see her portfolio and samples of her work, as well as references. You don't want a dress that looks "homemade"! Both bridal shops and reputable fabric shops can also recommend someone, but just make sure to check out her work first. If you are talented in sewing or have a friend or relative who is talented in sewing, this might be a way to save several hundred dollars, or it could add to the cost, depending on the cost of the fabrics and laces, as well as the skill of the seamstress. Patterns and fabrics for bridal gowns are readily available at your local fabric shop.

The J. C. Penney Catalog worked well for us. Many of the gowns in their catalog are manufactured by Alfred Angelo, one of the largest and oldest bridal manufacturers in existence. The catalog gowns are specially made for J. C. Penney and are not the exact ones found in bridal magazines, although styles are often similar. Because of the volume of gowns purchased by J. C. Penney, they get their own styles and lower prices from manufacturers. All gowns in their catalogs have the "J. C. Penney" label (but who is going to see the label when the bride walks down the aisle?). Their wedding catalog is excellent and also features attendant apparel and "mother of the bride" dresses.

There are stores in many big cities that rent wedding and bridesmaid gowns. Again, check the Yellow Pages under the "bridal," "rental," or "wedding" categories. Also check with tuxedo rental shops, as they may know of a source for rental gowns. Some places will even order in your "dream gown" for you, and you will be the first one to wear it. For a bride who doesn't attach a lot of sentiment to her gown and has no desire to pass it down to her daughter, this is a great money-saver. If you are renting a gown from stock, ask to see the gown and examine it carefully before you sign a contract to rent a specific gown. Some gowns have been rented and cleaned so many times that they are in very poor condition.

Bridal brokers also rent gowns. The best in the country is the Discount Bridal Service. They can be reached at (800) 874-8794 or (800) 441-0102. If you are in the buying market, this establishment has a network of representatives available in most major cities. The Yellow Pages also are an excellent source of discounted wedding gowns *only* if you know *exactly what you want and have previously tried on the dress*. With them, you can save anywhere from 20 to 40 percent when buying a gown.

Finally, be leery of saleswomen who make a huge fuss over the bride. They fuss and praise every bride-to-be. Remember there's a commission involved. Some saleswomen would say my dog Sasha is beautiful! A few questions you should ask are: Who is the manufacturer of the dress? If the dress has to be ordered, how long will it take to get in? What kind of financial terms are needed: all cash now or a percentage as a deposit with the remainder when the dress is delivered? If alterations are needed, what are the costs? How much does pressing (ironing) cost? And don't forget to ask what services are available at no charge.

Two years ago, I attended a wedding of the daughter of one of my close friends. Her gown was the same one her mother had worn thirty years prior. We all thought it was a kick that Dad got to walk down the aisle twice with the same dress. An heirloom dress can save you lots of money, and in some cases little or no alteration is needed. However, an old gown can be very

Money-Wise Tip

Use a credit card when putting down a deposit for a dress; then, if the dress isn't what you expected or were promised, or it doesn't get delivered in time, you may be able to contact the credit card issuer and receive a refund. If you paid by cash or check, you may have a major battle.

fragile. Make sure that it is taken to a *reputable* cleaner that specializes in wedding gowns so the fabric doesn't fall apart! If the gown needs alterations, most of the time the aged color of the fabric can be matched by "dying" new fabric in tea to give it a slight color.

Don't forget shopping at bridal outlet stores (look in the Yellow Pages) or consignment stores or thrift stores. It's amazing what people give away or finally turn over to a consignment shop. They realized that they won't wear this gown again and they need the money and the room in the closet. The previous owner gets some money for the clothing budget, and you find a real treasure and save on yours. Mothers of the bride and groom can do well in consignment shops too. To select a gown in a consignment-type shop (some cater only to brides) you need to be a patient and astute shopper—but you may find a real "gem" among some of the "garbage."

THE SUPPORTING CAST

One of my favorite weddings was that of one of my employees. Her bridesmaids wore dresses that they could actually wear again. Unfortunately, most bridesmaids are asked to buy dresses that are relegated to the back of the closet after the wedding. Look around, there are plenty of good styles that can be purchased for under $100. Don't forget the bridal department store sections, as well as catalogs and discount malls. Also consider rentals. If you must have your attendants wear expensive apparel that will only be appropriate for another wedding or at a costume party, do them a favor and offer to pay a portion of the cost. Your daughter's friends usually can't afford to pop for a $150 dress that is unusable for anything else.

Weddings and men—either tuxedos or suits are in order. If it is a formal wedding the tux will be the choice. Whether you rent or buy is another case. If it looks as though the men in your life or family will be participating in several weddings within a year, it probably makes sense to buy. Tuxedos range in price from a few hundred dollars to several thousand dollars. We bought my husband a used tuxedo for $150 that has been worn many, many times since. Tuxedo rental establishments retire their suits after a given number of rentals. If you don't see many weddings or formal occasions on your calendar in the near future, rent by all means.

The cost for a rental will be under $100. Many places rent tuxedos for about $50, plus shoes (about $10). Formal shoes are an important part of the outfit, as everyone should match. Also, many stores offer the groom's tuxedo free with rental of perhaps five or six other tuxedos. Shop around for the best deal. It's also important to make sure everyone in the wedding party tries on his tux *before* the wedding, so any necessary adjustments can be made. If the wedding is informal or less formal than the tuxedo style, a dark suit is perfectly acceptable. The shirts and accessories for the men should be coordinated for continuity when suits are worn.

THE WEDDING SITE—HOUSE OF WORSHIP

Seventy-five percent of weddings are held within a house of worship. That leaves 25 percent in civil ceremonies, ranging anywhere from a local park to a judge's office. Churches usually offer their members a discount or even free use of their facilities for weddings. The requirements for religious ceremonies vary from one denomination to another. Most will require some type of premarital counseling. Some forbid the performance of interfaith marriage ceremonies on their premises.

When you book your site, make sure you understand what is included in the fee. The church may supply a wedding hostess, an organist, and, of course, the minister, but these people all get paid. Know what you are getting, as well as the cost, so there are no big surprises.

If you are not a member of the church where the the wedding is to be held, expect to pay more. Whatever is done, make sure you understand the restrictions, setup times, and cleanup requirements for your wedding party. Determine who the contact person will be prior to and during the wedding. What kind of financial expectations beyond the cost of the wedding site will there be? What additional equipment will be needed, such as microphones or lights? If your church is already committed for the day you must have, the minister may be more than happy to perform the ceremony off site.

COUNTRY CLUBS

Even though you may not be a member of a country club in your area, one may be available for a wedding. Many of these clubs scrape by, and they are more than happy to open their facilities, especially in off hours, to receptions. Consider business clubs and country clubs as well as social clubs. Many will allow you to bring in an outside caterer. Their facilities are often quite nice, and the red tape of hotel sales and catering departments will not be a factor.

CIVIC SITES

If you are interested in saving dollars, one of your best buys will be a civic site. Civic sites include gardens, parks, amphitheaters, recreational centers, museums, even colleges and universities. Outside of the low cost, other advantages include the ability to bring in your own food and caterer and, in some cases, an unusual or unique location. One of the disadvantages to choosing an unusual or popular site is that their calendar may be booked up months and, in some cases, years in advance.

Some will have restrictions and requirements. For example, there may be time and beverage restrictions; you may have to hire independent security guards; you may be required to "donate" a fee, sometimes hefty. These sites rarely have all the tables, chairs, china, and serving equipment you need. So, the cost of bringing in outside rentals will be a factor.

Another nontraditional setting is the bed-and-breakfast—many of them have extensive gardens that make lovely wedding and reception sites, and your out-of-town guests can stay there too.

Then, of course, there are private homes—yours or a friend's or relative's. The costs depend on how many guests you have, what items need to be rented, what foods will be served, etc.

One friend had a wedding in a favorite park and had a potluck picnic dinner—everyone bought their favorite dishes. It was a wonderful event that was perfect for her very minimal budget and her enormous heart. No one cared that it wasn't an elegant sit-down dinner with vases of flowers everywhere. What was evident was that it was a wonderful, fun afternoon and evening shared with more than one hundred friends and relatives—as all weddings should be.

One of the more unique sites where my husband and I attended a wedding was at the new Denver International Airport in Colorado. The groom was a principal in the design and engineering of the connecting bridge between the main terminal and Concourse A. It is the only bridge of its kind in the United States. Travelers can cross over while planes taxi underneath.

The wedding was scheduled a week before the official airport opening (there were several planned dates before it finally opened, but that's another story). One hundred-plus friends gathered to celebrate the grand late-afternoon event.

The bride wore sapphire blue—a dress she has worn to several dress-up occasions since. Continental Airlines Club adjacent to the bridge was the site for the reception, which was catered by a Denver company.

We were treated to a glorious sunset on a one-of-a-kind site that allowed us to get a close-up view of the new airport with none of the hustle and bustle that regular travel creates. The wedding of Kristy and Mark is still talked about two years later—and the use of the airport and the airlines club didn't cost them one penny.

Often, remodeled or new complexes can create an unusual background. I attended a wedding in a shopping mall after hours—there were unlimited dance floors! Check around and see what is being built in your community. Merchants love the idea of publicity, especially if it is unusual. Costs can range from free to lots of money. Sharpen your negotiating skills.

OTHER SITES

There are endless options open for the wedding ceremony and reception, and your choice of a religious or civil ceremony doesn't limit the range of site choices. The home wedding is a popular choice. Home weddings can range from thrifty to posh. Some couples have a very private civil ceremony and a big bash reception at a later date. Weddings have been performed in planes, in hot air balloons, under the sea, on cruise ships, and on mountaintops. Many sites that host receptions also offer you the option of holding the ceremony in their facilities. There are, of course, wedding chapels and civic sites that are designed specifically for weddings. The choices are limited only by one's imagination. For any site other than the church you attend, get all the details in writing and signed by someone in authority.

WEDDING FLOWERS

Every bride needs a bouquet, right? Right! But what can help break your wedding bank will be the components of the bouquet. Granted, there are specialists in weddings out there who can help you, but you can do some of the work yourself and save a lot of money. For example, stay away from major holidays—Valentine's Day comes to mind. The winter months are also expensive for bringing in fresh flowers. Avoid the exotic lilies and orchids. Consider eliminating the big traditional bouquet. A single, elegant orchid or lily could be picture perfect. Ditto for the bridesmaids. Some brides are using silk flowers instead of fresh ones, or they use the artificial variety for at least the more expensive center flowers.

Don't forget corsages for the mothers and grandmothers and boutonnieres for the fathers and grandfathers. Often the person who handles the wedding guest registry, the organist, and vocalists (both male and female) are given flowers to wear. Depending on who attends, there may be other "important" guests who get flowers.

There are some low-cost options for floral arrangements within the church or your chosen site. Ask if there's another wedding scheduled the same day as yours. If so, contact the party and ask if they'd like to share the cost of flowers other than those that will be worn or carried. At some weddings the pews are decorated with greenery and even flowers. Many dollars can be saved if you have volunteer help set out your florals and greenery. If anyone within the wedding party has a flower-arranging thumb, he or she might be induced to help arrange and set up flowers at a much reduced price.

Consider renting green shrubbery (real or artificial), such as ferns, as fillers for the sanctuary or for the home wedding. There are a number of companies whose business is to supply office buildings, restaurants, and hotels with plants. These plants are rotated in and out to maintain their perfect appearance.

A bride who enjoys crafts and creativity might consider taking a short class on silk flower arranging (offered by many large craft stores) so she can do her own flowers, which will save a considerable amount of money. One of the nicest things about using silk flowers as opposed to fresh is that they can be done far in advance of the wedding to avoid the last-minute rush.

If you are considering a wedding around Easter or Christmas, most sanctuaries are already decorated for the season with either Easter lilies or poinsettias. Why not use them as a major backdrop and skip any other floral arrangements, except for what the bride and bridesmaids carry?

If you are using a florist, make sure you get a proposal, in writing, that specifies what kind and how many flowers will be used. Make sure the proposal identifies each item, such as the bride's bouquet, the bridesmaids' bouquets, corsages, and boutonnieres. Ask if there are delivery and setup costs and how much they are. Most important, have the florist put in writing the date and time you can expect the flowers to be ready for pickup or delivery.

Before deciding on a florist, ask to see photographs of weddings they have prepared recently and ask the cost for what they show. Make sure that you get good references and you are able to view, in person, some of the florist's actual work. Many florists take the cookie-cutter approach: Every bride gets the same kind of bouquet, and the arrangements for the wedding site look a bit funereal.

Many families have the floral work for the wedding party done by a florist and handle all the rest on their own. In larger cities, discount floral operations can supply you with flowers and greenery in bulk. Again, get things in writing and locate a van that is air conditioned to pick up the flowers.

INVITATIONS

The average couple pays anywhere from $200 to $300 for stationery needs. Expect to put down a minimum deposit of 50 percent. Besides the invitations, some brides include a reception card which identifies the location and time of the reception and a response card which asks the invitee to say yea or nay and how many. To save some money, it makes sense to put the location of the reception on the wedding invitations if the reception is open to everyone who is invited to the wedding. I also think it makes good sense to include a response card with a return envelope, which should include return postage to assure prompt response. You will want to have your invitations in the mail at least four to six weeks before the wedding so you know how many guests to plan for at the reception.

You will need to do some shopping around comparing bridal stores, department stores, stationers, and printers for your final invitation product. One way to save a lot of money is to avoid the traditional engraved card and use the modern thermography. Engraving has been around for a zillion years. In this process a metal plate leaves actual indentations on the paper. You can feel the engraving. Thermography is a process that is similar to the process used on today's business cards: Raised ink gives the appearance of engraving. Most people cannot tell the difference. Because of improved technology, thermography has become popular and can save as much as 50 percent on the invitations. Ask around and make sure that you can get actual samples of the process and of the types of papers and print styles. Here's another place to use your credit card as extra insurance in the event you are not pleased.

Again, through word of mouth, you will be able to save quite a bit of money working with someone who works from his or her home selling invitations—usually about 20 to 25 percent off the "book" price. You will also receive terrific personal service from a home business. Check your order carefully and ask for a copy to take with you. Always order at least twenty-five more invitations than you think you need. Whereas the cost will be minimal for the extras with your original order, a reorder of only a few invitations can cost almost as much as your original order.

PHOTOGRAPHY

One of the best ways to find a good photographer is from a recently married couple. They'll tell you in a nanosecond if they had a good experience and if it was reasonable financially. Another resource is to go to the church or site and talk to the person who coordinates events, such as the wedding hostess. She is going to know who works well and who doesn't. This is not the time to let your fingers do the walking through the Yellow Pages. You need good references for the person who is going to record your memorable event.

Don't forget to tap into friends and family members. Some of the best photos I've seen of weddings are the candid ones. Some ways to save money include avoiding peak wedding times—Saturday evening is one of the most preferred dates of the week. Many photographers charge a premium price for a Saturday booking.

Another way to save money is to avoid some of the photo frills—having photos taken prior to the day of the ceremony can be very costly. Do yourself a financial favor and have all photos made at the time of the wedding and reception. Another way to save money is to have a professional photographer present only for the wedding and to turn your family and friends loose at the reception with the candid cameras. Finally, when it comes time to encase your treasured photos, shop around for the photo album. Prices can range from $75 to several hundred dollars for the wedding style album.

A fun idea for the wedding is to provide guests (for example, one on each table) with a "disposable camera." Ask the guests to take photographs and then leave the cameras for you to develop. You can get some fantastic candids this way!

At my daughter's wedding we made mistakes with the photographer. He turned out to be a personal friend of the vocalist, and she was trying to do him a favor. Granted, he did take some good pictures, but he also took several bad ones. We paid too much money for what was produced.

To avoid the pitfall we fell into, ask to review a complete album from a wedding that he or she has done in the recent past (at least within the last year). Ask if there is a limit to the number of rolls or exposures he will take before, during, and after the wedding. If the photographer is sick, who does he or she use as a backup? Finally, make sure what the costs are.

Many photographers offer packages. Be realistic. Is the package—e.g., sixty to eighty pictures—the right fit for the size of your wedding? If you have more than one hundred guests, it's not going to be enough shots if you intend for the photographer to do the wedding plus the reception. If you have friends and family handling the candid shots at the reception, it may be enough.

WEDDING CAKES

At every wedding there is a cake and sometimes two if a groom's cake is desired. Make sure you know what you are buying. Cakes come in all kinds of shapes, sizes, and tastes. Bakeries that specialize in cakes are usually pretty good about showing you extensive photographs of the real thing. Rarely are there any hidden expenses within the quoted price. Make sure you understand what the total cost will be, including any delivery or setup charges. Expect to pay anywhere from $1.00 to $5.00 per serving, depending on what type of cake is selected.

How do you find a really good cake? Draw on friends' or your own recent experience at weddings you have attended. New trends in the cake area include different flavors and even types of cakes within the layers. Some weddings have the cakes decorated with flowers, either fresh or artificial, besides the traditional icings. If this is something that appeals to you, make sure the cake is available in time to get this done by you or someone else. Some bakers are glad to provide this service for free or a nominal amount.

Make sure you ask how long the cake is prepared in advance. The last thing you need is a dry cake.

After the bride and groom have their pieces, the cake will have to be readied for your guests. Some additional "icing" to your cake costs is the possibility of a cake-cutting fee. Be sure to allow for this when planning the reception.

Here's a money-saving tip for cakes. If you are expecting two hundred and fifty guests, have your fancy display cake prepared to serve perhaps one hundred; have your baker prepare a sheet cake in the same flavors to serve one hundred and fifty. The cost is much less for a sheet cake, and after it's cut up in serving pieces, no one is the wiser!

MUSIC

Weddings mean music is in the air—from harpists to dance bands to records and DJs. There is something for everybody. Most weddings call for different music for the ceremony than for the reception. Most churches have an organist or a music coordinator who can help with the selections before and during the ceremony. Costs will vary anywhere from $50 to $150 per musician per hour. If the wedding is at home or at another site, taped music is often the choice. A string quartet is also a nice choice, but more costly.

For the reception, you usually have a choice of a live or canned performance, the live being a singer/pianist, a quartet, or a band. You might want listening music or get up and knock 'em down with dancing music. Prices can range from a few hundred dollars to several thousand dollars. Many couples contract with a DJ who carries a type of jukebox filled with tapes, albums, and CDs. As a rule a DJ will be much less expensive than a live band. The cost is generally only a few hundred dollars. Another advantage is that they rarely take a break. Your music continues throughout the reception. And, assuming they are playing what you love and the crowd enjoys, you get much more entertainment for your wedding dollar.

The best place to find your entertainment is through word of mouth and personal experience. Ask people you know and trust and whose tastes are similar to yours. Try to recall weddings or events that you have personally attended that were enjoyable. You will need to contract with your music provider(s) in writing. If you go "live," make sure that the musicians that you saw and heard will be the musicians who show up for your wedding. Live music requires that you clearly understand how long they will play, how much the charges are, how music will be selected, and how many breaks they will take and for how long.

LIMOUSINE

All brides have to get to the church and from the church on time. In most cases, family members arrange to arrive on their own. It is after the wedding when a limo usually comes into view. If you decide to hire a limo, a driver comes with it. The average cost will range anywhere from $60 to $100 an hour, with a minimum of a three-hour rental time. And, remember, there's usually a gratuity on top. The best place to look for limos, outside of personal experience and referrals, is in the Yellow Pages under "limousines" and "wedding services."

Ways for you to save money include using a company that has a short minimum time requirement. Ask if the company has a pick up/drop off service. Definition: you hire them only for driving the wedding party to the reception. Why pay for time when the car is idle? An interesting option for a summer wedding would be horse-drawn carriages.

Money-Wise Tip

It is wise to check with the Better Business Bureau to see if there have been any complaints against the limo company you are considering. The last thing that you want is for them not to show up.

THE RECEPTION

Prepare yourself; you will spend money on the reception. You can have anything from snacks or hors d'oeuvres to a sit-down meal—but this is where the checkbook comes out. Understand what you are buying. Are you paying a flat fee for the entire afternoon or evening, or are you charged per hour with only a limited number of hours available? Reception sites vary in what you will be allowed to do. Some allow you to bring in the food and, in some cases, your beverage selections. Or they may require you to use their product exclusively. As a rule, if you are using their food services, there's not a charge for the use of the facilities.

Ways that you can save money include having the reception in the early part of the day, such as a brunch or luncheon instead of dinner. Dinner receptions will probably cost you twice as much as brunch or luncheon. If the site that you choose for your ceremony has facilities for the reception, you can use a caterer and usually reduce the per person costs charged by the traditional hotel site. In fact, most places that allow you to use your own caterer will be less expensive than a site that requires you to use its in-house services.

Many wonderful receptions have been held at a home, possibly yours. Wedding tables and chairs and often utensils and china can be rented. If you have a big enough group, and depending on the time of year, a tent can be pitched. Do yourself a favor and make sure you have someone come in to do the cleanup. When considering a site, make sure you probe the following questions.

- How many guests will the space accommodate?
- Is there adequate parking for guests to self-park, or do valets need to be hired?
- If your reception will be at a site other than where the ceremony is performed, what does the rental fee cover and for how many hours?
- Will there be any overtime charges?
- What are the cleanup requirements, if any?
- If you can bring in an outside caterer, are there restrictions, including cooking?
- If you are planning on dancing and having music, are there appropriate facilities available, including a dance floor?

- What else is happening at the site of your wedding? The last thing you need is a competing wedding or event that is using a band that could conflict with the program or music that you plan on having.

HOTELS

There are certainly advantages and disadvantages for each type of reception site. When you book your reception at a hotel, you don't have to worry about tables, chairs, serving pieces, dance floors, etc. When Sheryl's reception site bailed out on us, we were fortunate to find a hotel that did hundreds of weddings a year. Their efficiency saved us hours of agony, although we had to pay for it.

The choice of a hotel usually means that everything is included in the price quoted to you. Hotels are the efficient choice for taking care of parties that involve many hundreds of individuals. Many hotels aggressively go after the wedding business and offer special wedding packages. Ask for details. Some hotels have turned the wedding reception into an art form.

Money-Wise Tip

If you are bringing in out-of-town guests, book them at the hotel that is handling your reception. Discounts can usually be arranged for room rentals, and many hotels throw in the honeymoon suite as a perk. The Hyatt Hotel did this for my daughter.

This all sounds good, but there are disadvantages. The decor in many hotels is boring. They also are, as a rule, expensive. Most catering representatives in a hotel are on commission. The more money you spend, the more money they make. Their druthers would be for you to select foods that are more expensive. This means that they may try to steer you away from the less costly chicken dishes and suggest prime beef or a shellfish. If you plan on serving liquor, hotels grossly overcharge. This is one of the areas where they make big profit. Finally, never assume that anything is free. Hotels can charge extra for ice carvings, corkage fees, cake cutting, and extra food attendants. When in doubt, ask, and get your answers in writing.

Let's Eat

Several times throughout this chapter I have mentioned a caterer. What are some of the things to look for in a caterer? First of all, get references. Draw from your own experience or that of people that you know well. Reception sites that don't have in-house caterers often have lists of caterers that they recommend. Don't bother to look in the Yellow Pages. This is definitely a time to count heavily on personal references.

Ask if you can talk to contact persons for several of the weddings that they have done in the last six months, and specify weddings that are similar in size to yours. A good question for these contacts is, "If you had your druthers, what would you change about the wedding?"

When it comes to deciding on the menu, eat your way through it. Most caterers and hotels will allow you to sample items that you are considering. Take several friends so that you get feedback from multiple sources. Keep in mind that you will save money if you avoid items that are labor-intensive. Fancy dishes and unique hors d'oeuvres may take a lot of preparation and thus be very costly.

To save money, besides having a luncheon reception and avoiding the dinner, stay away from expensive food items such as shrimp, prosciutto, and the like. If you have the option to provide the beverages, shop at discount outlets for same and enlist friends or relatives to help serve. Most likely, you will save a lot on labor costs.

Caterers have fixed expenses that you are going to pay whether you have fifty people or five hundred. Never assume that if you have fewer guests your catering costs will necessarily be a lot less. Other questions to ask your caterer:

1. Will the food be prepared on site, or will they bring it in?
2. What flexibility do you have, if any, to change times and dates?
3. What are the options on their menus?
4. Do they write a contract? (They should.)
5. Do they have a license to be in the catering business?
6. How will the staff be dressed during your reception?
7. Who will be the supervisor in charge during the reception? I think it is a good idea if there is a representative from the catering firm who at least stops in for the reception to make sure that everything is running smoothly.

One of the plusses of catered wedding receptions today is the advent of the food station. Instead of a long winding line at the buffet table, your guests can sample food at several food stations that offer them a variety of foods. Food usually stays hotter, and the long lines are a thing of the past. Consider this idea for wherever you decide to have the reception.

There are two other costs that you could be hit with from either the reception site, the hotel, or the caterer—a cake-cutting fee and a corkage fee. Corkage fees usually involve liquor, although I have seen corkage fees charged for sparkling waters or any liquid that is not supplied directly by the reception site. Some places charge several dollars per bottle. When you have several hundred people, this adds up.

The other exorbitant fee is the cake-cutting fee. Some facilities charge anywhere from fifty cents to several dollars per guest to have their staff cut and serve your cake. If you have staff involved in serving, you are already paying a mandatory gratuity, so you should be able to avoid this extra charge by simply saying no. Or, you can put some family members or friends in charge and tell the hotel you will not pay extra for a cake-cutting service.

In Conclusion

Too often weddings get played out of proportion. Everyone involved gets frustrated and a little angry when they can't understand why they couldn't have the simple small wedding they originally planned for. The answer is, they can. But to maintain that, a strategy needs to be set out which identifies possible pitfalls as the process moves along. You need to be sure you have set a realistic budget and expectations—and that you stick with it. I have attended small weddings, including my own with sixteen participants, that were lovely with minimal dollars spent, and I have attended huge affairs with hundreds of guests that cost many thousands of dollars where it seemed like World War III was about to erupt. The choice will be yours.

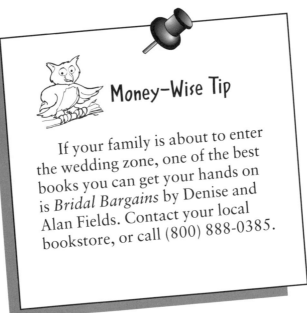

Money-Wise Tip

If your family is about to enter the wedding zone, one of the best books you can get your hands on is *Bridal Bargains* by Denise and Alan Fields. Contact your local bookstore, or call (800) 888-0385.

In the end, weddings are a celebration of a love a couple has for each other. There is no reason why the bride, groom, and parents shouldn't have a great time. And there is no reason why they should take on the national debt in the process.

Chapter Seventeen

LEAVING THE NEST

When your child leaves the nest, it is a momentous event. An element of surprise may be a factor when your kid (or you) announces that it is time for him or her to set up housekeeping on his or her own. Surprise may be unavoidable, but in this chapter I will give you some ideas to help you and your teen accomplish a successful takeoff. Flaps up? Here we go.

Our daughter Shelley was in her third year of college when she broached the subject. She had never wanted to live in one of the dorms on campus. But now, an apartment of her own began to look quite inviting. Shelley was a responsible young adult and had always been the most responsible of our children. At twenty-two, she had a year to go to complete her degree. She balanced her checkbook, saved, worked after school and on weekends, maintained good grades, pitched in around home, earned her allowance, and paid all her debts. Both my husband and I said "Bravo" when she announced she was ready to start out on her own.

The previous year had been a bumpy one for our family; my son Frank had died in an accident. Shelley's dedication to her schoolwork and other activities never faltered, even though she was grieving for her cherished brother. Her ability to handle adversity and maintain her previous level of performance indicated to both to John and me that she was indeed ready to try her wings and live on her own. And we felt sure that we had little to worry about. She was ready to jump ship.

Ah, but a complication surfaced—Sheryl said "me too." Whereas Shelley was always responsible and conservative, her younger sister was the exact opposite. Sheryl didn't lack intelligence; her problem was that she was reckless and headstrong—definitely an impulse person. If she saw it and wanted it, she was going to get it. Sheryl, who was then attending her first year of college, perked up her ears when her older sister started making noises about going out on her own. Sheryl thought hooking her independence declaration onto Shelley's was the perfect way to go.

Sheryl started her campaign—she came, she saw, and she would conquer. Did she make her wishes known to John and me? No way. She astutely discerned that Shelley would be her ally. She used one of the typical kid ploys—gang up on the parents. She convinced her older sister that she would be lonely living alone and that she wouldn't have as much spending money. Wouldn't it be a "lark" if the two of them lived together in an apartment? They could split all the costs fifty-fifty and spend more time with each other. Sheryl hooked Shelley's conservative and responsible side and her emotional side. She convinced her sister that this would be the perfect and right thing to do. And fun, to boot.

Sheryl told Shelley she was sure that Mom and John would supply some of the necessary ingredients for their new nest—surely they wouldn't have to buy everything themselves. And they each had a complete bedroom set that they could take with them. They would have such fun shopping around at garage sales for miscellaneous living room furniture and some type of table to use for meal times. A united front emerged.

When the two girls sat down with us to tell us about their plans, both John and I were skeptical. Sheryl was the kid who had completely messed up three different bank accounts. The only solution was to close them and start all over, because none of us could figure out what she had done.

We were primarily concerned about their schooling. Both girls assured us that we had nothing to worry about on this score. They would both be working part-time, and they had each applied for student loans. We finally decided to give it a go. The primary factor in our decision was that Shelley was a capable and responsible young adult. John and I fantasized that it would nice to be alone at last—an end in sight to the day in, day out responsibilities of parenting.

The girls managed to make it work for six months, but their lifestyles and their choices of friends just didn't seem to mesh. I suspect that the biggest problem evolved from the difference in their individual approaches to making the joint venture work smoothly. Both of the girls got new roommates. Shelley stayed in the original apartment. Sheryl moved, renting a room in a co-op house.

Today, ten years later, after a few more roommates and some ups and downs, both are responsible adults. They pay their bills on time and, yes, they still have their opposite personalities.

OUR RULES

Long before the girls took their leave of our home for one of their own, we had set out some guidelines, anticipating their (and our) eventual desire for emancipation. We told the three kids that, when they graduated from high school and/or turned eighteen, they had some options if they wanted to continue to live at home with us. Continued attention to their family member/ household responsibilities would be required, regardless of what they chose. And they would pay for their extra personal items through allowance and outside earnings.

- Choice #1: They could go to school full-time, and we would cover their room and board at home and their tuition.
- Choice #2: They could attend school and work part-time, but they would have to pay rent. We would pay tuition.
- Choice #3: They could work full-time, pay a larger rent, and also help pay for the food and utilities they used.
- Choice #4: They could sit on their jobless duffs and get out of contributing to their upkeep and use of household space. This choice, one which so many kids seem to manipulate, was not an option in our household. If selected, it was immediate grounds for expulsion.

Shelley understood the concept perfectly well. During her first three years of college, she worked part-time and covered all her personal expenses, including clothing and entertainment. In addition, she was able to save.

Our son Frank was another story. He graduated from high school a year before he died. Frank had no enthusiasm about going to college, at least not yet. He thought working might be OK. His attitude was later, rather than sooner. Right then he was too busy hanging out with his pals and having a good time, and he didn't have time to look for a job. So, he didn't have the money to pay for room and board as our household rules called for.

I used to get out the classifieds and highlight jobs from the daily newspapers and leave them on his bed. One time, I even noted a position for a chimney sweep. When he didn't respond to any of these "hints," I became more aggressive. I called the army, navy, air force, and marines for enlistment information. Frank developed quite a mailbag!

Nothing seemed to get his attention. We warned him twice and he ignored us.

THE HOUSEHOLD "PINK SLIP"

To really get his attention, I felt we had to be more innovative. I told him that we were going to have a "last supper," and he could choose the menu for the meal that evening. After we all had dined sumptuously, he was told he had to leave. First he laughed. "You can't be serious," he said. Then it finally dawned on him that we were dead serious. He got mad and threatened that if we kicked him out of the house he would sleep in front of our house in a sleeping bag or in his truck. He'd show us; he'd embarrass us in front of the neighbors.

His threats didn't phase us; he had broken the rules, and it was time for the consequences. We told him, "Sleep away."

True to his word, he camped in front of our home for three days and nights. We weren't impressed, and neither were the neighbors, but one of his pals was. Frank was offered the couch at his buddy's home. That night his friend's mother called about the boy on her sofa. I explained our rules to her and what had led up to Frank's ouster. I also told her that he was welcome to come home, but he had to either go to school or get a job. The choice was his. Within twenty-four hours, Frank had called me at my office and asked for an appointment. When he showed up that evening, he announced that he had found a job. And he asked if he could come home.

Ah, the parent has power after all. We told him that he would be more than welcome to come home, but there would be some conditions. During the next hour we wrote up a contract to be signed by Frank and John and me. We reiterated the household rules and came up with a dollar amount that he would pay toward rent and food and utilities. In addition, I was able to get a commitment from Frank that he would save half of every paycheck.

In the beginning of this chapter, I shared that Frank had died in an accident. This happened a year after we made him leave. Did/do we have any regrets about our position in handling Frank's non-work/non-school scenario? Absolutely not.

As parents, we have not a clue how long God will share His children with us. Each day must be taken one at a time. Both my husband and I are quite comfortable that we did the best job we could with the "tools" we had at the time. No one can rewrite our lives. We must learn and move on.

So, how did Frank do when he came back? Quite well. He lined up a full-time job, and he grew in maturity as new responsibilities were added. He also saved money for the first time in his life—almost $2,000. When

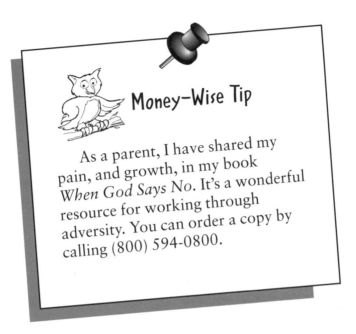

Money-Wise Tip

As a parent, I have shared my pain, and growth, in my book *When God Says No.* It's a wonderful resource for working through adversity. You can order a copy by calling (800) 594-0800.

Frank died, I divided his savings between his sisters. It was that $1,000 that enabled Sheryl to buy her first home in Denver, Colorado.

Throughout this book, as in this chapter, I have shared stories of how John and I met the challenges of parenthood and grandparenthood, and how we got our youngsters ready to deal with the money maze. Your experiences won't mirror ours, but my hope is that our experiences will encourage you to be candid with your kids about money. It's a tragic mistake when parents don't talk about all the money issues that will face their kids as adults.

I will say it again. One of your primary roles as a parent is to propel (and sometimes you do have to push) your kids into a position where they can break away from their dependency upon you. In the latter years of their teenhood, you as the parents should be actively unveiling the money maze. Teens are busy. They get distracted. And sometimes they think their parents are aliens. It's often hard to get their attention.

They don't hang on every word you say like they did when they were little ones. But you must make sure that you get their attention regularly about money issues and that you track their progress. They need to have the opportunity to succeed and to fail while you're still in their financial picture. They won't get a rose garden out there; better they understand that sooner than later when it can really hurt.

Your New Assistant

One of the smartest things I did with my kids when they hit the mid-teens was to enlist their help in paying our family bills and generally running the household. I covered this more fully in an earlier chapter. They came out of this exercise with a clear understanding of what it cost to run our household—invaluable information for their own future nest. They got important, hands-on experience with checking accounts, budgets, shopping wisely, etc. And, they also learned why a savings program is imperative for those times of financial crisis that hit everyone. And they learned that savings are a must in reaching the goals of pleasurable events like vacations or buying a car. Even leaving home.

Money Steps

If your teens do not have their own checking accounts, they should. Ditto with a savings account. Granted, you may have to be a cosigner, depending on the requirements of the bank you deal with, but do it anyway. Then spend the time to see that they learn all the ropes by getting them to set their account(s) up on the computer. They will be able to see exactly how they spend their money and where it comes from.

There are several programs that anyone can learn. I favor the ease of Quicken by Intuit; there are versions of this program that are compatible with most computers. Teens love computers, and you will love their balanced checkbook. Plus, Quicken will introduce them to other types of financial reports—such as profit and loss statements. Quicken is available for under $30 at stores that sell software.

One for the Money, Two for the Show...

Below is the *Leaving the Nest Money $ense Quiz*. When your son or daughter can answer yes to all twenty-five questions you can be confident that your efforts to educate your teen about the money maze have been successful. You have instilled the fundamentals of a *Money-Wise* adult. But first, take the test yourself, giving the responses you think they are likely to give. You will have some idea about the degree of penetration your money counseling has had in their minds.

Leaving the Nest Money $ense Quiz

1. Do you know how to open a checking account? Yes ____ No ____
2. Do you know how to balance a checkbook? Yes ____ No ____
3. Do you know how to open a savings account? Yes ____ No ____
4. Can you name three types of savings vehicles, other than a savings account? Yes ____ No ____
5. Would you know how to stop payment on a check if you needed to? Yes ____ No ____
6. When you run out of checks, do you know how to order more of them? Yes ____ No ____
7. Do you understand all the entries on monthly bank statements for both checking and savings accounts? Yes ____ No ____
8. Do you know the difference between a bank, a savings and loan institution, and a credit union? Yes ____ No ____
9. Do you know what interest rate is charged on the unpaid balance of your credit card or on one of your parents' credit cards? Yes ____ No ____
10. Have you been saving 10 to 25 percent of all money that you receive from parents, gifts, and outside jobs? Yes ____ No ____
11. Do you have money left over at the end of your pay period after all your expenses have been paid? Yes ____ No ____
12. Do you know who to call if you lose a checkbook or a credit card? Yes ____ No ____
13. Do you know how to use an ATM card? Yes ____ No ____
14. Do you know how to get cash in an emergency—day, night, or out of town? Yes ____ No ____
15. Could you make up a livable spending plan for yourself without your parents' assistance? Yes ____ No ____
16. Does your income cover every expense in your spending plan, plus 10 percent? Yes ____ No ____
17. Do you have three months' living expenses in the bank (don't forget taxes)? Yes ____ No ____
18. Do you understand how to read a simple contract, such as the one found on the back of a credit card application, or the conditions of a lease? Yes ____ No ____

19. Do you know how to get car insurance? Yes ____ No ____
20. Do you know what penalty or penalties are assessed when you make a late payment on a credit card? Yes ____ No ____
21. Do you know what a credit report is and how to get a copy of yours? Yes ____ No ____
22. Do you buy on impulse? Yes ____ No ____
23. Do you know how and when to file federal and state tax returns? Yes ____ No ____
24. Do you know what an IRA is? Yes ____ No ____
25. Do you know what traveler's checks are and how to get them? Yes ____ No ____

How to Score: Give every Yes answer 2 points. Give No answers 0 points.

If your teen scores:

40 to 50 points—Help him pack his bag; he's ready to leave home or perhaps even support you.

26 to 38 points—He's on his way but still needs input from you. He can read this book, so get him his own copy.

24 and below—You both need to wake up fast; otherwise, he will never be ready to leave home. You may have to support him the rest of your life.

As you can see, there are a lot of queries in the preceding quiz. All pertain to important money skills that your child will carry throughout his or her life. As your child gets ready to leave the nest, you want to make sure that he or she leaves on solid footing.

THREE TO GET READY . . .

Here some other money and credit-related areas you should cover with your teens. Do they understand how to complete applications for: a new job, a loan, an apartment, car insurance, phone and utility service? Do they know how to prepare a tax return? Have they read the fine print on credit applications, apartment leases, and insurance policies?

Tell your teen to go out and gather up examples of each. Then, spend time with him until you feel he fully understands the terminology and the implications of the answers when he fills in the blanks. Discuss the deposits that are required when renting an apartment and for the phone and utilities for this apartment. The youngster must know when and under what conditions these deposits are returned. Many young adults who are conscientious about their credit and their money get cheated by the system, simply because they didn't have all the facts and know how to use them.

As your child gets ready to leave the nest, now is the time to set up a realistic living budget. Below is a sample budget that you can use as a guideline. The objective is to help your soon-to-be-emancipated child get a firm grip on the concept that outgoing moneys can't exceed incoming moneys.

LEAVING-THE-NEST BUDGET

Income:
Jobs _____
Investments _____
Money Gifts _____
Parental Assistance _____
Other _____

Total Income:

Basic Expenses:
Food _____

Rent _____

Utilities:
Gas _____

Electricity _____

Water and Sewer _____

Garbage _____

Cable TV _____

Phone _____

Other _____

Transportation:
Car Payment _____

Auto Insurance _____

Gasoline _____

Repair and Maintenance _____

Misc. Car Expense _____
    (Traffic Tickets, Deductible/Accidents)

Bus/Mass Transportation _____

Bicycle _____

Other _____

Medical:
Insurance Premium _____

Doctor _____

Dentist _____

Medicine/Drugs _____

Other _____

Education Expenses:
Tuition _____

Books _____

Fees _____

Supplies _____

Other _____

Entertainment/Miscellaneous:

Clothing _____

Food _____

Movies _____

Sports _____

Vacations _____

Other _____

Gifts _____

Church & Charities _____

Total Expenses:

What else should your about-to-leave child know about? Everything. Everything that I have put down and everything I haven't. Think about how you spend your time and money. Consider laying out what a typical week looks like for you. How you spend your time—work, visiting with friends and family, community activities, church, cleaning, errands, shopping— what obligations you incur.

Most parents will experience a time when their kids are anxious to be on their own. Sometimes it's only because they want their own place, free from parental direction. Freedom, they think, will be wonderful—no one to answer to but themselves. And to this end, they have found the perfect job and the perfect place to begin their own life of freedom. But then the cost of living becomes, for some of these newly emancipated kids, a rather stark reality. One possibility is the roommate who was sharing the rental costs with your kid in an exorbitantly expensive apartment, who has now moved out. Your kid is left holding the bag. A suggestion to avoid this mishap: Do not let anyone move into a sharing arrangement unless there is at least one month's deposit in an agreed-upon interest-bearing account.

Each year, major magazines such as *U.S. News & World Report*, *Forbes*, *Newsweek*, and *Time* publish articles about the best places to live in America. There are many qualifiers used to crown a city or state as "the best," and two of them are the availability of affordable housing and affordable base living costs. A reasonable and growth-oriented economy is usually tied to overall affordable living costs.

I now live in Colorado, but I lived in my native state of California for forty-four years. The last eighteen of these years were spent in the Bay Area of northern California. It is not uncommon for a one-bedroom apartment (with a carport) to rent for $850 per month in this area. Hopefully, your kid doesn't attempt to live in an area as costly as this the first time out.

When they decide to leave home, post high school or post college, there usually is a rude awakening when they face the costs of housing. One unexpected expense is the deposits required. They can't have a phone or utilities without a deposit. Most landlords require at least two months' rent in advance, plus, in some cases, a damage deposit for pets and kids. This is why it is important that they did the math that shows what they can afford from their net present earnings to spend on the monthly costs to live on their own.

Young adults rarely have a nest egg to cover all the front-end costs required to move into their own place. Here's where the "6 Ps" come in—Prior Planning Prevents the Probability of Poor Performance. Your family spending plan sessions of the past have laid the foundation for your children's first full-blown adult spending plan. So, *before* they commit to the time they will officially leave the nest, call a family powwow. Help them prepare for successful emancipation with some *in depth* prior planning.

ASK THESE QUESTIONS:

- *First, and most important, what dollars do they anticipate each month from their job?* This is their net, after tax, income.
- *What are the fixed costs of living on their own?* Rent, phone, utilities, car insurance (and a car payment, if applicable), any debt from student loans or credit cards. Oh yes, there's also food.
- *What do they plan to spend for non-fixed costs?* Entertainment (an item that often "blows the budget"), clothes, haircuts, gasoline, auto repair and maintenance (new tires can break their bank), gifts, vacations, long-distance phone calls, and dry cleaning and laundry. They will probably not think of renter's insurance. But they should at least consider it if they have costly audio and visual equipment and computers they are taking with them to their new place.
- *What about savings and charity?* Where do these items fit in?

I strongly suggest you have your son or daughter read the following chapters from this book: the Introduction; Money Talks Within the Family; Your Insurance IQ; Creating a Wall Street Wizard; Where There Is a Will, There Is a Way; Savings; and The Boomerangers Are Back. In addition, get your daughters their own personal copies of *Money Sense*, which details everything they need to know about credit, dealing with professionals, even buying a house.

As a parent, your goal is to launch a responsible and self-reliant adult into his or her community. *Raising Money-Wise Kids* is meant to help you launch your children. If you follow the guidelines suggested within this chapter, as well as the entire book, you should have no problem. You have done the best you could with the tools you have. Good luck.

. . . And go!

Chapter Eighteen

THE BOOMERANGERS ARE BACK!

When I speak publicly, one subject about kids always pops up—an empty nest that fills again. I recommend to my audiences that they sell the house and get one that is too small for the kids to move back to. This comment always gets a big laugh, and some have commented to me that they wish they had thought of this a long time ago. Many newly adult children of the nineties appear on their parents' doorstep, bags in hand. And some appear with their *own* children in tow. This happens just about the time parents have settled into a peaceful existence that offers them time for themselves—at last.

Boomerang kids—you did your job as a parent, taught them how to fly the nest, and now life has broken one of their wings. They want to come home. One of the most common times that kids boomerang is immediately following college graduation. The perfect job hasn't been found yet, or they have decided to pursue a graduate study program. Surveys of never-married adults between the ages of twenty and twenty-nine show that more than 50 percent of them live with their parents. And depending on which studies you look at, between 30 to 40 percent of adult children return to living under their parents' roof at least once.

HELLO, MOM, I'M YOUR NEW TENANT

Let's admit it, once the kids are gone, your life changes! And you love a lot about it. The benefits include: laundry duty that doesn't take a whole day, grocery tapes that aren't a yard long (new challenge: can you make spaghetti sauce for *only* one or two?), one-page phone bills, no bass speakers vibrating you awake at 1 A.M., and you can sleep—no more need to wait up and worry where they are and when they will be home. This is a life you can get accustomed to.

But some kids do ask to come back home. The reasons are myriad: The roommate vamoosed, a marriage has failed, a job was lost, illness took its toll. Your kid is wounded in some way and wants to lick those wounds under your roof. Guaranteed, your life will change again if you say yes.

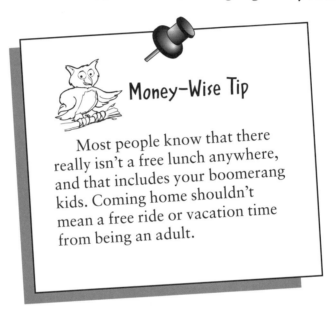

Money-Wise Tip

Most people know that there really isn't a free lunch anywhere, and that includes your boomerang kids. Coming home shouldn't mean a free ride or vacation time from being an adult.

One of the biggest mistakes related to me by parents of boomerang kids is that they haven't set guidelines for the new life with their adult child under their roof. Rule setting is tough to do. These "kids" are used to their autonomy by now and don't respond to parental authority in the same way they used to. And they may also be parents to one or more children.

Additionally, when your kid announces, "Mom, I'm coming home," there is often the stress of immediacy involved. They need (or think they need) your help NOW. You may be tempted to react emotionally in such a situation and take them in your arms and put no parameters on the move-in. Don't do it! They can have your unlimited love and emotional support in their time of need, but not your unlimited or unrestricted financial support. It's boundary-setting time.

Some kids quickly solve the problem(s) that brought them home, and some really never had a problem in the first place. But the fact is that they are living in your home now. The rationale may then become, Why leave a great, comfortable place, why take on another possibly problem roommate, where else can I get such a good financial deal that I get from Mom and Dad?

Granted, moving back home can be hard on your child. Her grand lifestyle and the public image she values so highly are gone. She has to move into her old room that still has the flowered wallpaper and the stuffed animals of yesteryear. But these issues are minor when you consider the ones that you as a parent are forced to deal with in redefining the relationship with your now very adult, independent child. Sticky issues pop up in the areas of privacy, moral standards, lifestyle, and money.

Before They Move In

The best formula for success is to hammer out the guidelines and the agreements you will have with your kids before they officially move in. Talk over the following issues with your adult kid, and make a contract (you may want to put it in writing, and both of you need to sign it):

- *What is the kid's financial situation now, and what does he anticipate it to be over the next few months?* If the kid is unemployed, what is being done to find new work must be discussed weekly.
- *What options does the child have, if any, for living accommodations besides the parental residence, both now and in the future?* Your home may not be the best choice after all.
- *How long does the kid need to live at home, and when can he leave again?* Pin this one down; for example, two months from now the youngster will be gone, no matter what.
- *What space in your home will you surrender to the adult child?* This is a crucial question. You like your life as it is, and this is your home now. Don't give them carte blanche, even if they bring your grandchildren home with them. You want them to be comfortable, of course, but not so comfortable that they want to *stay forever*.
- *What rent will I charge for living in my home?* You must keep the reality of life in front of your adult children by charging them for rent and food, even if they have to pay you back at a later date. This doesn't mean that you should charge the "market" rate for rent—be reasonable. Consider either a percentage of present income or a sliding scale, in case they get a raise or a better job. By your charging for living

expenses, they will be more eager to spend *their* money on *their* place and will do it, you hope, sooner rather than later.

A side note about this rent income and the tax implications: The IRS does not require you to declare as income any rental money received from your child.

- *What household duties will you require of them while they live with you?* They must help with the extra work they create and should not be "on vacation" in your home. This is not the "old days." They will not get paid for the required duties. No more allowances paid on Saturday morning.

You have every reason to expect them to keep their areas in the type of condition that were normal for you (i.e., their use of your guest bath requires "apple pie" order at all times). Be specific if you expect them to assist you with any cooking or housecleaning activities. If they don't follow through, don't do it yourself. Consider hiring it done and charging the fee to their account.

- *What about expenses other than food and rent?* You are not an ATM machine. You may have an unemployed kid at home, or some emergency could arise that he can't cover. Keep a ledger of all money expended, and let him know that these are loans that are to be paid back within a very short period of time and before he treats himself to any new toys or entertainment.

Money-Wise Tip

If you lend money to your adult kids, don't lend anything you would not be willing to convert to a gift, if need be, in the future. Family loans have a poor repayment history. You don't want to repossess your kid, do you?

- *What are the rules about phone and automobile usage?* If your child will be living with you for several months and is working, you could have him install his own phone line. If your child uses your automobile, he must share in all costs—insurance, car payments, gasoline, and repairs. Or, you could look at the lowest rate for a rental car and charge him a reasonable per diem rate. Guaranteed, this will get his attention.

- *What about your kid's kid(s)?* You will be sorry, later, if you don't set rules at the outset in this special case of grandchildren living in your home. Don't become a full-time baby-sitter—hands off is usually best. But if the grandchild is out of line a lot of the time, your philosophy should take over—it's your home and your sanity, after all.

- *And finally, what time do each of you need alone in the home?* You both need your space because you both have been used to it. Set times for each of you to entertain friends at home without the other present. You need your life and they need theirs. Your adult child's friends must adhere to your rules for behavior of guests in your home. Do you allow overnight stays? *This is your choice, not theirs.*

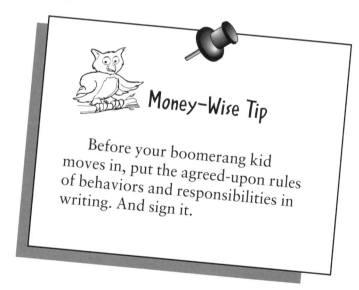

Money-Wise Tip

Before your boomerang kid moves in, put the agreed-upon rules of behaviors and responsibilities in writing. And sign it.

MANAGING THEIR MONEY DURING A FINANCIAL TIME-OUT

When queried about their reasons for returning to the homestead, most kids will say "money." When they do move back home, promises are made to you and to themselves that, in a very short period of time, they will be back on their feet and ready for living on their own again. It all sounds good, but it is easy to get sidetracked. You both want to avoid turning a short-term move into a long-term stay.

Sit down with them, and get a firm grip on a financial plan of action. Believe it or not, parents who charge rent and require their kids' contribution to routine household expenses are doing the best thing possible for both parties. They are once again encouraging their kids' future independence, both financially and emotionally.

In this effort to get them back out on their own, don't overlook the possibility of "sweat equity" or bartering. There are ways for them to live rent-free, and these can be very much in line. For example, if your daughter is going to law school and is also working part-time at a law firm, she may be covering her tuition, health insurance, and personal expenses. She can do some chores around the house or the yard in lieu of paying rent.

When kids suddenly are relieved of the obligation to pay for their own living expenses, they might begin to treat themselves to more goodies than they could afford when they were on their own—entertainment, clothing, and toys. It's time to blow the whistle. They moved back home because they needed a financial time-out.

I'm sure that their move back home—whether it was welcomed with open arms or reluctantly allowed—was not done with your agreement that they would be allowed to redirect their money into "fun" endeavors. If this occurs, a not-so-gentle reminder should be forthcoming from you. Tell them you agreed to a temporary stay and that a pass on expensive hair-dos, weekend trips, dinners out, and the like is expected from them.

Setting Up a Lease

If you have adult kids at home, either Boomerangers or Misfires (adult kids who have never ventured out on their own), it makes sense to have a different set of ground rules. Adult kids living at home should have responsibilities and behaviors that reflect their adult status. They aren't "just the kids" anymore.

Below are a series of questions intended to serve as a guide to setting up a room-and-board status for your adult child. There are no right and wrong answers to these questions. Rather, these questions are meant to probe into both sides of the issues involved.

Parents' Lease Worksheet

1. Should rent be charged? Yes _____ No _____

2. How much should your child pay? $ _____

3. Should there be a different charge if your child is employed or unemployed? Yes _____ No _____

4. If employed—how much? $ _____

   If unemployed—how much? $ _____

5. How long will the lease term be (weeks, months, years)?

   _____

6. Is it renewable? Yes _____ No _____

7. If renewable, for how long (weeks, months, years)?

   _____

8. Will your child have her own phone or use yours? Yours ___ Hers ____

9. Will you charge for utilities? Yes _____ No _____

10. How will you allocate utility charges, by percentage

    (i.e., 25 percent of each bill) or a fixed dollar amount?

    Fixed _____ % _____

11. How much will the utility charges be?

    Phone _____

    Gas & Electricity _____

    Water & Sewer _____

    Trash Collection _____

12. Does your child have her own car? Yes _____ No _____

13. Will your child use your car? Yes _____ No _____

14. Who will pay for insurance, maintenance, and gas?
    Parents _____ Child _____

15. If your child has her own car, will she park it in the garage or driveway or on the street? _____

16. What household chores will your child be responsible for? Make a list for indoors and outdoors.

17. How often do you want these chores done? Include on list.

18. Is your child allowed to have pets of her own? Yes _____ No _____

19. If your child brings in any additional pets, who will care for them in her absence? Parents _____ Other _____

20. Will your child eat only groceries she has purchased? Or will your child consume your groceries? Child's _____ Parents' _____

21. Will your child reimburse you for food by percentage (e.g., 25 percent of each bill) or a fixed dollar amount, or other? % _____ Fixed _____ Other _____

22. If your child eats at home, will she assist with the preparation of meals? Yes _____ No _____

23. Will your child do her own laundry? Yes _____ No _____

24. Can she use your TV and sound systems? Yes _____ No _____

25. If yes, will there be any time or program restrictions? Yes _____ No _____

26. Will she be allowed to entertain friends in your home? Yes _____ No _____

27. If yes, what types and what number of guests are allowed? _____

28. Are there to be any curfew rules? Yes _____ No _____

29. Will overnight guests be allowed? Yes _____ No _____
    How long can a guest stay? _____

30. If your child ignores or violates her agreement with you, what are the consequences?

Parents' signatures _____

Child's Signature _____

Most parents will go out of their way to help and support their kids. But roles begin to shift when the adult-to-adult relationship becomes a reality. So I suggest that you set this new relationship in motion when your child graduates from high school, whether or not college is in the picture. Flexibility and good negotiation skills are important factors in the parent/child-tenant arrangement.

LEASE VIOLATIONS

If your rules are ignored or violated, what will your policy be? By now, most parents know that their kids can be master manipulators. Yours are probably no different. The last thing you need is open warfare in your own home.

So, from the start, set out the consequences of noncompliance, just as you did when your child was a "little one"—cause and effect—and then be sure you stick to them!

- When a first-time infraction occurs, a verbal warning is in order.
- The next time, a written and/or financial penalty should be levied.
- The third time, evict him. If he and his things are not out in the required number of days, you can put the belongings in storage or simply out on the front lawn.

This may sound a little tough. But, by now, your kids are supposed to be grown-ups, aren't they? The advance planning, as cited in the previous pages, will most likely prevent such dire events in your home. Simply, if you define areas of agreement and concern in writing, you have introduced your now adult child to the real world. It's called performance and accountability.

PROTECTING THEIR (AND YOUR) PRIVACY

You may want to close your doors once in a while. For that matter, so will they. And if your son or daughter is receiving mail at your home, it's difficult not to know more than either of you would like about their business. You both deserve more privacy than was present when she was living with you as a child. She is an adult now and you are no longer a full-time parent. You were also emancipated. The lack of needed privacy can cause tempers to flare on both sides. Hone your negotiating skills.

Money-Wise Tip

If your kid brings bill collectors home with him too, refer him to CCCS (Consumer Credit Counseling Service) at (800) 388-2227, or refer to other similar services mentioned in chapter 2—Modeling Made Easy.

If your kids' attitudes and/or behavior bug you and seem inappropriate under your roof, tell them. It is critical for your kids to know, up front, what you can and cannot accept. If you feel negatively about what they do or say in your home, silence is not golden. Touchy areas include: Their friends, male and female—love interests could bring out the worst reaction in you. Their finances—if they are not model citizens, you will probably "see red." Their personal habits—loud music and smoking make you crazy. Their kids—a set bedtime is a must. You as a grandparent can have the fun of reading a bedtime story, but you've earned your stripes already in enforcing the bedtime regime.

Make it very clear what you can and cannot accept. A lot of unnecessary negative transactions with your adult child can be avoided if they adhere to three simple rules:

1. Keep your area and areas you use neat.
2. Respect each other's privacy.
3. Think before you speak or act.

When kids move back home, the bottom line is that it's *your* home and you have the final word. If your kids don't agree with the final word on any subject, they should pack up now. (And return your keys.)

Money-Wise Tip

If your boomeranger is under twenty-four years of age and was a full-time student for five months of this calendar year, you can claim him as a dependent—it doesn't matter how much he earns. But he can't claim his own deduction.

A FINAL WORD

No single book about such a broad topic can hope to cover everything a parent needs to know. *Raising Money-Wise Kids* is just the beginning of a long journey in learning the *Money $ense* approach to your and your child's financial well-being.

The money maze can be quite exciting. It can also be terrifying. How will you prepare for the trip? How will you negotiate the many and inevitable detours and obstacles that block your path? Your answers will be the determining factors in whether your kids turn out to be money wise or money dumb.

I've shared with you my many years of success (and failures). It's now time for you to create your family's *Money $ense* legacies. The work won't be easy. But do your best. And if you falter or make some mistakes, forgive yourself. Most of all, have fun.

AN INVITATION FROM THE AUTHOR

I'd love to hear from you. What ideas did you like best in the book? Do you have any questions about teaching your kids about money or any of the topics included (or not included) in *Raising Money-Wise Kids*?

How about success stories? What were the "ahas" that either confirmed your beliefs or were wake-up calls that helped you and your kids get on track? What about other areas that you think would be great to have a book on for your family—for the adults, for the kids?

Write and let me know. Your opinions are always valued and welcome.

Dr. Judith Briles
P.O. Box 22021
Denver, CO 80222-0021

If you are interested in information about other books
written from a biblical perspective,
please write to the following address:

Northfield Publishing
215 West Locust Street
Chicago, IL 60610